The Twelve Caesars

The Twelve Caesars

The Twelve Caesars

Michael Grant

CHARLES SCRIBNER'S SONS

New York

10065

Library of Congress Catalog Card Number 75–7533
ISBN 0–684–14402–6

Contents

Illustrations

Maps

Acknowledgements

I owe thanks to Mr Stewart Perowne and Messrs Hodder and Stoughton Ltd, and to Mr P. L. K. Wait of Messrs Methuen and Co. Ltd, for sending me advance copies of forthcoming publications. The editorial arrangements of Mrs Susan Loden and Miss Olivia Browne of Messrs Weidenfeld and Nicolson Ltd have been excellent. I am also grateful to Mrs Bezi Hammelmann, Mr D. E. L. Haynes and Mrs Hilary Walford for their assistance, and to my wife for invaluable and indispensable help of a great many kinds.

In quoting English translations, I have sometimes ventured to introduce minor modifications, usually in the interests of consistency or comprehensibility.

Acknowledgement is due to Robert Graves for permission to quote from his translation of *The Twelve Caesars* by Suetonius, and to the Loeb Classical Library (Harvard University Press, William Heinemann) for permission to quote from the Loeb Suetonius I and II and Dio's *Roman History*.

Gt.St Bernard Pass

A L P S

Mt.Genèvre Pass

Julian Alps

TRANSPADANA

Mediolanum

CISALPINE GAUL

VENETIA

Vicetia

R.Po (Padus)

Cremona

Patavium

Placentia

Bedriacum

LIGURIA

Brixellum

Hostilia

R.Po (Padus)

AEMILIA

Mutina

ETRURIA

Luca

Pisae

Florentia

R.Rubicon

UMBRIA

Ilva

PICENUM

Planasia

Corsica

Mevania

Ferentium

R.Tiber

Narnia

Reate

Sabini

Aquae
Cutiliae

Rome

SAMNIUM

Ostia

Marsi

Aricia

Anagnia

Velitrae

LATIUM

Antium

Volsci

APULIA

Luceria

Sardinia

Pontia

Capua

Beneventum

Pandateria

CAMPANIA

Puteoli

Neapolis

Mt.
Vesuvius

LUCANIA

Brundu

Misenum

Herculaneum

Pompeii

Tarentum

BAY OF NAPLES

BRUTTIUM

Capreae

N

Naulochus

Rhegium

0 miles   50   100   150

0 km   100   200

Sicily

Syracuse

ITALY

Introduction: The Significance and Strangeness of the Caesars

This book seeks to provide short biographies of the Twelve Caesars: Julius Caesar and the first eleven Roman emperors who followed him. It therefore deals with the same period as Suetonius' *Lives of the Caesars* (*De Vita Caesarum*). In attempting to cover the same ground as he did, I am not, of course, prompted by any mad thought of equalling the Roman biographer. For how could one begin to equal a writer who continues to be marvellously readable after more than eighteen centuries? On the contrary, my imitation of his subject, and of its chronological limits, is intended as a humble tribute to Suetonius. But I also propose, and I hope this will not seem presumptuous, to try to show the somewhat different appearance the subjects of his absorbing *Lives* present after the passage of so many hundreds of years.

Those dozen men were a fabulous series, the theme of countless legends. Every sort of enormous achievement and bizarre fantasy is conjured up by their names. Moreover, although the long roll-call of emperors continued after them into a still far distant future, there is a certain completeness about the Twelve. Suetonius himself felt this, since otherwise he could have gone on to write about the three later emperors he had known – or at least about one or two of them, since there were obvious difficulties in the way of describing the current occupant of the throne. But he gracefully renounced this endeavour in the final chapter of his final *Life* – declaring that the last of the Twelve,

Domitian, shortly before his death, dreamt that a golden hump grew out of his back, portending the upright, moderate rule of the emperors who would shortly succeed him. Moreover a raven perched on the Capitol, and cawed *All will be well*.

What Suetonius was virtually saying was that the subsequent rulers were too good, and therefore too dull, to be worth going on with. Besides, although there were still some pretty strange rulers in the centuries to come, the Twelve he dealt with had already, between them, exhausted almost the entire range of possible idiosyncrasies, attainments and talents. They can claim a certain monumental, self-contained comprehensiveness, as the later Roman poet Ausonius appreciated when, for the information of his son Hesperius, he composed memorial lines about the selfsame Twelve.

Suetonius, who was born in about AD 69, may have come from Hippo Regius, near the present Annaba in Algeria. Another writer, the younger Pliny, who liked him very much, intervened with a friend, Baebius Hispanus, to secure him a little property in Italy:

My friend Suetonius Tranquillus [he wrote] wishes to buy a small estate which I hear a friend of yours is trying to sell. Please see that he has it at a fair price, so that he will be pleased with his purchase.

There is indeed much about this property to whet his appetite if only the price suits him: easy access to Rome, good communications, a modest house, and sufficient land for him to enjoy without taking up too much of his time. Scholars who take to the country, like himself, need no more land than will suffice to clear their heads and refresh their eyes, as they stroll around their grounds and tread their single path, getting to know each of their precious vines and counting every fruit tree.[1]

Later, however, Suetonius left that earthly paradise to accept a series of appointments at the imperial palace, culminating in three important secretaryships. It is intriguingly reported, though the writer who tells the story is far from reliable, that the emperor Hadrian dismissed him from the last of these jobs, and that his patron the praetorian guard commander lost his post at the same time, because of disrespectful or over-familiar behaviour towards the empress Sabina. Her sour expression and grim hair-do, as displayed on the coinage, inspire us with some sympathy for Suetonius, especially as her husband Hadrian was heard to remark that he would have been happy to get rid of the irritable woman had not his position made this impossible. Suetonius no doubt returned to his Italian rural retreat, but his dismissal proved unfortunate, since his later *Lives*, on which he was still engaged at the time, suffer from the unavailability of the imperial archives that had enriched the earlier biographies with valuable information.

Posterity paid the *Lives of the Caesars* the great and well-deserved compliment of regarding them worthy of preservation, although the far more elaborate works from which their author had derived his material were allowed to perish. But the compliment was somewhat grudging, since the work only survived by a thread. For although Suetonius remained known for a long time at Constantinople, western Europe seems to have preserved just one single isolated copy. It is from that one copy, now lost, but studied by the ninth-century Frankish scholar Einhard at the monastery of Fulda, that all our existing manuscripts are directly or indirectly derived.

Three editions of the *Lives* were published in Italy in 1470–1 – two in Rome and another in Venice. Then, in the 1530s and 1540s, translations into continental languages multiplied. Montaigne quoted Suetonius more than forty times, modestly declaring (as any modern Suetonian student must repeat with infinitely more justified diffidence), 'I make others say for me what, either from want of language or want of sense, I cannot myself so well express.'

England then produced a wonderful, lively Jacobean translator, Philemon Holland (1606), though he by no means shares the succinctness of his original:

> Philemon with translations doth so fill us,
> He will not let Suetonius be Tranquillus.

The best modern English translation is J. C. Rolfe's rendering in the Loeb edition, published more than sixty years ago. G. W. Mooney translated the last six lives in 1930. Robert Graves' Penguin version (1957) is entertaining, but has to be used with caution.

Biography, judged Virginia Woolf, 'imposes conditions, and those conditions are that it must be based upon fact' – fact that can be verified by its readers. But she was setting an inaccessibly high standard for the life of any individual who died nearly two thousand years ago. Indeed Voltaire even considered it 'a monstrous piece of charlatanry to pretend to paint a personage with whom you have never lived'. As for the Caesars, some modern scholars scarcely regard it as practicable to attempt their biographies at all, and deliberately refrain from doing so. This warning enjoins great humility upon those unwise enough to ignore it. They can only derive reassurance from the fact that even Suetonius himself achieved his results without actually knowing the Caesars in person. When the very last of them came to the throne, he was only twelve years old – so that his acquaintance with all of his predecessors must have been entirely second-hand. Yet no one will suggest that he failed to make them come alive.

Pliny wrote to the emperor Trajan that Suetonius was not only a very fine scholar but also a man of great integrity. A later classical writer allotted special praise to his accuracy. Indeed it is generally agreed that he had the firm intention of getting at the truth – and the comments of his great contemporary, the historian Tacitus, on other writers who had dealt with these same themes show what a distinctly unusual merit that was. Suetonius, that is to say, is exempt from the usual bias of ancient historians in favour of the senatorial class. He refuses to follow the ancient tradition demanding that the lives of princes must either be panegyrics or venomous attacks; and he does not, unlike most writers of the time, write a biography with the determination that his subject must be wholly good or utterly bad. He is also refreshingly free of the moral, rhetorical, uplift which lessened the credibility of so many ancient biographies, including the works of his Greek contemporary Plutarch. Suetonius is drily indiscriminate, apparently indifferent: one of the ancient world's nearest approaches to objectivity. He can analyse a problem very efficiently, as he reveals on occasion. But such displays are unpretentiously infrequent, because on the whole he conceives it his task merely to place the evidence in front of us, for and against, side by side, without judgement or prejudice. As a result, G. B. Townend rightly observes: 'There is something solidly authentic about his emperors, even if individual stories remain suspect. He allows us to construct our own figures from his materials, and we feel that the results are real.'

Nevertheless Suetonius' veracity is subject to undeniable limitations.

In particular, he is extremely superstitious. As Pliny confirms, he believed determinedly in prophetic dreams. Omens, too, attracted his credulous fascination, as his work repeatedly testifies. For example, he records with interest the uncanny atmosphere in Augustus' nursery at Velitrae (Velletri), where the local inhabitants believed that the emperor had been born. People were afraid to enter this room, reports Suetonius, because strange things had happened to those who had made the attempt before.

And, verily, this was confirmed by this occasion. For when the new landlord and possessor of that farm-house, either by chance and at unawares, or else to try some experiment, went into it, there to take up his lodging, it happened that in the night, within a very few hours after, being driven out from thence by sudden violence (he knoweth not how), he was found in manner half-dead, together with bed and all, before the door.[2]

Other writers, too, recounted heaven-sent miracles with equal gusto. Indeed ancient annalistic tradition required that they should not be left unrecorded, and poets were equally susceptible to their dramatic force.

> When Caesar died, the great sun pitied Rome,
> So veiling his bright head, the godless time
> Trembled in fear of everlasting night;
> And then were portents given of earth and ocean,
> Vile dogs upon the roads, and hideous
> Strange birds, and Aetna quaking, and her fires
> Bursting to overflow the Cyclops' fields
> With flames whirled in the air and melted stones.
>   Thunder of war was heard in Germany
> From south to north, shaking the granite Alps;
> And a voice also through the silent groves
> Piercing: and apparitions wondrous pale
> Were seen in dead of night.[3]

Very often poets and historians who told these tales believed in them, or some of them. 'I hesitate', remarked Tacitus, 'to be sceptical about events widely believed and handed down.' Yet those words hint at a certain caution, and the debate for and against such credulity continues throughout his works. Almost everyone else was far more openly credulous – like Suetonius. Professional astrologers abounded. One Roman government after another, seeing that a horoscope might contain infinite potentialities for subversion, tried to throw these men out: they were expelled in 139 and 33 BC, and then again in AD 16, 52, 69 and 70. But the very quantity and frequency of such expulsions show how futile they evidently were.

Of all the Twelve Caesars, perhaps the only one who wholeheartedly disbelieved in omens was the first, Julius Caesar; though Galba may also have tended in that direction. Augustus was sceptical about some reports – though not always prepared to admit as much. But he keenly believed in others. Tiberius was deeply involved with the astrologer Thrasyllus, and it was because of astrological predictions, magician's rites, and interpretations of dreams that the first treason victim of the reign, Libo, came to a bad end. Even the very tough Agrippina the younger was frightened by the births of half-bestial children, and of a pig with the claws of a hawk: and when Claudius died (probably by her own hand), she refrained from announcing her son Nero's succession until the propitious moment forecast by the astrologers. Vespasian was keen to publicize all the signs that had pointed to his imperial destiny. Vitellius, like Augustus, scoffed at such signs on occasion, yet believed that many others were authentic. Otho took an astrologer with him to Lusitania. The horoscopes of potential rivals were keenly scrutinized by Domitian.

So portents and prodigies played a massive part in Roman history. We may smile at Suetonius for believing so many of these stories (though which of us harbours not the smallest superstition of any kind whatever?). All the same it was understandable, and even useful, that he should include them in his account, since they influenced events, directed them and created them.

Another aspect of Suetonius' *Lives* which we may feel inclined to take with a pinch of salt, or disinfectant, is his emphasis on sexual aberrations. Were the Caesars really as peculiar as all that? Some of his descriptions, notably the account of Tiberius' aquatic sports, are so pornographic that the Loeb editions modestly leave them in the highly descriptive Latin. 'We may remark', says Gibbon, 'that Claudius was the only one whose taste in love is entirely correct': that is to say, he seems to have been 100 per cent heterosexual – and this was unique.

In writing of such matters Suetonius did not display the burning indignation of Tacitus, or indulge in Juvenal's satirical invective. He just piled on the details – either because he was carrying out his usual practice of quoting the good and the bad with indifferent impartiality, or more probably because he enjoyed that sort of thing: as befitted the man who had also written a book *On Famous Whores*. J. Wight Duff was appalled by this '*chronique scandaleuse* based upon tittle-tattle about the emperors and compiled by a literary man with the muck-rake'. G. W. Mooney criticized Suetonius' practice on the grounds that 'modern standards of taste demand the omission of all that is unsavoury'. Duff and Mooney were writing in 1927 and 1930, not in the 1970s when references to such matters are less often impeded by any such delicacy.

If the stories were true, we do not need Freud to tell us that they are important; because even a man's public life, as modern politicians have found, can easily be affected by what he does in private. Galba was not quite right to say it mattered to nobody what he did in his own free time. Pliny the younger, in order to praise Trajan – though he was on delicate ground in view of that emperor's allegedly pederastic tastes – elaborates the point that 'it is a man's pleasures which tell us most about his true worth, his moral excellence, and his self-control ... it is our leisure moments that betray us.'

But were these stories of erotic eccentricities true? Not necessarily. And this is not because such monsters could never have conducted the government of the empire – that is a naïve view, because their peculiar practices may have helped them to get on with their work. Nevertheless the stories remain doubtful for another reason, because the imperial palace, which kept itself fairly secret, was the sounding-board of incessant whisperings. These rumours, like the portents, are of importance to the historian, even if they may not be true, because they show what people were saying.

Nevertheless there may also be more factual truth in Suetonius' accounts of these amorous adventures than is often believed. Admittedly there is sometimes, where gossip is concerned, smoke without fire. Yet, in the words of E. A. Freeman: 'The peculiar qualities which are picked out for exaggeration are pretty sure to show what a man's character really is.'

Besides, ever since the days of the later Roman Republic at least, a high degree of sexual freedom had been the prerogative of Roman nobles, male and female alike: when marriage and divorce are coldly manipulated as high politics, that is what happens. When Nero expressed his conviction that chastity and purity just did not exist, although this sentiment may to some extent reflect his own wishful thinking, he was accurately describing an upper-class society which had smaller barriers against wide-ranging immorality than our own.

When one of the members of this society became emperor, such flimsy obstacles as existed came down altogether. In the words of the younger Pliny, himself a man of decorous behaviour: 'It is rare and almost unknown in a prince to think himself under any restraint – or to welcome it if he does.' This knowledge that the possibilities open to him were literally unrestricted could hardly fail to influence the conduct of an emperor, unless he was quite exceptionally self-controlled. In our own time, custom and law, between them, impose considerable sexual restrictions; or, if drop-outs choose to reject these, their freedom is likely to be restricted by financial stringency instead. A Roman emperor was unimpeded, to any appreciable extent, by either custom, or law, or lack of funds. In the unlikely event of anyone today being equally unhampered, one may wonder whether he or she might not likewise throw numerous inhibitions overboard. That is what many of the Caesars, surely, did, and although Suetonius' prurient descriptions are rich in imaginative detail, they may nevertheless, in their main lines, not be too far removed from the truth.

As J. W. Mackail remarked: 'There perhaps never was a series of biographies so crammed with anecdote.' Some of these anecdotes, the ones which seem to throw most light on their subjects and what was thought about them, are reproduced in the present book, for they make the Rome of the Caesars come to life. Moreover Suetonius, when he wishes, is also a master of narrative on a larger scale. We are told that he was a slow producer: but his stories rush ahead with great rapidity. His account of the death of Nero, for example, is a masterpiece of moving, dramatic presentation. He was also addicted to the fashionable pseudo-science of physiognomy, of which the most famous exponent was his own younger contemporary, the sophist Antonius Polemo of Laodicea (near Denizli in Turkey). When the philosopher Plotinus later declared that the face gives a glimpse of the soul, he was saying what Polemo and Suetonius had thought; and Suetonius' descriptions of the personal appearances of the Caesars are memorable.

In composing his biographies, unlike the more chronologically minded Plutarch, he generally interrupts the straightforward account of his subject's life by a selection of material, classified according to topics, which deals successively with the man's various characteristics. In this rather schematic pattern we may detect the grammarian and antiquarian at work, for Suetonius possessed both of these interests. Nevertheless a host of vital characters leaps out from his pages. Yet they are characters of rather too static an appearance, since, in keeping with the ancient idea that a man's inner nature remains unchanging from birth to death,* little attempt is made to reflect psychological developments or alterations. Biographers of Franklin D. Roosevelt often discuss whether illness had made him a 'changed man' at the end of his life. The ancient biographers and historians would not have admitted that any such real, basic, change was possible. Certainly people sometimes seemed to act in inconsistent fashions: Suetonius was quite happy to endow his characters with a mass of strangely inharmonious features at one and the same time. This fits in with his general, and quite explicit, reluctance to reconcile contradictory statements, or even offer rulings on discrepancies. He does not attempt to make all these separate data and details add up to a consistent, coherent account; and one sometimes suspects that he has not really made up his mind what these men were really like. This is, of course, tantalizing. Yet the discordant personages which emerge may not be so wrongly presented after all. For that is how many people are, and not least the Caesars who were subject to so many almost intolerable pressures of contradictory kinds.

To us those pressures are probably the most interesting things about them. A biographer, to quote Virginia Woolf again, must 'give us the creative fact; the fertile fact; the fact that suggests and engenders'. The fertile fact, for the Caesars, relates to power. They are absorbing not only, and not so much, because of the weird stories which gathered around them, but because they were human beings who became enormously powerful. It is important to know just how they handled this power, and how it affected them.

Now the answers to these questions may not necessarily emerge from Suetonius: and that is one of the reasons why one can summon up the courage to try to rewrite his biographies from a somewhat different point of view. For, on the whole, he does not grapple with the power problems the Roman rulers had to face – nor indeed, the circumstances of the varying epochs in which they exerted that power, nor the growth, administration and defence of the empire which occupied a great deal of their energies and time. A biographer of national leaders, one would

---

* Tacitus's interpretation of Tiberius's character in this way is discussed in Chapter 3.

feel nowadays, ought to say rather more about the stage on which they performed, and consider the ways in which their characters affected, and were affected by, their public careers upon that stage. Suetonius, however, does not really consider this to be part of his job. If his readers want such material, involving background information about Roman institutions and history, then he feels that they should go elsewhere – to the historians.

For ancient biographers suffered from a strong traditional inferiority complex, accepting the current view that they were quite different from historians, and not only different but a lesser breed. The only Latin biographer before Suetonius whose works in part survive, Cornelius Nepos, is full of apologies. 'I am well aware', he writes to Cicero's friend Atticus, 'that a great many people will look upon this kind of writing as trivial and unworthy of the roles played in life by men of eminence.' Indeed Nepos even shies at attempting a systematic account of a well-known personage's achievements 'in case I may appear to be writing history rather than giving an account of his life'. Suetonius, for his part, was all too well aware of an enormously distinguished contemporary historian, namely Tacitus. And he therefore wisely decided not to compete with Tacitus at all, abandoning systematic chronology so as to get away from Tacitean history altogether, and seeing himself as a researcher and a scholar rather than as a creative historical writer.

This divorce between biographers and historians persisted. It is true that, since the sixteenth century, leading handbooks on historical method have generally regarded biography as a legitimate form of history. But there have been notable dissentients, for example Eduard Meyer and R. G. Collingwood. And even in our own time, Richard Holmes can still begin a review of A. O. J. Cockshut's recent book *Truth to Life* with a searching series of questions relating to this problem:

Is biography really an art, really a form of imaginative literature? Or is it only one of the secondary genre, honourable but parasitic, like criticism or the documentary? Do biographers really have the stature of novelists, say, or dramatists? Or are they essentially craftsmen, tradesmen – journalists, or out-of-office politicians, or retired diplomats, or raffish dons? . . .

Biography is in fact one of the occult arts. It uses scientific means – documentation, analysis, inquiry – to achieve a hermetic end: the transformation of base materials to gold. While its final intention is the most ambitious and blasphemous of all – to bring back a human being to life.[4]

By this standard Suetonius is an occultist of wily skills.

Nevertheless, it must be admitted that there is something lacking in the magic. True enough, he duly brings the Caesars back to life. But the resurrected figures he presents to us cannot surely, without some further explanation, be the men who wielded all that immense authority. For we are not shown them operating in any such context at all.

Still, the situation is not hopeless, since we also have Tacitus. He deals with many of the same men, but works, very often, in a diametrically opposite manner, omitting private biographical material and considering his subjects almost exclusively from the standpoint of their power. He hates power, and finds it a horrible denial of freedom, a seed-bed of cruelty and evil of every sort. Yet he believes that the alternative of civil war is even worse. So the imperial might has to be endured: and its progressive consolidation, under whatever names and forms, is the main theme that is apparent in his vision of the Twelve Caesars.

Since Suetonius is so much more forthcoming than Tacitus about the picturesque details of his characters, and Tacitus is so far more enlightening about their power, our problem of relating the Caesars' personalities to their exercise of authority might seem to be largely solved by a judicious blend of the two writers (with a certain admixture of a third, later, surviving historian, Dio Cassius, who concentrates on politics from valuable first-hand experience but with notable anachronisms).

And this, indeed, is what countless modern historians, and historical novelists, have thankfully decided. But their decision has been premature, for something more than a combination of Tacitus, Suetonius and Dio is required.

Indeed, Tacitus, in his different way, is just as inadequate as Suetonius. True, his genius as a writer and thinker is soaring and startling. His unforgettable, unequalled artistry means that the study of the emperors cannot even begin without his aid and inspiration. When Lytton Strachey declared that 'the first duty of a great historian is to be an artist: uninterpreted truth is as useless as buried gold, and art is the great interpreter', he might well have been writing with Tacitus in mind. Yet Tacitus' estimates of character are misleading. 'He is not a just writer', remarked Thomas Hunter (1752), 'though we allow him a great wit. He is void of Candour, wants Judgement, exceeds Nature, and violates Truth.'

In particular the absorbing earlier part of the *Annals*, relating to Tiberius, is unique among serious historical writings for all the dramatic techniques, biased interpretations and unjustified innuendoes which distort its veracity. Tiberius is allowed to get away with nothing. To quote a single small example, even when he declined divine honours voted to him in Spain, Tacitus cannot accept the obvious interpretation – that the emperor was unassuming enough to deprecate such pretentiousness – but explains how 'most people thought it was uneasiness. It was also ascribed to degeneracy, on the grounds that the best men aimed highest . . . "Contempt for fame", it was said, "means contempt for goodness."'

All that is entirely uncalled for. And indeed Tacitus himself, just before those phrases of insidious demolition, had quoted the speech of Tiberius explaining his views: and it is a speech which, to an unbiassed eye, reflects authentic modesty. For Tacitus was far too good a historian to conceal the facts – even when they directly contradict his own interpretations. In consequence he treats us to continual, glaring discrepancies between these facts, which are conscientiously stated, and the quite unjustified impression he then chooses to give of them. The greatest of human tragedies, it has been said, is a theory killed by a fact. But Tacitus kills his own theories with the very facts he himself obligingly provides.

So his character sketches, for all their incisiveness, are often dismaying. At times their brilliance is merely that of colourful lay figures – often based on the character types created by earlier historians such as Sallust. The imperial minister Sejanus is a stock villain, empresses are standard villainesses, Tiberius is the Tyrant of declamations and dramas, an implausible monster of Cruelty, Injustice, Suspiciousness, Craftiness and Sensuality.

In spite of all his allurements, then, Tacitus is not enough. Indeed Tacitus and Suetonius and Dio Cassius together are not enough – not nearly enough. When they have all had their say, we still have to make fresh endeavours to find out what sort of men the Caesars really were.

Besides, all this emphasis on the man at the top is nowadays regarded as somewhat out of date. We are still allowed to try, in William Roscoe Thayer's words, 'to discover how the human will – that force more mysterious than electricity – shapes and directs the deeds of men'. But Tacitus, for example, seems to have gone too far along this path. For he saw the history of Rome, and of Roman power, as the history of a series of men. Admittedly he was prepared on occasion to concede that, whereas rulers changed, the system did not – and kept things going. Nevertheless, inheriting the keen Roman interest in personality, he accepted, indeed partly created, the humanist view that the dominant factor in history is the will of the individual. To him characters mould events, and not the reverse. He saw Caesars as Marvell in 1650 saw Cromwell, who

> Could by industrious valour climb
> To ruin the great work of time,
> And cast the Kingdoms old
> Into another mould.[5]

A century after Marvell, this presentation of history was denied by Montesquieu, who remarked that if Julius Caesar and Pompey had never existed other ambitious men would still have destroyed the Roman state. To Goethe, too, any personage must needs be the reflection of his times; if born a decade later or earlier, 'he would have become an entirely different being'. During the nineteenth century both the extremes in this controversy found strong expression. In 1841 Thomas Carlyle, in his book *On Heroes, Hero-Worship and the Heroic in History*, reasserted the significance of the individual. 'As I take it,' he declared, 'Universal History, the history of what man has accomplished in this world, is at bottom the History of the Great Men who have worked here.' But Friedrich Engels on the other hand went back to the opinion of Montesquieu, declaring that Napoleon, for example, 'did not come by chance, and if he had not come another man would have taken his place'.

Today's historians, disgusted by Hitler and other autocrats of our own century, feel more sympathetic to Engels' point of view than to Carlyle's. 'Very few revolutions', points out Professor Arnaldo Momigliano, 'are explained by their chiefs. The study of the leaders is necessary, but by itself is not enough.' And this standpoint has been firmly extended to the Caesars. Sir Ronald Syme, for example, one of those who are doubtful about the validity of imperial biography, denounces 'fancied oppositions of personality, and artificial contrasts in policy ... Far too much

13

attention goes to the emperors as individuals.' Certainly, the ancient writers were too intent on seeing everything in terms of personalities, and concentrated excessively on the melodramatic, rhetorical figures whom they themselves had conjured up out of the sometimes recalcitrant facts. This sort of over-emphasis stands in need of redistribution. The continuity of Roman policy depended, not on a single man, but on the almost unconscious consensus of the whole governing class. And in any case the personal malevolence of ferocious emperors only affected a limited clique, comprising the relatively few men who came within his personal orbit. Even Tacitus himself admitted as much. Yet at the same time he added a qualification, on the lips of a Roman general, Cerialis, addressing rebellious Gauls: 'Whereas tyrants wreak their will upon such as are nearest to them, those emperors who are well spoken of benefit you as much as they do us, though you live far away.' For rulers *could* make themselves felt over all the vast range of the imperial territories. Syme, too, although doubting whether they often actually achieved the total redirection of social movements, allows that they may have 'accelerated or retarded' them.

Even to do so much was an enormous performance, affecting the lives of thousands and millions of people. Yet some of the Caesars, surely, did a good deal more even than that. Although, had Julius and Pompey never been, the Republic would still have fallen to someone else, the *way* in which it fell was that of Julius, and his choice of method bequeathed enormous consequences to the future. As for Augustus, the effect he himself exercised on the Roman world, and subsequent civilization, was gigantic. Rightly did Tiberius, at his predecessor's funeral, lay stress on 'the deeds which are in a peculiar sense those of Augustus himself, deeds which have never been performed by any other man'. For Augustus' personality was the greatest impetus and determinant in every aspect of his age. Claudius, too, exerted a highly individual effect. And Vespasian and Domitian established two different, opposed, methods of imperial rule of which their successors followed one or the other for centuries.

These were major personal influences upon history, and there were others. If we are seeking for modern analogies, the governments of near eastern countries are in some ways closer to the government of ancient Rome than any west European regime of today is likely to be. But students of the Presidency of the United States, too, are not likely to be altogether unwilling to minimize the influence of individual personalities upon the course of events.

Perhaps, then, the current tendency to attribute developments to general trends rather than to the characters and abilities of the Caesars is in danger of going a little too far. The task of trying to find out what the leading personalities were like remains extremely important; and it is in the hope of making an infinitesimal contribution to this task that I have written the present book.

Yet the various deficiencies of the ancient literary authorities make this aim exceptionally difficult to fulfil. Certainly Tacitus, Suetonius and Dio Cassius all relied on authorities contemporary, or nearly contemporary, with the events they were describing. But the works of those contemporaries and near contemporaries are lost, and so we cannot judge them for ourselves. However we can be quite sure that they, no less than their extant successors, were uneven in quality, and subject to strong political biases and falsifications – as Tacitus caustically observes.

Besides, even if they only lived a hundred yards away from the emperor, that did not mean that they were in a position to know what was really going on in the palace. As we have already seen, unconfirmable rumours seeped out of it continually – and very often that was all the writers had to go on. Dio Cassius, who was personally familiar with the imperial court of the Severan dynasty (AD 193–235), describes this situation with feeling.

Formerly, as we know, all matters were reported to the senate and to the people, even if they happened at a distance. Hence all learned of them and many recorded them; and consequently the truth regarding them – no matter to what extent fear or favour, friendship or enmity, coloured the reports of certain writers – was always to a certain extent to be found in the works of the other writers who wrote of the same events and in the public records.

But after Augustus' time most things that happened began to be secret and concealed, and even though some things happen by chance to be made public, they are distrusted just because they can not be verified. For it is suspected that everything is said and done with reference to the wishes of the men in power at the time and of their associates.

As a result, much that never occurs is noised abroad, and much that happens beyond a doubt is unknown, and in the case of nearly every event a version gains currency that is different from the way it really happened.

Furthermore, the very magnitude of the empire and the multitude of things that occur render accuracy in regard to them most difficult. In Rome, for example, much is going on, and much in the subject territories, while, as regards our enemies, there is something happening all the time – in fact, every day – and concerning these things no one except the participants can easily have correct information, and most people do not even hear of them at all.[6]

And Nero's friend Petronius, who was intimately acquainted with palace life in the time of the Twelve Caesars themselves, depicted this proliferation of unreliable rumours with even greater vividness:

> People would rather swallow a lighted candle
> Than keep a secret that smacks in the least of scandal.
> The quietest whisper in the royal hall
> Is out in a flash buttonholing passers-by against a wall;
> And it's not enough that it's broadcast to the nation –
> Everyone gets it with improvement and elaboration.[7]

How, then, can we defend ourselves against all these dubious reports, and sift out whatever grains of truth can be detected in them?

For one thing, we can check the historians and biographers against hundreds of more or less casual references in ancient authors who were not compiling systematic histories at all. Robert Graves, defending himself against the charge that his historical novels *I Claudius* and *Claudius the God* depended entirely on Tacitus, Suetonius and his own 'vigorous fancy', protests that he consulted a whole list of these additional writers; and he did well to do so.

But he could have done more. For there is one great advantage that we modern students of these subjects possess – in contrast with the ancient writers who were not deeply interested in such matters. That is to say, labours in various specialist fields enable us to consult a large number of original documents for ourselves – inscriptions, papyri, buildings, works of art and coins. Inscriptions supply the exact words of emperors, for example the highly individual and revealing utterances of Claudius. Papyri cast light on many obscure places and themes. Great complexes of buildings show us the emperors' chosen bequests to posterity. The achievements of sculptors include an extraordinary series of imperial portraits. Coins add to them, as well as providing an enormous range of governmental publicity, much of it demonstrably inspired by the personal aims of the emperor himself.

What is the snag about all this evidence? Certainly it needs handling with a great amount of caution. For it is all, or almost all, imperial propaganda. Yet that, in itself, makes it infinitely valuable – because so much of our literary material is *anti*-imperial propaganda. It is only fair to weigh the one kind of source against the other. Neither is necessarily true – but by a judicious combination of the two we can truly begin to build up a picture of what the Caesars were like.

Indeed in two senses the coins and other documents are more valuable to the biographer than the surviving literary authorities. First, they are actually contemporary. And second, being for the most part direct emanations from the palace, they display the precise means deliberately selected by the government itself to illustrate the personalities and policies of the Caesars, and their attitudes to imperial authority.

The task, therefore, of writing about these rulers is challenging and exciting. True, nothing approaching complete success is attainable. Yet we do have a chance, even after all this time has passed, of reaching certain conclusions about these extraordinary and immensely powerful men. This is what I have tried to do, and I shall be happy if the pages which follow stimulate others to fare better.

There were certain permanent features in the situations of all the Caesars which influenced their behaviour almost all the time.

Every one of them depended for his throne and his life upon the army. The army, of course, had other functions as well, since it was indispensable for the defence of the empire, and was also employed on the extension and expansion of the imperial frontiers which continued steadily reign by reign.* But the necessity of maintaining forces large enough to perform this function meant automatically that they were also large enough, and their commanders powerful enough, to offer a perpetual threat to the security of the rulers themselves.

Apart from a few exceptional men among them who took this menace remarkably lightly – Julius Caesar and Vespasian are conspicuous examples – it was never out of their minds for long at a time. Indeed unceasing consciousness of the peril very often formed the principal guideline of all their policies. When external wars arose, the question of who should take the active military command was a terrible dilemma. The Caesars could not afford to take their eyes off Rome and the rest of

* Compare Maps 1 and 2, pp. xii and 28.

the empire by taking command themselves. And yet it was an equally grave hazard to place a large expeditionary force under the command of someone else.

Another ever-present danger faced them from the senate. For centuries this body, although technically no more than advisory, had been the real head of the Republican government, advising the state officials on domestic and foreign policy, finance and religion, offering guidance on legislative proposals, and providing the principal element of corporate continuity in Roman affairs. The senate as a whole had not, it is true, normally been an independent originator of policy, which was decided in the private councils of a few of its leading members, chiefly those who had at one time or another been successful in the annual elections to the pair of consulships, the senior office of state. Yet many other senators, too, were among the political and social elite of ancient Rome. They were also the plutocratic elite, since membership depended on a minimum financial qualification (the next richest class were the knights). From the time of Sulla, who was dictator in 82–1 BC, entry to the senate was obtained by holding a junior state office, the quaestorship, so that it become a body of ex-officials. Distinguished from other citizens by tunics with a broad purple stripe and by red leather shoes, the senators enjoyed immense prestige with the Roman people and army, whose commanders, active and retired, were among their number.

There had come a time, however, when senatorial authority began to be questioned. The first serious menace appeared in the second century BC, from noble politicians such as Tiberius and Gaius Sempronius Gracchus who threatened to go over the heads of the senators to the Assembly of the People. Most serious of all, however, was the subsequent emergence of generals who, with armies behind them, increasingly took matters into their own hands. Then, under Julius Caesar and the emperors, the senate passed into a perpetual state of subordination. However the great families who had hitherto shaped the destiny of Rome were unprepared to accept this development, since it conflicted with their personal, inherited, inordinate ambitions. Each successive ruler in turn, though wooing these arrogant men with tempting marriage alliances, invariably failed to win their unreserved loyalty. In consequence they continued to present a grave hazard. One Caesar after another suffered from the recurrent and often justifiable nightmare that some sinister alliance between a general in the field and a group of his fellow-senators at home might bring him down.

The rulers were also frightened of the urban populace of Rome – with less reason, on the whole. At no time had Rome ever been a democracy, since the Assembly of the People, though technically the sovereign body of the Republic, had invariably been dominated by the vote-controlling powerful and rich. Under the Caesars the Assembly, although Augustus and others meticulously observed its outward forms, became even more of a cypher, and displayed no traces of political initiative whatever. The people, remarked Juvenal, were absolutely indifferent to affairs of state. Yet they needed careful watching all the same, since they could easily start riots and demonstrations at public ceremonies and shows, or on any other occasion when they could get a hearing from the emperor. Claudius, for example, on the occasion of a food shortage, was assailed with rude remarks and pelted with bread.

More bread was one of the official solutions to the possible security problem of the Roman populace. It was a twofold solution, the famous 'bread and circuses' – applied to keep them happy and quiet. 'Bread' meant free food, or money to buy food, such as Nero boasted of on his coinage. 'Circuses' meant bigger and better public entertainments. All emperors vied with one another to enlarge and extend the Games – with the single exception of Tiberius, under whom even the gladiators complained that they were not given a chance.

'It is in *your* interest', said the dancer Pylades to Augustus, 'that the people should devote their spare time to us entertainers – if they do so, they will not bother about subversive politics.' According to the orator Fronto, Trajan never failed to pay meticulous attention to the stars of the theatre, circus and arena, because he knew that spectacles are necessary for the contentment of the masses. He was even of the opinion, according to the same authority, 'that the excellence of a government is shown in its amusements'. Or at least they helped to guarantee its security.

This treatment of the Roman populace was successful. The government's nervousness about their loyalty turned out, on the whole, to be unfounded. From time to time, it is true, the city mob showed signs of becoming unruly. But in the last resort they always remained controllable. The proof is that, despite recurrent official fears, it was never they who brought any of the Twelve Caesars down – and scarcely any of the subsequent Caesars either, whose violent deaths came to them from quite other sources. The inhabitants of the capital, despite their perilous proximity to the palace, proved the least of the dangers to imperial security.

The perils from army and senate, on the other hand, were far more menacing. Such plotting, remarked Tiberius, is a favourite pastime of subjects, and he declared that he, as their ruler, *was holding a wolf by the ears*. All except the very few rulers who despised such timidities were eternally preoccupied with security. The historians and biographers report a hundred measures that were taken to guard against the various perils. The praetorian prefect Macro would not even let Caligula fall asleep at a dinner-party, but 'would wake him up, in the interests both of propriety and of his safety, since a sleeping man is an easy prey for conspirators'. And every emperor took antidotes to poison.

For there were plots the whole time. Whether posterity has attached to an emperor the label 'good' or 'bad', he was a target of these seditious attempts all the same. Or were they only suspected plots, and not really authentic at all? It is never easy to tell – as the historian Dio Cassius was well aware:

> It is not practicable, of course, for those on the outside to have certain knowledge of such matters. For whatever measures a ruler takes, either personally or through the senate, for the punishment of men for alleged plots against himself, are generally looked upon with suspicion as having been done out of spite, no matter how just such measures may be.

The last of the Twelve Caesars, Domitian, had spoken in similar terms· The lot of a ruler is singularly unfortunate, he remarked, since when he discovers a conspiracy no one believes in it until he has been killed.

It was very difficult for a ruler to stop thinking of the perpetual danger at any time whatever. Almost Augustus' last words, on his deathbed, were a cry that forty young men were carrying him off.

To be a Caesar was also appallingly hard work.

This is a prosaic fact not always sufficiently emphasized by their biographers, ancient or modern. Some ancient writers, however, do not fail to make the point. Horace commiserated with Augustus on his gigantic responsibilities. And upon Tiberius at Capreae, stressed

Plutarch, 'the cares of imperial rule poured in from every quarter of the world'. Tiberius had forecast that the job would be a wretched and toilsome servitude, and he felt later that his prophecy had been perfectly right.

Claudius chose Constantia, hard-working perseverance, as a special virtue of his own for self-advertisement on the coinage. Vespasian forgave conspirators with the remark that aspirants for his job were fools not to realize what an enormous burden it was. Pliny the younger praises Trajan because he needed so little sleep. 'Thanks to his frugal diet', said Marcus Aurelius about his own predecessor Antoninus Pius, 'he could remain at work from morning till night without even attending to the calls of nature until his customary hour.'

The nineteenth-century moralist Samuel Smiles may sound ridiculous when he praises Shakespeare as 'a close student and a hard worker', and Napoleon and Wellington because they, too, were unfailingly industrious. Yet in speaking of the Caesars there is a good deal of truth in this approach. For, as Dio points out, 'affairs of the state had become so vast that they could only be administered with the greatest difficulty'. The rulers of Rome had to work almost incessantly in order to survive.

Yet the state did not provide the Caesars with any administrative assistance. The situation that resulted was anticipatory of the modern system in which, said President Woodrow Wilson, 'men of ordinary physique and discretion cannot be Presidents and live, if the strain be not somehow relieved'. It is relieved by presidential assistants and, although this system can, as recent events have shown, produce highly unsatisfactory results, at least the assistants, in Clint Rossiter's words, 'give the incumbent a sporting chance to stand the strain'.

Roman emperors, too, were plainly compelled to lighten their burden of work by bringing in friends, counsellors or secretaries. Corneille enlarges on the miseries of Augustus when such a friend let him down.

> O God above, in whom henceforth shall I confide
> The secrets of my heart, the burden of my load?
> Take back the power on me bestowed
> If, given men to rule, I am of friends deprived!

For the difficulty was to make sure you got hold of the right man. 'The chief need of the monarch', said Seneca, 'is an *honest* adviser.' But the difficulty of fulfilling this condition meant that all too frequently disaster ensued. It was like the problem of the army all over again. You had to have the imperial aides, and yet if they were powerful enough to do their job, they were also powerful enough to present a grave danger. The whole history of the Caesars could be written in terms of the men in whom they wisely or unwisely placed their trust.

But in any case the imperial secretaries and other advisers did not take on so much of the work as might nowadays be expected. 'Sovereignty cannot be shared,' the Jewish philosopher Philo imagines the Roman people as saying: 'nature's ordinance on this point is unchangeable.' And Pliny the younger tells Trajan, 'You do not have to have a partner, unless you want to.' Both these writers were thinking in terms of actual co-emperors, but the same applied to imperial counsellors and friends. Since there was one ruler and one only, their part was interpreted as an essentially subordinate one.

The ancient tradition did not comprehend sophisticated arrangements for the delegation of work. When, for example, a letter arrived for one of the Caesars, it was brought directly in for his personal perusal, and after reading it he wrote out or dictated a reply. The practice of President Herbert Hoover, who personally read and approved every letter sent by the Budget Bureau to executive agencies, would have seemed to them quite appropriate. Augustus dismissed one of the governors of his provinces because he spelt in an illiterate fashion, writing *ixi* for *ipsi*: the story shows not only that the governor had written the dispatch himself, but that the emperor himself had read it. We hear of Caligula flushing with anger as he looked through a report from his governor of Syria.

Ancient letters were not signed, but the Roman rulers added personal notes or greetings to their secretaries' drafts. They also set down a very great deal in their own hand. Augustus wrote part of his will, and Tiberius wrote the whole of one copy of his. Nerva addressed Trajan with his own hand to announce his adoption as his heir, and Trajan wrote with his own hand to the senate when he came to the throne. It was also regarded as proper that rulers should themselves compose their own public statements, written or verbal. Nero was the first to need 'someone else's eloquence'; in other words Seneca had to be employed to draft his speeches. Domitian could not express his own pronouncements in the correct form, so that others had to do it for him. But this was evidently a matter of comment: the Caesars usually did such work for themselves.

They were continually pestered, in person, with requests and petitions, in a manner which is unfamiliar in western countries today. Some of these petitions were in writing, and it was noted as distinctly unusual when Trajan, on principle, refused to answer any of these applications. The philosopher Euphrates handed Vespasian a request for gifts, expecting him to read it in private, but he read it aloud there and then.

The rulers also had to listen to innumerable verbal pleas. Indeed, if they were conscientious, the receipt of a written petition often prompted them to demand supplementary explanations by word of mouth, summoning the applicants from far off to provide them. When Tiberius asked Augustus to give Roman citizenship to a Greek client, the emperor answered that he would not grant the request unless the man appeared in person and persuaded him that his application was well founded.

The public considered that this sort of interview was very much the ruler's duty. A woman once accosted Hadrian with a petition while he was on a journey. He replied: 'I haven't time.' But she shouted after him, 'Well, stop being emperor, in that case!' And so he immediately turned back and gave her a hearing.

This was all part of the gruelling accessibility of the rulers, which greatly exceeded what is required of their counterparts today. Exceptionally accessible men such as Vespasian and Trajan are noted and praised. 'At last,' says Pliny the younger about Trajan, 'there is an end of closed doors and crowds of delegates waiting on the palace steps.' And those who like Tiberius hid themselves away were correspondingly blamed, and became the targets of malevolent rumours.

Emperors had to give receptions and make social calls and attend anniversaries and dine out and advise their friends and listen to recitations. Augustus personally taught his grandsons and ate with them. Even when he was on the point of death, he still managed to watch a party of young men doing their training at Capreae, and consented to attend a party in their honour.

A Caesar also had to spend an immense amount of time displaying himself in public at the Games and other shows. Jérôme Carcopino analysed the significance of this.

A salutary contact was thus established between the ruler and the mob, which prevented him on the one hand from shutting himself off in dangerous isolation and prevented them for their part from forgetting the august presence of the Caesar.

The moment he entered the circus or the theatre or the amphitheatre, the crowd leapt spontaneously to their feet and greeted him with a waving of handkerchiefs, as the faithful today greet the Holy Father in the Basilica of the Vatican, offering a moving salutation that had the modulation of a hymn and the accent of a prayer.

At a time when the Assembly was silent and the Senate merely repeated the lesson prescribed to it, it was only amid the merriment of the Games that public opinion could take shape and express itself in petitions suddenly echoed by thousands of voices demanding from Tiberius the Apoxyomenus of Lysippus,* and obtaining from Galba the death of Tigellinus.

The emperors developed skill in canalising this mass emotion and directing its currents, and often succeeded in transferring to the multitude the responsibility for acts of vengeance which they had already planned but preferred to execute under an appearance of popular duress.

And the rulers not only had to attend the Games frequently, to the detriment of their other occupations, but had to look as if they were enjoying these spectacles. Tiberius manifestly did not care for them at all, so that his conscientious attendance failed to stand him in good stead. Julius Caesar was sharply criticized, when he came to a public show, for reading or answering letters and petitions while the performance was going on. Augustus showed a much more ostentatious, and indeed genuine, appreciation of such entertainments and never allowed his attention to wander. If he had to leave before they were over, he excused himself and designated someone else to preside. But even when he was suffering from a fatal bowel complaint, he still managed to attend the five-yearly festival at Neapolis (Naples). Caligula sometimes arrived at the theatre before dawn. When he was attending the Games, he usually went out for a bath and lunch, and then came back. That was no hardship for him, because he was an addict, but even if he had not been, it would still have constituted a good political investment to waste his time in this way. Trajan created an excellent impression by sitting at the circus on the same level as his subjects, instead of upon an elevated dais.

•   •   •   •   •

* Tiberius had taken this famous statue, and another, for the decoration of his bedroom.

The Caesars were also expected to stand by their friends personally in lawsuits. But what seems strangest of all to our own ideas was their central and wearing role as judges. 'This is indeed', declares the younger Pliny, 'the true case of a prince' – the most essential of all his functions. Every ruler was obliged to spend an immense amount of his time deciding personally upon the multifarious problems of litigants and defendants. When Augustus, once again at the very end of his life, wanted to escort Tiberius to Beneventum, we still read of 'contestants detaining him on the judgement seat by bringing forward case after case'. Maecenas, on an earlier occasion, is seen fighting his way through the crowd which surrounded the emperor as he gave judgement. The imperial tribunal, according to Carcopino,

suggests the familiarity and popular tumult which surround the justice of an eastern pasha seated on his divan in the patio of his seraglio. . . What seems inconceivable to us is that the Romans should have tolerated this exhausting system with no attempt to modify or lighten it.

Are we to believe that their heads and nerves were more resistant to strain than ours?

It is possible that they were. But even so, they were not resistant enough, as the rest of this book will show; perhaps no human heads or nerves could have stood up to everything that they had to endure.

Part 1

From Republic to Empire

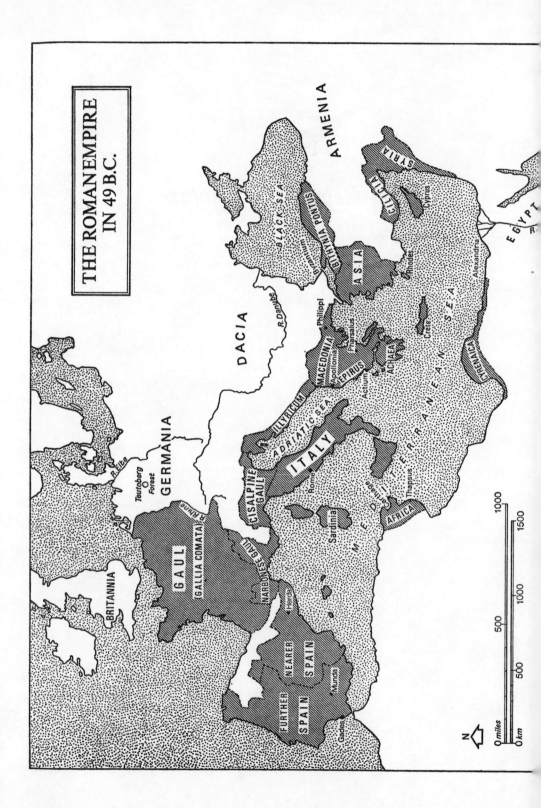

THE ROMAN EMPIRE
IN 49 B.C.

GERMANIA

BRITANNIA

GAUL
(GALLIA COMATA)

NARBONESE GAUL

CISALPINE GAUL

FURTHER
SPAIN

NEARER
SPAIN

Ilerda

Munda

Gades

Teutoberg
Forest

R. Elbe

R. Rhine

R. Danube

DACIA

ILLYRICUM

ITALY

Rome

Sardinia

AFRICA

Thapsus

MEDITERRANEAN SEA

ADRIATIC SEA

MACEDONIA

Apollonia

EPIRUS

ACHAEA

Actium

Philippi

Pharsalus

Crete

BLACK SEA

BITHYNIA PONTUS

Byzantium

ASIA

Rhodes

CILICIA

SYRIA

Cyprus

CRENAICA

EGYPT

R.

ARMENIA

N

0 miles   500   1000

0 km   500   1000   1500

I

Julius Caesar

Gaius Julius Caesar, born in 100 BC, was the son of a moderately distinguished member of an ancient but not very rich patrician family. His father's sister was the wife of the great general Marius, and Caesar himself married the daughter of Marius' successor Cinna. In about 76 she bore him a daughter, Julia, before dying about eight years later. Meanwhile Sulla, the conservative enemy of the radicals Marius and Cinna, had been dictator (82–1), and Caesar, after holding a variety of minor posts, became known as an opponent of Sulla's pro-senatorial order. In this capacity he supported the successful military commander Pompey and the millionaire Crassus, and achieved the first major success of his career by gaining election as Chief Priest in 63.

Three years later, snubbed by the senate after his governorship of Spain, he established a virtually autocratic compact with Pompey and Crassus, the informal First Triumvirate. In 59 Caesar, with this backing, secured his first consulship, in which he ruthlessly overrode opposition and disregarded the vetoes of his pro-senatorial colleague. Then, between 58 and 51, he conquered the whole of central and northern Gaul as far as the River Rhine, which he briefly crossed. In 55 and 54 he conducted two armed but unproductive reconnaissances of Britain.

During this period, however, the triumvirate, although shored up by the Conference of Luca (Lucca) in 56, began to fall apart owing to mutual jealousies. The death in 54 of Caesar's daughter Julia, who had become the wife of Pompey, removed a bond between the two men, and their confrontation was sharpened by the disappearance, in the following year, of Crassus, who was slain by Rome's eastern enemies, the Parthians.

After lengthy preliminaries civil war broke out between Caesar and Pompey in 49, and the end of the Republic was at hand.

Crossing the Rubicon from his Gallic province on 10 January, Caesar speedily overran Italy but failed to prevent Pompey from evacuating his forces to Greece. Before following him, Caesar turned to Spain, where he defeated the Pompeian army at Ilerda (Lerida). After returning briefly to Italy, Caesar left for the Balkans on 9 August overwhelmed Pompey at Pharsalus in Thessaly, whereupon the defeated leader fled to Egypt and was murdered by the government of the boy-king Ptolemy XIII. Caesar followed to Egypt and, after establishing Ptolemy's half-sister Cleopatra as his mistress and the queen, fought the Alexandrian War against the forces of the young monarch, who was defeated and killed (47). Next Caesar crushed the hostile King Pharnaces in Asia Minor – the operation which occasioned his boast 'I came, I saw, I conquered'.

Later in the year he moved to North Africa where, after four months' military operations, he crushed Pompey's sons Cnaeus and Sextus and their generals at Thapsus (Ras Dimas). He returned to Rome to celebrate his triumph, and shortly afterwards Cleopatra came from Egypt to join him. But Caesar did not stay in the capital long, departing for southern Spain where, in March 45, he fought his last battle to destroy the surviving Pompeian forces at Munda, east of Seville. Pompey's elder son Cnaeus was killed, but his brother Sextus escaped.

In such time as Caesar was able to spare from fighting, he undertook a mass of important administrative reforms. During the last months of his life, however, the rapidly intensified absolutism of his rule became disturbingly apparent to the conservative nobility who had hoped in vain for a reversion to oligarchic Republican conditions. The climax was reached in February 44 when Caesar was appointed perpetual dictator.

On 18 March he had intended to leave for the east and conduct massive campaigns against the Parthians, in order to avenge his fellow-triumvir Crassus. But three days earlier he was murdered by a group of sixty conspirators, including Marcus Brutus, Gaius, Cassius and Decimus Brutus Albinus.

Julius Caesar's appearance scarcely seemed that of a conquering general.

Caesar is said to have been tall, fair, and well-built, with a rather broad face and keen, dark-brown eyes. He was something of a dandy, always keeping his head carefully trimmed and shaved; and has been accused of having certain other hairy parts of his body depilated with tweezers. His baldness was a disfigurement which his enemies harped upon, much to his exasperation; but he used to comb the thin strands of hair forward on the top of his head, and of all the honours voted him by the Senate and People none pleased him so much as the privilege of wearing a laurel wreath on all occasions – he constantly took advantage of it.

His dress was, it seems, unusual: he had added wrist-length sleeves with fringes to his purple-striped senatorial tunic, and the belt which he wore over it was never tightly fastened – hence Sulla's warning to the aristocratic party: 'Beware of that boy with the loose clothes.'[1]

Equally disconcerting, and indeed unnerving, was Caesar's extraordinary charm. Whenever he chose to exhibit it, the people in whose company he found himself were overwhelmed by the fascinating manner, amusing conversation and hilarious good humour of this supremely courteous, cultivated, urbane man.

But the gift which contributed most largely to his success was an abnormally energetic ability to get things done. This was conspicuously apparent in the occupation of warfare in which he excelled all his rivals.

Caesar was a most skilful swordsman and horseman, and showed surprising powers of endurance. He always led his army, more often on foot than in the saddle, went bareheaded in sun and rain alike. If he reached an unfordable river he would either swim or propel himself across it on an inflated skin, and often arrived at his destination before the messengers whom he had sent ahead to announce his approach.[2]

In light, four-wheeled carriages, bumping and jolting along highly imperfect roads and tracks, Caesar could cover a hundred miles a day, twice the pace of an average traveller. And while he was on his way he did not just look out at the countryside; for he composed a two volume work *On Analogy* during a crossing of the Alps, and a poem 'The Journey' on an exhausting twenty-seven-day land journey from Rome to southern Spain. These works, if he wrote them down in person, had to be composed in daytime, since the light cannot have been good enough to write after dark. But perhaps he dictated them, because he often spent the nights in his carriage or litter, so as to be able to get on with his work. 'I have heard', reported the elder Pliny, 'that Caesar was accustomed to write or dictate and read at the same time, simultaneously dictating to his secretaries four letters on the most important subjects or, if he had nothing else to do, as many as seven.'[3] He also spent a great deal of time on his judicial duties, administering justice with the utmost conscientiousness and strictness. And yet, despite these and innumerable other occupations, he also managed to make himself as accessible as he could.

The point was that he could do everything with extraordinary speed. The orator Cicero, who hated him utterly, described his rapidity at the beginning of the Civil War as something horrifying and monstrous. Caesar lived at a faster tempo than the people who had to contend with him, and this gave him an enormous advantage, offering the widest scope to that capacity for the unexpected, unpredictable action, which his friends found such an irresistibly attractive feature of his talents.

Such were the qualities which enabled him to dwell self-confidently, even complacently, on his own luck (*fortuna*). 'Let the dice fly high!' he is supposed to have cried out, as he made that fateful crossing of the Rubicon: and it was just the sort of thing he was likely to say. A curious large number of the emperors who followed him enjoyed gambling games as a relaxation, but to the ancients Julius Caesar, above all, was the gambler with fortune itself, throwing dice for the mastery of the world.

At first sight Caesar's attribution of his successes to good luck sounds like modesty. But it was not. Luck seemed to himself and his contemporaries the intangible something which conferred real greatness, and cast an aura of the supernatural around human achievements. Besides, just as the early Benedictines, when they said 'work is prayer', implied that praying had to be followed up by hard endeavour, so Caesar, too, took pains to point out that luck did not come by itself, but had to be won by grasping its gifts at the right moment. 'If things do not go as they should', he remarked to his soldiers in 48 BC, 'we must help fortune by efforts of our own.'[4]

In most of what he did – though not quite everything, as we shall see – clear vision of this kind was Caesar's outstanding characteristic: the product of exceptional brain-power guided by a will of steel. Even Cicero, when he saw Antony trying to step into the dead dictator's shoes, knew that the anti-climax was absurd. 'Your ambition to reign, Antony, certainly deserves to be compared with Caesar's. But in not a single other respect are you entitled to the same comparison ... His character was an amalgamation of genius, method, memory, culture, thoroughness, intellect and industry.'⁵

Cicero goes on to admit that Caesar's achievements in war, though he regarded them as disastrous for Rome, were nothing less than spectacular. His conquest of Gaul was a decisive act in world history, by which central Europe was opened up to the Mediterranean civilization. To some of his contemporaries – in spite of the Roman taste for aggression – it was clear enough that he had deliberately, gratuitously and illegally launched a major foreign war to satisfy his personal ambitions, and had then prosecuted it with unequalled brutality and treachery, slaughtering, he himself claimed (with some, but not total, exaggeration), as many as 430,000 Germans on one day. What could not be denied, however, was that the conquest of Gaul was a marvellous, portentous, feat of arms. True there had been crises and set-backs, but they were temporary, and they were overcome. Starting with a veteran army less than forty thousand strong, he won in the end with utter decisiveness. In the subsequent Civil War, too, there were grave emergencies – in Epirus, Alexandria and southern Spain. But once again he proved totally victorious. Given these results, it seems useless to criticize Caesar's strategy and tactics from a modern armchair.

His army was the most potent, effective, responsive martial instrument the world had ever seen. Its traditional talents were raised to a new red-hot capacity by its commander. The weapons that his forefathers had placed in his hands he exploited with incomparable skill; and in a whole number of different specialist fields – camp-building, armaments, tactics, intelligence training methods, and command structure – he added numerous innovations of his own. As a general, he was as versatile as he was perilously incalculable: not only a frightening military intellectual whose versatility posed a perpetual riddle to his opponents, but a man who was totally committed, determined and indefatigable – physically courageous beyond measure, and, in the words of the poet Lucan:

> Thinking naught done while aught remained to do ...
>   His manhood knew
> No rest – his only shame to lose a fight.
> Keen and untamed, where hope or anger called,

33

He turned his hand, nor quailed to stain his sword . . .
To make a path by havoc was his joy.[6]

Caesar's successes were largely due to his personal relationship with his troops. Their two mutinies at Placentia (Piacenza) in 49 and in Campania in 47 BC – emergencies which enabled Caesar to display that expertise as a military orator which played such an important part in an ancient commander's life – were only minor incidents in a long, close, association with his troops which was almost amorous in its mutual intensity. He knew exactly how to treat his men, when to loosen the rein and when to tighten it, and they followed him loyally for year after year – not only because they admired his glamorous personality, but because they deeply respected his military skill.

They needed him too; because, when the time for their demobilization finally came, it would be he, and no one but he, who could secure them their rewards. And he needed them because it was only through their support that he could ward off personal ruin from himself. Ever since that first consulship of 59 BC, in which he committed many illegalities, his political enemies had been lying in wait. As long as he held office as a commander or state official, they would not be able to lay hands on him. But as soon as he reverted to private life, they could prosecute him and bring him down to utter ruin. And this they were determined to do.

During the course of the Civil War he was perfectly frank in admitting that the reason why he was fighting was to avoid this fate. Or rather, he was perfectly frank for part of the time; because his excellent propaganda machine also thought up many high reasons of state and morality to explain his defiance – the sanctity of the tribunes, the liberty of the people, and so on – just as Pompey piously asserted that he, for his part, was defending the authority of the senate. Nevertheless Caesar also went so far as to admit that he was waging the Civil War *for the sake of his personal position* – meaning, he explained, that after he had won such great distinction in Gaul, he owed it to himself to resist the ignominy his political enemies had in store for him. Soon after he had crossed the Rubicon, he admitted and emphasized this personal motive to a Pompeian deputation. 'My position', he told them, 'has always been of prime importance to me, even outweighing life itself. It pained me to see the privilege conferred on me by the Roman people being insultingly wrested from me by my enemies.'[7] On that occasion he was treating it as a matter of honour, and honour was a vital element in the Republican aristocratic tradition in which he had been brought up. Yet when he surveyed the victorious, corpse-strewn battlefield of Pharsalus, it was in terms, not of honour, but of saving his own skin that he redefined the point. 'Despite all my achievements', he cried to his friends, 'I should have been condemned, if I had not appealed to my army for help!'

This was true enough. However, as later rulers realized, it is not always profitable, in the long run, to admit that what you are doing is being done from purely egotistical motives. Besides Caesar was now proceeding to pile new illegalities upon old ones. It was illegal of him to cross the Rubicon, because as governor of his province of Gaul, which included Cisalpine Gaul (now northern Italy), he was not permitted by the constitution to cross the border stream, the Rubicon, into Italy. For this reason, when he traversed the little river, he performed special religious rites, in order to dispel fears of sacrilege because of the blasphemous nature of his unconstitutional action.

But what aroused far greater horror was the fratricidal bloodshed of the Civil War which was thus unleashed. And for this he could not be altogether exonerated. To the poet Lucan, a hundred years later, the bloody carnage of Pharsalus seemed Caesar's fault:

> Man nor arms could stay
> The crash of onset, and the furious sword
> Clove through the stubborn panoply to the flesh,
> There only stayed.
> One army struck – their foes
> Struck not in answer; Magnus' swords were cold,
> But Caesar's reeked with slaughter and with guilt.
> Nor Fortune lingered, but decreed the doom
> Which swept the ruins of a world away.[8]

And yet the defects of the Republican cause which opposed him were equally bad, or even worse. The poet Lucretius, writing in the 50s BC, had seen around him a society sick of feuds and utterly weary of violence. The Roman noblemen of these years seemed to have lost their earlier talent for government altogether. The constitution they stood for was totally failing to control the ambitions of the individuals to whom they were obliged to entrust armies; and the nobles themselves were, for the most part, a murky lot.

For several decades before the Civil War, therefore, the senate's constructive achievement had been non-existent. Not surprisingly, Roman thought, throughout this entire period, was inclining towards the idea that the Republic needed some sort of 'guide' (*rector*). Not, indeed, anything so drastic as a monarch. Yet the idea that some sort of leadership would have to be found is prominent, for example, in Cicero's essay *On the State*. Indeed, after the Ides of March Brutus wrote to Cicero blaming him and people like him for their despair of the Republic which had positively encouraged and tempted Caesar to grasp the supreme power for himself.

Although the Rubicon is only a trivial brook, its crossing by Caesar was a decisive moment, since it meant that the illusion of an aristocratic, senatorial, basically civilian Republic was gone for ever. From now on Caesar was autocrat in all the territories under his sway, and during the next four years he gradually brought the entire empire under his control. 'With the army of the Roman people', declared Cicero, 'he subjected the Roman people to oppression and enslavement!'

The constitutional methods Caesar employed in order to exercise his supremacy were varied. He accepted an extensive array of titles and offices. Augustus' subsequent, prudent, concern to economize as much as possible in outward manifestations of power held no interest for him at all.

One ominous title he adopted was '*imperator*', which had hitherto meant 'general' but was now employed by Caesar to mean '*the* general'. Moreover, in succession to his notorious first consulship of 59 BC, he allowed himself, as absolute ruler, to be elected to a whole series of further tenures of the office, in 48, 46, 45 and 44. This had its administrative conveniences, since the consuls enjoyed easy means for getting things done; but the continued repetition was out of keeping with traditional practices. The strain became particularly conspicuous in 46, when the senate enacted that, having resigned from his consulship during the course of the year, he should have the seat of honour between the two consuls, and should speak first, if he wished to, in every senatorial debate. Furthermore his assumption, at the same time, of a somewhat vague 'prefecture of morals' – or rather, of customs, traditions, institutions – gave him an enhanced version of the powers of the antique Republican censors, who, elected every five years, had possessed the right, during their eighteen-month tenure, of controlling membership of the senate.

Yet these powers were secondary and unnecessary – and therefore over-emphatic – because the basis of Caesar's rule, and a basis from which he could take action in any direction that he pleased, was the dictatorship.

This, like the office of censor, was an ancient feature of the Roman constitution. But the men traditionally appointed as dictator 'to carry on affairs', empowered to control all other officials and exempted from vetoes and appeals, were appointed by the senate (on a consul's nomi-nation) in emergency situations only, and never for more than six months at a time. In the third century BC the importance of the dictator-ship had declined, and it came to be used increasingly for comparatively minor purposes such as the conduct of elections or the celebration of festivals. The office was momentarily revived as an important instrument of state during the invasion of Italy by the Carthaginian Hannibal in the Second Punic War. But after the third year of that war, 216 BC, the dictatorship was never again utilized for its original purpose, because the senators did not like its overbearing powers. From 202 onwards even dictators with more limited functions ceased to be appointed.

In the early first century BC, however, the dictatorship appeared once again. After Sulla had won a terrible civil war against the followers of Marius, he arranged in 82 for the Assembly of the People to pass a law appointing him to this office so that he could claim he was occupying it by popular consent. And there were other novelties too: Sulla's appoint-ment was 'for the purpose of making laws and setting the state to rights', and it was of indefinite duration. However, at the end of 81, after energetic legislative activity, Sulla abdicated from his dictatorship, and, after a further year as consul, retired into private life. Soon afterwards he died.

His measures had not been designed to suppress the senate but to allow time for the re-establishment of its authority. Yet, during the thirty years that followed, the Sullan regime gradually foundered, and when people like Cicero began speaking of the need for the Republic to have a guide they were sometimes prepared to envisage the return to a temporary, orthodox, dictatorship. And this was one of the constitu-tional solutions which Julius Caesar first envisaged – though he had to bring it about in an unusual manner. After his Spanish campaign of 49 he wanted to secure election as consul for the following year. This was what he had aimed at all along, and this is what his enemies had tried to keep from him. But the consular elections for 48 could not be held since the consuls empowered to hold them had fled to Pompey. In their absence, therefore, Marcus Aemilius Lepidus – who was praetor, the office next in seniority to the consulship – was requested by Caesar to arrange for the Assembly to nominate him as dictator.

How the powers of his office, on this occasion, were defined is not quite certain, but the purpose for which he used it was to conduct the consular elections for the next year – at which he was both returning officer and successful candidate. At the end of the year, on becoming consul, he duly abdicated his dictatorship.

He became dictator for the second time in October 48, after defeating Pompey at Pharsalus, and for the third time – probably by popular election – after returning from North Africa in 46. This time his powers were certainly of a comprehensive nature, resembling Sulla's: and a sinister novelty lay in their conferment for not less than ten years. However there were still, apparently as a concession to public opinion, annual renewals of a formal nature, since at the beginning of the fatal year 44 Caesar called himself dictator for the *fourth* time, as his coins specifically record.

Then, at some date between 20 January and 15 February of that year, he assumed the office of 'Perpetual Dictator'. This was a very different matter from the dictatorship of Sulla, who, although appointed for an indeterminate duration, had in fact very quickly resigned. Caesar's new title showed explicitly that he had not the slightest intention of acting likewise. Indeed he commented that Sulla, by resigning, showed that he did not know his ABC.

The novelty was tremendous. None of the previous eighty-three dictators had held office more than temporarily, and to do otherwise directly negated and violated the traditional character of the office. How did Caesar's mind work when he made himself perpetual dictator? It cannot have escaped his notice that what he was doing would shock the traditionalists. But either he must have concluded that this did not matter, since it was pointless to attempt to cloak or conceal his unmistakable autocracy, or he may have reckoned that the perpetual dictatorship, even if it strained and stretched the constitution, still did not actually break it.

All such conclusions, however, were miscalculated. Caesar had gravely underestimated the desire of the aristocracy to avoid dotting the i's and crossing the t's of absolute rule. He had also failed to appreciate that what he might have described as straining or stretching the constitution others would undoubtedly regard as shattering it to pieces. A perpetual dictatorship was unthinkable, in official terms because it permanently abrogated the sovereign rights of the Roman people, and unofficially because it meant that *never again*, at least in Caesar's lifetime, would the nobles be allowed to compete with the dictator, or with each other, for the real control of the state, and the pickings that went with it. As Cicero asserted later, this was a dictatorship 'which had already usurped the might of tyrannical authority'.

Recent history, it was true, had proved the total inadequacy of the old Republican institutions for the conduct of Rome's huge and wealthy empire. Something had to be done. But what Caesar did to remedy this was totally unacceptable to the other leading men of the state. His outstanding intellect, at this juncture, displayed an astonishing and fatal lack of foresight. He did not apparently see, or did not care, that this abrupt formula of the dictatorship, with all temporal limits removed, was not subtle or sophisticated or outwardly unpretentious enough to be endurable by an upper class with an ancient tradition of political self-expression. Dio Cassius rightly stresses that Caesar's failure to reject the office of perpetual dictator brought disaster upon himself. For he paid for the miscalculation with his life. The perpetual dictatorship was a peremptory cause of the senatorial conspiracy which brought about his murder.

But it was by no means the only cause. The almost numberless distinctions that the senate itself voted him, whether he accepted them or not, 'decked him', in the vivid words of the historian Florus, 'garlanded for the sacrifice'. Indeed more than a few senators may have maliciously voted for this accumulation of honours in the deliberate hope of making his position seem outrageous, and thus causing his death.

Other actions performed by Caesar actively contributed to this same result. In particular, there was the difficult, delicate question of his helpers.

The only helper that the state authorized a dictator to possess was an official deputy, described by the archaic and irrelevant title of Master of the Horse. This deputy, who ranked with the praetors, derived his powers from the dictator, and the commissions of the two men came to an end at the same time. Caesar's Masters of the Horse were Antony (48–7) and then Lepidus (46–4).

Antony, during his tenure of the office, acted unwisely, and Lepidus was a mediocrity. But even if they had both behaved satisfactorily the practical assistance which a single deputy could contribute to the gigantic amount of business piling up on the dictator's table was negligible. He could not have obtained part-time help from the consuls and praetors, who continued, it is true, to exist under a dictatorship, but had distinct, though subordinate, spheres of their own in the state administration. One attempt, it is true, was made to deal with this problem by a constitutional innovation, when Caesar, about to leave for Spain in 45 BC, arranged the appointment of eight prefects, with armed cohorts, to assist Lepidus to manage affairs at Rome during his absence – an unwelcome arrangement to the traditional ruling class, who felt by-passed. But for the most part Caesar, and his Master of the Horse if he was away, had to rely upon the services of purely personal appointees to help them carry on the business of the dictatorship.

There were precedents for this, on a smaller scale, since Republican notables had habitually employed their own personal advisers; and in recent years Pompey had made use of a small team of them. Moreover Caesar himself, while in Gaul, had utilized the labours of half-a-dozen private helpers who seemed, to exasperated Republicans, a sort of illegal inner council or even two councils – one of them accompanying him at his headquarters, and the other representing his interests in Rome. And after the Gallic War he kept these men on, assembling them in his own residence, or keeping them at work for him in their own homes. The personal staff of the proconsul of Gaul had become transformed into a sort of informal cabinet assisting the dictator.

Within this group, two men, both devoted to Caesar, and neither of them members of the senate, had become outstandingly influential. They were Oppius and Balbus, both members of the order of the knights which came next after the senators. Gaius Oppius probably belonged to a substantial family of Roman bankers; Caesar, in some wild and distant land, had once saved his life. Like his patron, Oppius was a writer, the author of *Lives* of Scipio and probably of Caesar himself, to which he added other biographies later on. But he spent most of the time doing political work for Caesar, on whose behalf, for example, we find him corresponding with Cicero.

Lucius Cornelius Balbus was a more exotic figure. Born in about 100 BC, he came from Gades (Cadiz in southern Spain), where he became the virtual ruler of his city. Although probably of Semitic extraction – Phoenician or Carthaginian – he was given Roman citizenship in 72 by Pompey, under whom he had served in a Spanish war. In 60 he acted as a highly effective go-between in the negotiations between Pompey, Crassus and Caesar which led to the formation of the First Triumvirate. A year or so later he was adopted by Pompey's tame historian Theophanes as his son, thus inheriting enormous wealth, which in due course enabled him to purchase estates at Tusculum and in Rome itself. During these years, however, Balbus was gradually shifting his allegiance from Pompey to Caesar, whom he served as aide de camp in Spain and then again during the Gallic War. Subsequently, in Gaul but mainly in Rome, he acted as manager of Caesar's most important interests, controlling his correspondence and access to his person, and leaving his own personal mark on every negotiation and intrigue that took place. In the Civil War he was ostensibly neutral, but in fact on Caesar's side, and after Pharsalus he and Oppius became the dictator's chief agents for the administration of public affairs. We catch a glimpse of him in a letter written by Cicero in 45 in which Caesar is seen working through-out the morning at his accounts, closeted with Balbus, and receiving no one else.

Indefatigable and inseparable, Oppius and Balbus were always on the job. In 49, for instance, when Caesar wanted a policy announcement to become widely known, he chose to frame it in a letter addressed jointly to this pair. And four years later, when Cicero drafted a letter to Caesar advising him how to restore the Republic, it was Oppius and Balbus who recommended the orator to revise it thoroughly before dis-patch, since his views stood no chance of receiving the dictator's favourable attention as they stood. Tacitus rightly saw in these two men the first knights, that is to say non-senators, in the history of Rome who became 'important enough to decide issues of peace and war' – proto-types of the powerful secretaries whom emperors were to employ in subsequent epochs.

The influential position of Oppius and Balbus made them exceedingly unpopular with the senators. Conservatives must have been overjoyed in 56 when Balbus, not without prompting from themselves, was prosecuted on the charge of usurping Roman citizenship. But with

Pompey, Crassus and a subservient Cicero to defend him, his acquittal was a foregone conclusion.

After Caesar, during the Civil War, had gone away to fight campaigns in North Africa and Spain, the most powerful people left in Rome were not his successive Masters of the Horse, or the special prefects appointed to assist them, but his own personal representatives Oppius and Balbus. Yet the nobles, who might, with difficulty, resign themselves to queueing up for interviews with the dictator, found it a grave humiliation to wait in the ante-rooms of jumped-up knights. In 46 Cicero had hopefully written to a friend: 'Caesar makes his own decisions, and does not rely on those of others.' But once he went away this was clearly true no longer. When, therefore, in the early days of 44, it became clear that Caesar was going away to campaign in the east for at least three years, the prospect of having Oppius and Balbus as virtual masters for all that time was appalling. Here, then, was another pressing reason for the conspiracy which brought about his assassination.

Meanwhile the dictator, with the assistance of these collaborators, had been rapidly pushing through a huge programme of administrative reforms, many of which show a keen desire for social justice.

One of the greatest problems of the age, for example, was the existence of numberless debtors, greatly augmented by successive periods of civil strife. The harsh laws customary in the ancient world permitted money-lenders to bleed these people white. Over a period of several years Caesar passed a whole series of legislative measures to relieve their position. Creditors, in certain cases, lost about 25 per cent of their entitlement. They had feared even worse, for the dictator had been suspected of planning a general, revolutionary attack on private property. But this never materialized. His debt-laws, though far-reaching, were politically moderate. 'Rather than rob you of your possessions', he assured property-owners, 'I shall do my best to be rich *with* you.'

Caesar also embarked on a novel programme involving the settling of Roman citizens *en bloc* in the provinces, a policy which traditionalists had always shied at. Over thirty of these 'colonies', with lands attached, were formed or projected. The granting of such plots of land, whether in Italy or elsewhere, to discharged soldiers was a prime necessity, on which Caesar's very existence depended. But he also enlarged these settlements by nearly a hundred thousand impoverished civilians from the capital, thus making it possible to effect a corresponding diminution of the grain dole distributed to its parasitic population.

In carrying out this large colonization scheme, he did his best to avoid the dispossession of existing owners of land, except for a few who had seized properties illegally in the time of Sulla. And so this, like many of Caesar's other plans, cost a great deal of money. Indeed Machiavelli expressed the opinion that, if the dictator had lived on, he would have been obliged to moderate his expenditure in order to escape otherwise inevitable disaster. Yet that is a doubtful conclusion, since Caesar, although he spent a large part of his earlier life feverishly trying to raise money, had by now reaped such an enormous financial harvest from the Gallic Wars that he was very rich indeed, as the celebrations of his Triumphs displayed with unprecedented lavishness.

Meanwhile, not only was he dispatching Roman citizens far and wide as settlers, but he also substantially increased the total number of citizens in the empire as a whole. Once again, however, he proceeded without revolutionary excesses – without, that is to say, destroying the historic character of the citizen body as a relatively small elite among the large populations of the empire.

In the course of this process, however, corruption was not unknown. For example, Caesar's own personal secretary Faberius, who had been able to afford a palace on the Aventine Hill, was believed to be only one of a number of people who had made huge profits from selling awards of Roman citizenship. Nevertheless such unfortunate incidents were only the almost inevitable by-products of a varied programme which, had it not been cut off by Caesar's death, would have taken shape as a coherent, comprehensive attempt to promote equitable government and economic expansion in Italy and the Roman world.

The dictator was intensely busy, almost busier than the human frame could stand.

Like many Roman rulers after him, he hoped to have the cooperation of the senate in his many administrative tasks. But this assistance was not readily forthcoming. So he raised the senate's membership from Sulla's figure of six hundred to nine hundred in order to make sure that his own supporters had a clear majority. As he himself remarked, 'even if bandits and cut-throats had helped to defend my position in the state, I would have rewarded even them with the gratitude they deserved.'

However the new senators, even if they included their quota of bandits and cut-throats, were mostly people of a very different stamp – solid officers and business-men and Italian municipal politicians. There were also just a few notables from outside Italy. They originated from southern Gaul, which was virtually Italian in culture, and indeed the new senators may even have been not Gauls at all, but men of Roman origin. But even so their importation stirred up the narrowest caste-prejudices among metropolitan conservatives, who made jokes about individuals in baggy Gallic trousers wandering round Rome and asking people where the senate house was.

With the senate thus adjusted to his plans, Caesar prompted it to issue many decrees to implement his policies. But there was so much work to be done that the prompting could not always be undertaken very tactfully. For example, he himself did not always find the time to attend the senate in person, and instead summoned small groups of senior senators to come and see him. Or, if he did manage to call a full meeting of the senate, he was quite likely merely to inform it of his decisions, which were then, without debate, forthwith entered in the records as senatorial decrees. Sometimes senators found their names recorded as witnesses to transactions of which they were wholly un-aware; for example, Cicero complained that he was receiving thanks from foreign princes he had never heard of, for honorific decrees of which he had no knowledge whatever. And so when someone happened to remark, gazing at the sky, that a certain constellation was due to rise in the sky during the following night, he made a bitter joke – 'No doubt it has received orders to do so!'

Caesar was also careless and high-handed about the hallowed pro-cedures for the annual election of state officials. In several years of his dictatorship the senior officials were not elected at all until the summer or autumn of their actual year of office, a whole year late. Moreover, on the last day of 45, one of the consuls died, and the dictator arranged the election of a successor for the last few hours of the year (without even bothering to get the procedure right). His purpose, no doubt, was to confer the prize of consular rank upon a loyal supporter. But Cicero commented that it was a peculiar term of office indeed in which no one had any lunch and the consul got no sleep.

Moreover a measure was now passed giving Caesar the right to recommend half the candidates in the election of all officials except the consuls; and the consuls, too, may have been included in this patronage in a subsequent bill. Such powers were very un-Republican – and unnecessary, too, since it was just as easy for him to control the elections informally through his supporters. One way and another, as Suetonius remarked, he could confer any office or honour he wished according to his pleasure. And then, to Republican ways of thinking, matters took a turn for the worse once again in 44, when Caesar was about to leave for the east, and his future acts were declared valid *in advance*. He was also granted authority to name officials for three whole years ahead; whereupon the consuls for both 43 and 42 were speedily elected within a matter of weeks or days.

So many things were happening which traditionalists found quite insufferable. The Caesar-hater Cato, alcoholic, unforgiving, impeccably honest, had killed himself at Utica after his side had been defeated in the North African campaign of 46. Yet Cato, as the arch-Republican, at once became a popular myth, and when Caesar gloatingly displayed a picture of his death at his Triumph the public received this with disfavour. Cicero and Brutus wrote eulogies of Cato, and the legend – still flourishing in the pages of Dante – rapidly took root and grew. Caesar was aware of this embarrassing spectre, and the eulogies directed towards it stung him into writing an abusive *Anti-Cato*.

On the whole, however, he did not let this political opposition upset him. Already at the beginning of the Civil War he had formed the unfamiliar idea of extending clemency to his Roman opponents – a sharp contrast to the brutalities he had inflicted on recalcitrant Gauls and Germans. And this merciful policy he persistently pursued, so that the senate dedicated a temple to the Clemency of Caesar, and it is to be seen on official coins. In pursuance of his plan the dictator took pains to concede Cicero's obsequious appeals for an amnesty to distinguished noblemen still in exile. Later, however, after the Ides of March, the orator was less fulsome: 'By a mixture of intimidation and indulgence,' he declared, 'Caesar inculcated in a free community the habit of servitude.' For although this clemency had proved a clever inspiration, it was not a traditional Republican virtue but the quality of a tyrant, which must have seemed a patronizing insult to the dignity of the nobles. Caesar knew he had enemies, but believed he could break their opposition by continuing to pardon them. It was a contemptuous attitude, and turned out to be yet another of the miscalculations that contributed to his downfall. Over two centuries later the emperor Septimius Severus pointed out its unwisdom, and the senate of his day, listening to him, trembled.

In his last few months Caesar's contempt seemed to separate him from the ordinary range of humanity since 'he allowed honours to be bestowed on him which were too great for mortal man.' Such honours even included his own enshrinement in the state worship, with a priest, Antony, devoted to his cult. It could be argued that this measure was in his honour rather than for his worship. Yet this was not a very substantial distinction, and no one could help thinking of the Greek monarchies of the east where the kings, all-powerful helpers or destroyers, were traditionally elevated to divine status in their lifetimes.

Because of such developments during those fatal last months the German historian Eduard Meyer suggested that Caesar was aiming at the creation of a new monarchical state on Hellenistic lines. But this theory is not borne out by the rest of our evidence. It is true that in 46 Caesar had been followed to Rome by his mistress Cleopatra, who may have borne him a son and remained in the city until his death: and Cleopatra was a thoroughgoing exponent of divine Hellenistic monarchy. Moreover she evidently supplied Egyptian experts to help him in a number of his governmental reforms. But there is no reason to suppose that she inspired him with any Greek monarchical ideas. At most she may have influenced him to treat his political enemies with even greater contempt than he had felt for them before – since that was her attitude to her own opponents at home.

However, even if Greek theories of kingship failed to intrigue Caesar, that did not mean that he shrank from becoming an autocrat. Already in 49 Cicero was writing to his friend Atticus, 'The man no longer refuses to be called a tyrant, in fact he practically demands it – and that is exactly what he is.' And three years later the orator was again sadly remarking, 'All power has been placed in the hands of one man.' Indeed Caesar, true to his denunciation of Sulla as a fool because he had not kept his dictatorship for life, was heard declaring that the Republic was nothing – a mere name without form and substance – and that since his word was now law, people ought to be more careful how they spoke to him. It was rumoured that he had harboured autocratic ambitions for years, and his supreme command in Gaul seemed to have made him unfit for anything else. When passing, on one occasion, through an Alpine village he was said to have remarked, 'I would rather be the first man among these humble mountaineers than the second man in Rome.'

However that may be, he was now the first man in Rome, divided by a vast gulf from those who came next. 'There is nothing I desire more,' he observed, 'than that I should be true to myself and others to themselves.' The historian Macaulay considered this to be the finest sentence anyone had ever uttered. Yet it surely displays an unconcealed feeling of personal superiority. At the outset of the Civil War he had at first tried to win the senate over to his plans by persuasion. However he was very soon heard saying that, if the senators would not cooperate, he would run the state on his own. Towards the end of his life, when consuls and senate came to him with a mass of honorific, flattering, grovelling, pronouncements, he did not even bother to rise to his feet to receive them.

This unhappy incident, which his advisers failed to explain away satisfactorily, took place outside the temple which he was building in honour of his alleged divine ancestress, Venus. Already twenty-five years earlier, Caesar had publicly boasted that the blood both of gods and kings flowed in his veins. There had been no kings at Rome since their ejection nearly five centuries earlier, and kingship was detested as the very antithesis of everything the free Republic stood for. Yet now Caesar's image was seen standing among the statues of those antique, semi-mythical Roman monarchs. He was also voted various outward emblems and trappings that were reminiscent of this ancient royalty. Moreover his portrait began to appear on the Roman coinage, as had never fallen to the lot of any living Roman before.

It was hardly surprising, in these circumstances, if word began to circulate that he intended to revive the kingship in his own favour. Comic songs accusing him of these regal ambitions were going the rounds, and on the pedestal of the statue of Lucius Brutus, the legendary personage who was believed to have expelled the last of the kings of Rome, someone wrote a verse declaring that he had virtually become their successor:

> Brutus was elected consul
>   When he sent the kings away;
> Caesar sent the consuls packing –
>   Caesar is our king today.[9]

All this may have seemed a subject for jesting among the masses of the population. But to the upper class it was a deadly serious matter. 'What made Caesar most openly and mortally hated', wrote Plutarch, 'was his passion to be king.' Such suspicions undoubtedly added fuel to the hatred felt for him by senators. But to suggest that Caesar actually intended to make himself king was incorrect. He had no need whatever to take such an unpopular step, since his perpetual dictatorship already gave him all the powers he wanted. It was one thing to accept a lot of titles and honours, but even the negligent Caesar saw it would be quite another matter to assume the kingship.

So he deliberately scotched the rumour. At the festival of the Lupercalia on 15 February 44 it was arranged that Antony should offer him the royal diadem in public, so that he could publicly reject it, and place his rejection on record.

On 18 March he was due to leave for the east, for his campaign against the Parthians; and on the way back it was supposed that he might destroy the Dacian empire, centring on the lands that form the modern Rumania. As we have seen, he did not expect to return until 41.

Caesar had already undertaken a great deal of useful legislation in Rome. But there was still a gigantic amount that needed to be done, and it was a strange decision to shelve it all. This plan to leave the capital and stay away for years reveals the workings of Caesar's mind and character as vividly as anything he ever planned. Plutarch's diagnosis was that he urgently wanted new glory 'as though he had exhausted the rest – a kind of rivalry with his own self'. And, after all, fighting was the most exciting indulgence he could find for himself. It was his own chosen field of action, where he would be freed from grumbling Republicans, and enlivened by the heady stimulus of an admiring soldiery. He was a man of fifty-six who had lived too hard, and was showing signs of wear. Yet he was only too ready to live the Gallic War all over again, in order to get away from the stifling atmosphere of the capital into an open-air world where his mastery over men and events could be allowed the fullest expression.

However to leave Rome at this juncture, and to go so far away for so long, was the height of irresponsibility. It was the ultimate assertion that, for all Caesar's greatness, his statesmanship was flawed by startling defects.

To the Roman nobles, his imminent departure brutally underlined their subjection to the perpetual dictatorship. For them it was the ultimate blow. Already a year earlier the eminent jurist Servius Sulpicius Rufus had written to Cicero, 'Think how unkindly fate has already treated us, robbing us of things that should be as dear to men as their children – country, reputation, position, our whole career.' And now the last phantom vestiges of the old noble rule had been ruthlessly dissolved. The tyranny could no longer be endured.

Caesar knew he was not loved by the former governing class. How could he be, he said, when he had to keep even a good man like Cicero waiting for an interview? Surely it needed only a minimum of foresight to see that conspiracy must be in the air. Yet Caesar's reaction was remarkable. He had previously employed a personal bodyguard of tough Spaniards. But instead of increasing the numbers of these guardsmen, he decided, in spite of remonstrances from his advisers, to dismiss them from his service altogether. Nobody would benefit from killing him anyway, he remarked, since his murder would only bring chaos. Was he not introducing a new justice and efficiency into the Roman world? Besides, he was totally unafraid of death, and aristocratically disdainful of measures designed to defend himself against it. In this he resembled General De Gaulle, but differed from almost all the other Roman Caesars, who mostly went in continual fear of assassination. When all the senators swore to protect his life, he can scarcely have regarded their oath as an adequate substitute for his bodyguard. But he did not care.

And so the plot began. There had been attempts on his life before, and a good deal of talk about others. One of his generals – Gaius Trebonius – had hinted to Antony that some violent change might be necessary; though Antony had not responded. Now, however, the fatal step began to be seriously discussed.

The prime mover was Gaius Cassius Longinus, a stern, proud nobleman who had come over to Caesar's side after Pharsalus. His idealistic brother-in-law Marcus Brutus, who had likewise transferred his allegiance from the Pompeians at that time, was persuaded to join the plot – out of loyalty to the memory of Cato, and of his own legendary ancestor who had expelled the ancient kings. Another conspirator was Brutus' distant relative Decimus Brutus Albinus, one of Caesar's most prominent and favoured officers. It was significant that the dictator had failed to keep the loyalty of his best lieutenants such as Decimus – and Trebonius, who likewise took his place among the prospective assassins.

During a series of secret talks these individuals were joined by various small groups of malcontents, and a single body of sixty conspirators was finally formed. We know the names of twenty of them. In the Civil War nine had fought for Pompey and seven for Caesar in Gaul. Their individual, personal, motives were various. But Marcus Brutus spoke for all of them when he said: 'I hold slavery and the sufferance of indignities in deeper loathing than all other misfortunes.'

And so came the Ides, and the fatal blows were struck. As the slayers brandished their daggers around their screaming victim, only two out of all the senators who had recently sworn to protect him tried to intervene; and they tried in vain.

Caesar's prophecy was fulfilled. His assassination brought prolonged chaos and anarchy. Ever since that fateful day, the rights and wrongs of the deed have been disputed. Was it a noble act of tyrannicide, or a brutal murder? Had the dead man, in the short period of his supremacy, merely destroyed the old order, or creatively started a new one?

To the first question no simple answer is possible; intolerable as the nobles found Caesar's autocracy, they themselves, previously, had governed the empire a very great deal worse. To the second question, the reply is that, although he had indeed destroyed the Republic, his formula for its replacement was so ludicrously unacceptable to the very men whose cooperation, or at least toleration, was indispensable that a new order was scarcely even in sight. As a warning, therefore, to all who came after him, his murder was invaluable. For the catastrophic experiment showed his successors, when the first of them began to emerge, what they must *not* do, if they wanted to survive.

In spite of all his unique assemblage of talents, Caesar's reliance on the perpetual dictatorship, and his decision, at the end, to abandon the capital for a prolonged period, reveal that he just did not reflect what was possible or impossible in Roman politics – or he did not trouble to apply the knowledge to his own position. Besides, two years before his death he had already been heard saying: 'My life has been long enough, whether reckoned in years or in renown.' He felt he had come to the end of the road, and the Parthian campaign was only a desperate expedient to open it up in a new direction.

During this last period of his life he was subject to outbursts of intense impatience and irritation. After his Triumph in 46 he himself hauled a grumbling soldier off by the scruff of the neck to execution, and offered up two others for human sacrifice. Moreover, in spite of his Olympian indifference to Republican opposition, he allowed yapping young tribunes of the people (the traditional guardians of popular rights) to infuriate him, first in 46, and then again in Janury 44 when his tough treatment of two such officials, although mitigated on second thoughts, revealed that his nerves were seriously frayed.

This condition was caused not by the fears which tormented later rulers, but by another of their troubles, prolonged and incessant over-work. Moreover, Caesar was far from well. About his alleged night-mares we need not trouble, since it was traditional to attribute these to tyrants. But at intervals ever since 49 Caesar had also suffered from fits of giddiness, leading to convulsions and insensibility; and the ancient authorities seem to be right in describing this affliction as epilepsy. Bad health was the excuse made by his assistants when he failed to rise for that senatorial deputation; and on the fatal Ides, too, he was not well. The lapses of judgement and temper, major and minor, of his final years were seriously accentuated by ill-health.

In the previous autumn he had thought it advisable to make his will. The heads on his coins show a man who looks much older than the mid-fifties, and so do some careworn portrait busts. Frederick the Great, when he returned from the Seven Years War, was still only fifty-one, but had aged so noticeably that he was described as 'Old Fritz'. And Caesar, too, had lived so much harder than his health permitted that he deteriorated in mind as well as in body before his time.

After Caesar was dead Cicero wrote to Atticus that if he had gone off on his Parthian expedition, he would never have returned. The orator may well have been right – not because Caesar would have been defeated, since that is a might-have-been on which we cannot pro-nounce, but because his powers were declining too far and fast for the process to be reversed. When the assassins struck, they slew a man whom the terrible burden of ruling the Roman empire had already begun to destroy.

2

Augustus

Born in 63 BC, Gaius Octavius, the future Augustus, was the son of a knight from Velitrae (Velletri near Rome). His father, whose career had been sponsored by Julius Caesar, rose to be a senator and a praetor, but after his death the young Octavius was brought up by his mother Atia. Caesar, who was her uncle, introduced the youth to public life and adopted him in his will, thus making him his personal heir.

When this information was published after the dictator had been murdered, Octavius – or Octavian as he is generally known to us during these years of his rise to power – assumed his adoptive father's names Gaius Julius Caesar, and started the fourteen-year struggle to gain supremacy in the state. After siding with the senate against his chief rival Antony, whom he helped to defeat at Mutina (Modena in north Italy) in 43, a snub from the senate caused him to join Antony and Lepidus in the formal, autocratic Second Triumvirate, which organized the proscription and execution of many political enemies, including the orator Cicero. In October 42, in two successive engagements at Philippi in Macedonia, he and Antony overwhelmed Caesar's assassins Brutus and Cassius, who met their deaths – although ill-health and perhaps physical cowardice had prevented Octavian from playing a distinguished part in the battles.

During the next eleven years the Roman world was shared between Octavian, in the west – helped by the outstanding admiral Agrippa and the equally talented diplomat Maecenas – and Antony in the east, in association with Cleopatra, queen of Egypt. In 36 Agrippa suppressed the semi-piratical naval forces of Pompey's son Sextus Pompeius off Naulochus (Venetico) in Sicily, and then Octavian, after forcing Lepidus to retire into private life, fought campaigns in Illyricum and Dalmatia, the modern Yugoslavia (35–3).

But soon came the inevitable clash with Antony, heralded by extra-legal Oaths of Loyalty sworn to Octavian by Italy and the western provinces, and culminating in the naval battle of Actium (off north-western Greece), in which Agrippa was victorious (31). Thr suicides of Antony and Cleopatra in the following year left Octavian sole ruler of the entire Roman world.

Although owing to his control of the Roman army he preserved this mastery for the rest of his life, he began, after Actium, to prepare the way for an ostensible restoration of the traditional Republican government. In January 27 BC, three days before assuming the reverential name of Augustus, he 'transferred the state', to use his own words, 'to the free disposal of the senate and people'. At the same time, however, he retained the annual consulships which he had held for the past four years, and agreed to accept as his province for an initial ten years (continuously renewed thereafter) Spain, Gaul and Syria – in addition to Egypt, which he had annexed after his victory at Actium.

These regions included by far the greater part of the army, which was augmented at home by a praetorian guard to protect his own person. Its necessity was demonstrated by a series of plots and alleged plots and strained situations which revealed that the loyalty of the writers devoted to Augustus' aims was by no means universally shared. These early years after Actium were also characterized by real or imaginary threats from ambitious commanders. The bad health which dogged Augustus throughout his life led to serious illnesses in 25 and 23 BC.

In the latter year he resigned the consulship but retained his multiple province and apparently obtained some legal power enabling him to intervene, if desirable, in the other ('senatorial') provinces as well. He also assumed the 'tribunician power', a vague but popular echo of the ancient tribunes who had stood for the rights of the lower classes. His enormous prestige was further enhanced, in due course, by the chief priesthood (12 BC) and the title of Father of the Country (2 BC).

Agrippa was granted an eastern command (23 BC), and in 21 Augustus' daughter Julia was given to him in marriage. Although the ruler's power could not, officially speaking, be handed on, Agrippa's and Julia's sons Gaius and Lucius, adopted by Augustus on the birth of the younger boy in 17, gradually came to be regarded as the heirs to the throne. During these years Augustus undertook enormous feats of reorganization in every governmental field.

Meanwhile his stepsons Tiberius and Drusus the elder (the sons of his aristocratic wife Livia by a former marriage) were employed for major military

*campaigns beyond the western frontiers. When Agrippa and Drusus died, in 12
and 9 BC respectively, Tiberius remained the undisputed second man in the state.
After some years of retirement to the island of Rhodes* he was given powers in
AD 4 indicating that he was earmarked for the eventual succession.*

*However, the last decade of Augustus' life was darkened not only by family
troubles but by spectacular disasters in recently occupied territories, notably a
three-year rebellion in Illyricum (AD 6–9), and the destruction of Varus and three
legions by the Germans (AD 9). Nevertheless, with the help of Tiberius, Augustus
carried on for another five years, dying in AD 14 at the age of seventy-six.*

Julius Caesar's adoption of his young grand-nephew Octavian in his
will 'provided he had no son of his body' was a remarkable step. It is
true that adoption had been widely utilized by the great Republican
families in the absence of an heir. But Octavian was not yet out of his
teens and had already displayed signs of deplorably bad health: this had
caused him to miss the Spanish campaign of 45 altogether, only arriving
after the battle of Munda had been fought. Yet Caesar must have
discerned his altogether exceptional abilities. The dictator himself could
have no heir in any political, official sense, for the state offices he held
were not inheritable. But, equally certainly, the man whom he adopted
as his personal heir – leaving him three-quarters of his vast property –
was elevated to exceptional political significance.

Octavian was at Apollonia in Epirus (Albania) when he learnt of
Caesar's death: and he immediately decided to return to Italy and take
up his inheritance with all its possible implications. He appeared, at
first, insignificant in comparison with his rival Antony – who was
gravely disappointed about Caesar's will. Indeed Octavian's family
background by no means enabled him to compete either with Antony
or with any other of Rome's established political leaders. The Octavii,
although in comfortable enough circumstances, were a modest clan by
metropolitan standards, and their only substantial claim to fame was
their marriage into the house of Julius Caesar. By the same token, the
youthful Octavian's adoption by Caesar was his only claim to eminence.

He exploited this advantage with the utmost skill, notably in mid-
July 44, when, in the face of extensive opposition and with only a few
supporters behind him, he celebrated Games in honour of the Victory of
Caesar. In the words of his autobiography:

* The reasons for his retirement will be discussed in the next chapter.

On the very days of my Games, a comet was seen in the northern part of the sky for seven days. It appeared about the eleventh hour of the day and was clearly visible in all countries. The young people believed that by that star it was signified that the soul of Caesar was received among the immortal gods, on which account the sign of a star was attached to the head of the statue of Caesar which I shortly consecrated in the Forum.[1]

Octavian's advance to power had begun; and on 2 November Cicero wrote to Atticus:

On the evening of the 1st I had a letter from Octavian. He is doing great things. He won over to his side the veterans at Casilinum and Calatia. No wonder, he is giving them 500 *denarii* each. He is thinking of going round the other colonies. Clearly this means that there will be war against Antony with him as leader. Which are we to follow? Look at his name – but then at his age![2]

'His name and his age': his youthful years were an enormous handicap, but his name – Gaius Julius Caesar – already a remarkable asset, became more valuable still when, in January 42, he and the two men with whom he had now become allied in the Second Triumvirate, Antony and Lepidus, pronounced the murdered Julius a god of the Roman state. Octavian's exploitation of this development was displayed upon coins which show himself on one side, described as 'Caesar Son of a God', and Julius Caesar on the other, named 'the God Julius'.

However, the new divinity had not only bequeathed to Octavian this initial advantage, but had also left him the most difficult of dilemmas. For look what had happened to Julius. Now Octavian was equally determined to be an autocrat – yet he somehow had to avoid coming to the same violent end. In due course, therefore, it was imperative that the memory of Caesar should be quietly transformed. The poets sympathetic to Octavian – Virgil, Horace and Propertius – showed how this could be done. A veil is drawn over the illegalities of Caesar's life, or they are even implicitly and delicately deplored. On the other hand his godhead is emphasized, in order to stress the divine parentage of his adoptive son.

Meanwhile the danger of assassination still remained ever-present. For the Second Triumvirate, although the supreme power was now shared by three men, was every bit as autocratic as the dictatorship of Caesar. Well aware, therefore, of the unpopularity which this situation made inevitable, the triumvirs at once exterminated all the political opponents they could lay hands on, with Octavian, it was said, hanging back at the outset but then entering into the butchery with gusto. Thus inaugurated, the triumviral period remained a grim, unconstitutional time of bloody harshness. Throughout its duration Octavian devoted himself with remorseless single-mindedness to the pursuit of his own enormous ambition, through every means that came to hand – persuasion, corruption, fraud, treachery, execution and civil war.

From 42 onwards, despite outward demonstrations of solidarity, he pitted himself against Antony, whose financial superiority, based on the wealth of the eastern provinces and of Cleopatra's Egyptian kingdom, had to be counteracted by the most ingenious methods. One of them was the oath of allegiance sworn to Octavian in 32, with alleged spontaneity, by the populations of Italy and the west. For by this means he contrived to raise his position beyond and outside constitutional limitations and improprieties altogether, basing it instead upon a personality cult blending the firm loyalties of a military oath with the traditional Roman institution of *clientela*, according to which powerful patrons were bound by strong hereditary mutual ties to a host of more humble citizens, their clients. Earlier on Octavian had exploited Caesar's tentative use of the title *'imperator'* in a special, personal sense. In spite or because of his own poor endurance as a commander, of which something will be said later, he had adopted this designation as his very own name and prefix, an unchallengeable sign of personal victoriousness.

Nevertheless, when his relations with Antony gradually showed signs of irreparable strain – more through his own fault than Antony's – the senators still found it hard to decide which of the two men was going to win: even at the very last moment a considerable proportion of them still decided to take Antony's part. Later on the poets assigned a fateful inevitability to the outcome of Actium. From a military and naval point of view, however, it was 'inevitable' for one reason only, because of Octavian's good fortune and good judgement in employing an admiral, Marcus Agrippa, who was far superior in strategic and tactical talents to any commander on the other side.

Yet Octavian's principal official reason for declaring his victory at Actium to have been inevitable was because the gods and fate were held to have decreed that the west should defeat the east.

> Augustus Caesar stands
> High on the lofty stern; his temples flame
> With double fire, and over his head there dawns

His father's star. Agrippa leads a column
With favouring wind and god, the naval crown
Wreathing his temples. Antony assembles
Egypt and all the East, Antony, victor
Over the lands of dawn and the red ocean,
Marshals the foes of Rome, himself a Roman,
With – horror! an Egyptian wife.[3]

Virgil's picture is an accurate one in so far as the battle *did* decide that Octavian's insistence on Roman and Italian hegemony should prevail, so that Antony's and Cleopatra's ideas of a truer partnership between west and east, under Roman rule – ideas which the poet travesties – were suppressed. For the ambition pursued and gained by the victor of Actium was a world that would be ruled by the west. True, Virgil's *Aeneid*, like many other writings of the time, implies a good deal of praise for his ruler's hoped-for reconciliation between west and east. This was the doctrine which Augustus' artistic and religious policies implied by their careful incorporation of Hellenistic motifs into the main Roman framework, a process symbolized by his reliance on the divine sponsorship of Apollo, the supreme patron of Hellenic culture but, at the same time, an ancient deity of the Italians as well.

Yet although these attitudes, as Donald Earl remarks, display the hope of 'a new unity in which east and west supported each other in a relationship of mutual benefit', the west was unmistakably intended to be the dominant partner. Indeed Virgil, for all his careful insistence on reconciliation, makes this fully explicit in the words which are addressed to Aeneas in the underworld by the ghost of his father Anchises:

There are others, assuredly I believe,
Shall work in bronze more sensitively, moulding
Breathing images, or carving from the marble
More lifelike features: some shall plead more eloquently,
Or gauging with instruments the sky's motion
Forecast the rising of the constellations:
But yours, my Roman, is the gift of government,
That is your bent – to impose upon the nations
The code of peace; to be clement to the conquered,
But utterly to crush the intransigent.[4]

This message is quite unequivocal. The eastern provinces, inhabited by Greeks, remained by far the richest and most civilized and developed portions of the empire. Yet the Greeks themselves, over the past centuries, had manifestly failed in the essential art of governing – of establishing security and stability: and, in accordance with Augustus' profound conviction, they were to remain the political subordinates, as they had been under the Republic. And so the effective political rehabilitation of the Greek half of the empire had to be postponed for another three hundred and fifty years and more, until Constantine moved his capital to Constantinople.

The opportunity for a real, major, liberalization was quite intentionally missed and avoided by Augustus. This decision, however, was due not merely to his own small-town preferences. It was also based on his practical assessment of what could and could not be done. The extreme distaste which the Romans and Greeks reciprocally felt for each other's qualities could not be disregarded. Certainly many a Roman would have been able to protest 'some of my best friends are Greeks', patronizingly praising their dear old loyal Greek slaves and secretaries, and eulogizing the Greek culture of the distant past. Nevertheless dozens of surviving passages from ancient writings confirm that the sentiments which for the most part prevailed between the two peoples were hatred and contempt. Augustus himself, it is true, although he never wrote or spoke Greek really fluently himself, admired Greek culture, in his own chilly way, and by no means excluded all its living representatives from his friendship. But he had to recognize that anti-Greek feelings were widely prevalent: and in any case he himself felt as strongly as anyone else that the men who ruled the Roman empire ought to be Italians.

In consequence the exclusion of the Greeks from the centres of power was almost total. Not more than one single Augustan senator of Greek origin is known, and it was not until 120 years after Actium that the first oriental consul made his appearance. Under Augustus one Greek historian, Timagenes, was so outspoken in his criticism of Rome, and laid such stress on the virulence of anti-Roman feeling in the east, that the emperor broke off all relations with him and banned him from his house. Timagenes retaliated by throwing the work he had written about Augustus' deeds into the fire.

There were also recurrent troubles and riots in at least half a dozen Greek towns, resulting, in some cases, in the lynching of partisans of Augustus, followed by sharp official repressions. In AD 6 such commotions became widespread. Moreover – not that this was anything new – seditious underground literature was also in circulation:

> First of all
> Inexorable wrath shall fall on Rome;
> A time of blood and wretched life shall come.
> Woe, woe to thee, O land of Italy,
> Great, barbarous nation . . .
>
> With images of gold and silver and stone
> Be ready, that unto the bitter day
> Ye may come, thy first punishment, O Rome,
> Even a gnashing anguish to behold.
> And no more under slavish yoke to thee
> Will either Greek or Syrian put his neck,
> Barbarian or any other nation.
> Thou shalt be plundered and shalt be destroyed
> For what thou didst, and wailing aloud in fear
> Thou shalt give until thou shalt all repay.[5]

Admittedly it would be a mistake to exaggerate this discontent among easterners. Thousands of Greeks lived in unprecedented prosperity under Augustus. But it was *la solution économique* such as was complacently adopted by modern colonialist powers in pre-independence Africa. It was hoped and expected that prosperity would keep the Greeks quiet: and with that hope in mind Augustus, although he still allowed them to rule their own cities, felt able to pursue their deliberate exclusion from the upper reaches of imperial government.

However he did not make the narrow-minded mistake of supposing that Rome could dominate the whole empire by itself. Indeed there was something novel about his attitude, which envisaged a world ruled, no longer by Rome all on its own, but by Rome with Italy as its partner. Up to now Italy had scarcely existed, not only as a territorial unit, but even as a concept of any significance. It was little more than half a century since the Italians had been in active revolt against Rome; and the rich and populous north (Cisalpine Gaul) had only been fully incorporated into Italy a mere eleven years before Actium.

Italia had never previously caught the imagination of mankind. It had always been a land of prose. Now, on the other hand, on the lips of some of the most famous poets in the history of the world, it dramatically came into its own. Already before Actium Virgil, in the *Georgics*, had written a great eulogy of his Italian homeland.

> This land produced the Marsians, the Sabellian stock,
> Ligurians, friends of hardship, Volscians with short spears –
> hard manly tribes. It bore the noble Roman heroes,
> the Scipios, tough in war, and you, magnificent Caesar,
> who now victoriously in the furthest Asian land
> defend the citadels of Rome from the soft Indians.
> Hail, earthly paradise, mighty mother of crops
> and mother of men.[6]

In the *Aeneid*, too, Italy is Aeneas' goal, and the gods forbid him to settle anywhere else: 'This is my love, this is my fatherland.' To Horace, as well, the victorious ruler is 'the ever-ready guardian of Italy and imperial Rome'. And this was an idea which appealed deeply to Augustus himself, an Italian whose whole personality was deliberately devoted to the exaltation of Italy in partnership with Rome. This formula, which set its seal upon the centuries that lay ahead, represented a progress in liberalization to the extent that the dominant role was at least extended from the capital to Italy as a whole. But the extension went thus far and no further, because it was conditional upon the continued exclusion of every other part of the empire, and the east most of all, from the realities of power.

The corollary of Augustus' pro-Italian attitude, striking the same cautious balance between liberalism and narrowness, was a considerable but once again not excessive increase in the number of Roman citizens in the empire. 'Considering it of great importance', remarks Suetonius, 'to keep the people pure and unsullied by any taint of foreign or servile blood, he was most chary of conferring Roman citizenship, and set a limit to the liberation of slaves.'

But perhaps the biographer rather over-emphasizes Augustus' caution. For whereas the empire had contained 4,063,000 Roman citizens (not including women and children) in 28 BC, there were as many as 4,937,000 in AD 14. It is true that a recently discovered inscription gives the latter figure as only 4,100,900. But that perhaps represents the citizen population of Italy itself, so that we may suppose the balance of 836,100 to have been made up by the citizens who lived in the provinces. Augustus continued Caesar's policy of founding citizen settlements on provincial as well as Italian soil, though he abandoned the experiment of sending out impoverished civilian city-dwellers and devoted his settlements entirely to the numerous discharged soldiers for whom he had to find land, commuted, later in the reign, into cash gratuities. Although there was some confusion between his private resources and those of the state, for the first thirty-seven years after Actium the enormous cost of providing the veterans with these rewards was defrayed out of Augustus' own funds, which had fortunately been very much increased by the annexation of Egypt.

To make this provision for the demobilized troops was a task of the highest priority, for it related, once again, to Augustus' prime dilemma. Although he must avoid looking like an autocrat, his authority, just like Caesar's, depended wholly upon the army, which must therefore be adequately rewarded. Moreover, it must be maintained at sufficient strength to defend the empire. Augustus felt he could not rely on emergency conscript forces, for several reasons: conscription was unpopular, short-term soldiers tended to rely seditiously on their own generals, and it was impossible to give them adequate training. So he decided he must have a regular army, with long-term service. He also concluded that its appropriate strength was about 300,000 men, of whom half comprised Roman citizens forming twenty-eight legions while the other half consisted of auxiliaries of various origins who would become Roman citizens on their discharge.

Twenty-eight legions seemed a relatively small total – immediately after Actium he had disposed of sixty or seventy – and indeed it was too small to allow for any central strategic reserve. Yet a larger army would have been more than the empire's primitive agricultural economy could support. Besides Augustus, like other emperors after him, was incessantly obliged to weigh up the needs of national defence against his fears for his own personal safety. He himself could not spare the time to command his forces in the field, even if he had wanted to, and for nearly the whole of the last four decades of his life he never appeared at their head. That meant that he had to entrust their command to others. If, however, there had been a central reserve, its commander might have been tempted to revolt; and indeed a larger force on the frontiers, too, might have held out similar temptations to the commanders of such massive

61

legionary groups. Augustus possessed a unique capacity to make knife-edge calculations, and this problem subjected them to their most exacting test. The dimensions of the army on which he finally settled seemed to him to strike the best available balance between military inadequacy and security hazard.

But there were also other security hazards too. Attempts on Augustus' life were always to be expected. So he developed the personal bodyguards of earlier generals into a regularly constituted and well-paid praetorian guard, consisting of nine cohorts, each of five hundred infantry, together with ninety horse and a central mounted unit which was attached closely to the ruler's person. And he surrounded himself by an additional bodyguard of Germans as well.

Yet, for as long as he ruled as an unconcealed autocrat, the danger of his suffering Caesar's fate still remained pressing. Soon after Actium, therefore, he set himself the task of restoring the old Republican institutions. It was a particularly delicate task, because he did not, in fact, have the slightest intention of relinquishing the real power. The restoration was to be a conjuring trick, a feat of sleight-of-hand.

And yet Augustus may well have believed in what he was doing. When he said 'anybody who will not want the existing order to be altered is a good man and a good citizen', it sounded rather surprising, in view of his own massive innovations. Yet he may have been speaking sincerely. He had to produce a system which would work: which would on the one hand leave the empire under the strong unitary government it needed, but would also save Republican appearances and thus content the nobility sufficiently to rescue him from Julius Caesar's fate. To steer this perilous path between renewed anarchy and unconcealed despotism, to ensure that although everything had in fact changed everything must still look the same, might seem an impossible assignment. But so great were the political and diplomatic gifts of the *princeps* or leader – as he called himself – that he carried it out successfully, thus creating the Roman imperial system that we know as the principate.

In the year of the battle of Actium he was consul for the third time, and he went on holding this office continuously for a further seven years. But meanwhile, on 13 January 27 BC, he had ostensibly restored the institutions of the ancient state. At the same time, however, the state granted him the territories in which the greater part of the army was stationed. After that date, he himself declared, 'I excelled all in prestige [*auctoritas*], but had no more power than my colleagues in the various offices of state'. This idea of prestige, not legal or constitutional yet deeply rooted in custom and tradition, is very Roman and yet not unlike the Confucian system in which the effective guarantee was, once again, not so much juridical as social and moral. *Auctoritas* represented the sum total of the qualities in a man that command respect for his person and opinion, including his birth, wealth, personal achievement, talent and virtue: and the rulers endowment with this quality was now emphasized by the assumption of the etymologically related name 'Augustus', which was propitious and auspicious and hinted at superhuman greatness, while nevertheless suggesting nothing that could offend a Republican ear. Such were the astute means by which the first Roman emperor – as he later, in retrospect, was seen to have become – asserted his continued supremacy in the state without interfering with the operation of the meticulously revived Republican institutions.

Or rather, it might at first have appeared to a politically sensitive observer – and there were many such observers – that he *was* interfering to some extent after all, because he was still occupying a continuous series of successive consulships, and thus keeping them from nobles who would like these offices for themselves, and felt they were fully entitled to have them. So from 23 BC Augustus ceased to hold these continual consulships any longer. He did *not*, however, cease to control his provinces and his army. He retained them by a process which involved the divorce of *imperium* or power (which he kept) from office (which he had vacated), a constitutional principle which had already been tried out during the last years of the Republic. The 'tribunician power' which he accepted at the same time – once again without accepting the office of tribune – was not a power of any great practical importance, but a significant bid for the support of the populace as a whole, whom the tribunes had traditionally protected from oppression.

There were slight modifications of these arrangements later in the reign. For example, in 19 BC, without becoming consul again, Augustus was granted consular powers in Italy and Rome, so that his official powers of command were no longer limited to the provinces. But by now the main lines of this extraordinary formula were laid down. It was carefully tailored to Roman prejudices and instincts and predilections. And yet, declared Otto Hirschfeld: 'we cannot acquit him of the grave

reproach of having willed the impossible and set up the impermanent.'
Impermanency would scarcely seem to be the right description for the
line of Roman emperors founded by Augustus, which continued for
hundreds of years. But although the emperors went on and on, his own
system proved impossible to maintain. For this needed a man of his
ability to direct its operation. His successors, highly efficient though
many of them were, could not possess his unique talents: and the results
of their consequent failure to maintain Augustus' delicate machinery
became gradually clear under each of the remaining ten of the Twelve
Caesars.

The essence of the new principate was that the ruler should exercise vast
powers in a way which took account of public opinion – and especially
of the opinion of the senators. Not every senator, however, was prepared
to accept these acrobatic tricks at their face value. Certain nobles were
too hard-bitten to be taken in, and considered the whole scheme an
artificial sham. Certainly it was a sham that enabled them to save their
dignity, and hold the offices their forefathers had held before them. Or,
better still, if they happened not to be ancient aristocrats but new men
brought in because they had supported Caesar and Augustus, the new
order raised them to heights they had never reached before. Many,
therefore, were satisfied. But some were not. And among those whom he
had failed to win over there were grumbles and plots, or rumours of
plots.

Yet Augustus enjoyed an enormous advantage. By the time of Actium
the empire had been convulsed and ruined by decades of civil war. In
the eternal balancing of order against liberty, this was one of the epochs
of the world during which people were prepared to tolerate a certain
tilting of the scales towards order.

For civil war, even to extreme Republicans, was the ultimate horror.
As Virgil, before Actium, had cried out in his *Georgics*, it was a time of
justice thrown down, of fields gone to ruin, of men and women made
homeless and destitute. But Virgil saw a saviour who could rescue the
world from these miseries: and he was the future Augustus.

> Paternal gods! Ancestors! Mother Vesta!
> You that guard Tiber and the Palatine!
> Let not this young man fail to give us peace!

He had not failed: and the poets who commemorated his success were echoing a widespread, heartfelt, gratitude. One of its principal spokesmen was Horace:

> I celebrate, and with good cause,
> A day that banishes dark cares.
> While the world's bound by Caesar's laws,
>   I need not apprehend
>   War or a violent end. . .
>
> While Caesar stands guard, peace is assured, the peace
> No power can break – not civil dissension or
>   Brute force or wrath, that weapon-forger,
>   Misery-maker for warring cities.
>
> When Caesar's here the ox plods safe and sound;
> Ceres and gentle Plenty feed the ground
>   With fruitfulness; across
>   The uninfested seas
>   Men speed with bird-like ease;
> Honesty is afraid of its own loss.[7]

And the message was taken up by many others, in the east as well as the dominant west. Indeed, despite its relegation to the second place, the east had a tradition of special fulsomeness, which is reflected in this letter addressed by an Augustan governor of Asia to the cities of his province (9 BC):

The divine providence that guides our life has displayed its zeal and benevolence by ordaining for our life the most perfect good, bringing to us Augustus, whom it has filled with virtue for the benefit of mankind, employing him as a saviour for us and our descendants, him who has put an end to wars and adorned peace; and he being made manifest to us has exceeded the hopes of all who before brought good tidings, not only outstripping all benefactors before him, but leaving no hope to those who shall come after to surpass him; and the birthday of the god is the beginning of all the good tidings brought by him to the world.[8]

The eminent geographer Strabo, who likewise came from Asia Minor, emphasized that the monarchic rule of Augustus was a necessary precondition of this prosperity:

Italy – though it has often been torn by faction, at least since it has been under the Romans – and Rome itself have been prevented by the excellence of their form of government and of their rulers from proceeding too far in the ways of error and corruption. But it would be a difficult thing to administer so great a dominion otherwise than by turning it over to one man, as to a father. At all events, never have the Romans and their allies thrived in such peace and plenty as that which was afforded them by Caesar Augustus from the time he assumed the absolute authority.[9]

And the Alexandrian Jew Philo was equally enthusiastic:

This ruler, Augustus, who truly deserves the title of 'Averter of Evil', is the Caesar who lulled the storms which were crashing everywhere, who healed the sicknesses common to Greeks and barbarians alike. . . This is he who cleared the sea of pirate-ships and filled it with merchant-ships. This is he who set every city again at liberty, who reduced disorder to order, who civilized all the unfriendly savage tribes and brought them into harmony with each other. . . This is he who safeguarded peace, gave each man his due, distributed his favours widely without stint, and never in his whole life kept any blessing or advantage back.[10]

It was upon the firm basis of all this upsurging grateful emotion that Augustus was able to create that improbable structure which became forever associated with his name. The east, which was accustomed to autocrats, did not mind that he was autocratic. The west, or its upper classes, might have minded very much. But Augustus, borne along on the wings of an abundant relief that the wars were over, made his absolutism palatable to the majority of westerners by concealing it, just sufficiently, behind the imposing restored front of venerable institutions. 'I am as much for government by consent as any man,' observed Oliver Cromwell; 'but if you ask me how it is to be done, I confess I do not know.' Augustus, even if there were some who would not accept his solution, more nearly solved the riddle than Cromwell or any other absolute ruler.

His personal habits were simple. Renowned for his frugality, Augustus enjoyed simple foods like green figs; and unlike most of the later emperors of his house he was only a moderate drinker. He frequently gave formal dinner-parties, but was sometimes in the habit of eating alone before or after his dinner, though often what he ate was little more than a snack.

In all his social contacts he was genial and accessible – the very opposite, it would seem, to the traditional tyrant, with the praetorian guard kept as far out of sight as possible.

He did not, if he could help it, leave or enter any city or town except in the evening or at night, to avoid disturbing anyone by the obligations of ceremony. In his consulship he commonly went through the streets on foot, and when he was not consul, generally in a closed litter. His morning receptions were open to all, including ordinary people, and he met the requests of those who approached him with great affability, jocosely reproving one man because he presented a petition to him with as much hesitation 'as he would a penny to an elephant'.

He exchanged social calls with many, and did not cease to attend all their anniversaries until he was well on in years... When Cerrinius Gallus, a senator with whom he was not at all intimate, had suddenly become blind and had therefore resolved to end his life by starvation, Augustus called on him and by his consoling words induced him to live.[11]

Augustus 'allowed all who could make any useful suggestion to speak their minds freely'. He displayed the quality admired by the Romans under the name of *civilitas*, absence of unnecessary pomp. Genuinely preferring simplicity to luxury, he at first lived in an unpretentious part of Rome near the Forum, and then moved to a modest though tastefully decorated house on the Palatine (the excavated 'Casa di Livia'), where for forty years he slept in the same bedroom. A later ruler, Marcus Aurelius, said he had been taught by his unostentatious predecessor Antoninus Pius that an emperor could almost live like a private gentleman. The founder of the principate had already been imbued with the same idea.

True, there was a somewhat dismaying contrast between this homeliness and his soaring position, not to speak of the scarcely human designation 'Augustus'. Yet he was human enough for all that. For example, he hated early rising. When, therefore, he had an engagement scheduled for an early hour of the next day, he used to spend the night with a friend near its location, so that he could get up at the latest possible moment. Besides, his nights were often interrupted. For he suffered badly from frustration dreams, especially during the spring, and usually woke up four or five times during the night; to while away these wakeful periods he liked to have readers or story-tellers close at hand. Besides, urgent business might arise during the night hours, and in case of such sudden emergencies he always kept a toga ready in his bedroom. Because of his shortage of sleep, he often dropped off while he was being carried through the streets, or when his litter was put down owing to a traffic delay.

Augustus was an orator of 'imperial fluency and spontaneity', and gave very helpful encouragement to contemporary writers. Nevertheless his personal attitude towards literature was depressingly inclined to edification.

In reading the writers of both tongues there was nothing for which he looked so carefully as precepts and examples instructive to the public or to individuals. These he would often copy word for word, and send to the members of his household, or to his generals and provincial governors, whenever any of them required admonition.[12]

However Augustus also had his recreations. After the Civil Wars he had given up military exercises but thereafter he continued to play ball games for a time, although later he contented himself with riding or walking. He was also fond of gambling, like many other occupants of the imperial throne. Private letters he wrote to Tiberius on the subject have survived, and very boring they are.

We spent the festival of Minerva very merrily, my dear Tiberius, for we played all day long and kept the gaming-board warm. Your brother made a great outcry about his luck, but after all did not come out far behind in the long run, since after losing heavily, he unexpectedly and little by little got back a good deal. For my part, I lost twenty thousand sesterces, but because I was extravagantly generous in my play, as usual. If I had demanded of everyone the stakes which I let go, or had kept all that I gave away, I should have won fully fifty thousand. But I like that better, for my generosity will exalt me to immortal glory.[13]

We are also told that 'to divert his mind Augustus sometimes fished, and sometimes played at dice, marble and nuts with little boys, searching everywhere for such as were attractive for their pretty faces or their prattle, especially Syrians and Mauretanians'.[14] However his interest in these boys is unlikely to have been sexual, since, in spite of the inevitable rumours that he had been Caesar's boy-friend, and reports that he used to singe his legs with red-hot nutshells in order to make the hair grow softer for effeminate purposes, he was evidently a determined and continually adulterous womaniser. When, therefore, he organized propaganda attacks on Antony for his liaison with Cleopatra, Antony was able to retaliate with a letter uncomfortably full of statistical repartee:

What's come over you? Is it because I go to bed with the queen? But she isn't my wife, is she? And it isn't as if it's something new, is it? Haven't I been doing it for nine years now? And what about you, is Livia the only woman you go to bed with? I congratulate you, if at the time you read this letter you haven't also had Tertulla or Terentilla or Rufilla or Salvia Titisenia or the whole lot of them. Does it really matter where you get a stand or who the woman is?[15]

Terentilla, mentioned in the letter, is probably Maecenas' wife Terentia, who was widely alleged to be one of Augustus' mistresses.

Augustus employed brilliant sculptors who, by various gradations of tactful idealizing, made his interesting facial features into a sort of legend, or rather a whole series of legends embodying every aspect of his official personality. His actual appearance was described by Suetonius.

He was very handsome and most graceful at all stages of his life, although he cared nothing for any sort of finery. He was so uninterested in how his hair was dressed that he would set several barbers to work at once in a hurry, and he would have his beard clipped at one time and shaved at another, and while the barbers were working he would read or even write something. His expression both when he was talking and in silence was so calm and mild that a certain Gallic noble confessed to his own countrymen that it had softened him and prevented him from his plan of hurling Augustus over a precipice when, during a crossing of the Alps, he had been allowed to approach him under the pretext of talking with him.

Augustus' eyes were clear and bright, and he liked men to think that there was a sort of divine power in them. He was very pleased if anyone at whom he looked keenly lowered his face as if before the light of the sun. In old age he did not see very well with his left eye. His teeth were widely separated, small and dirty. His hair was slightly curly and yellowish. His ears were small. His nose protruded somewhat at the top and bent rather inwards at the bottom. His complexion was between dark and fair. He was short (although his freedman Julius Marathus, who kept his records, informs us that he was over five feet six inches in height), but this was disguised by the good proportions of his figure and only apparent if someone taller stood beside him.[16]

But Augustus also had an extraordinary record of sickness. It must be almost unique in history for a man who for so long bore such a burden of responsibility and overwork to have been so frail and unhealthy.

In the course of his life he suffered from several severe and dangerous illnesses, especially after the subjugation of Cantabria (northern Spain), when he was in such a desperate plight, from abscesses of the liver, that he was forced to submit to an unprecedented and hazardous course of treatment. Since hot fomentations gave him no relief, he was led by the advice of his physician Antonius Musa to try cold ones . . .

His body is said to have been spotty, with birthmarks scattered all over his chest and belly in the shape, arrangement and number of the stars of the constellation of the Great Bear, and with rough places like ringworm caused by the itching of his body and the constant vigorous use of the scraper. His left hip, thigh and leg were not very strong and he often limped, but he tried to strengthen them by treating them with a poultice of sand and reeds. He also sometimes found the forefinger of his right hand so weak when it was numb and contracted with cold that he could scarcely write even when it was supported by a horn finger stall. He complained of his bladder, too, and was relieved of pain only after he had passed stones in his urine. . . .

He also experienced some disorders which recurred every year at definite times. For he was commonly ailing just before his birthday, and at the beginning of spring he was troubled with an enlargement of the diaphragm, and when the wind was in the south, with catarrh. Hence his constitution was so weakened that he could not readily endure either cold or heat.[17]

All this meant that Augustus took immense care of his health. He sounds at times like an advanced case of hypochondria. It is true that in ancient times to catch pneumonia, for example, meant death. Augustus was all too conscious that this was so – and could by no stretch of the imagination be described as taking risks with his bodily welfare.

He made good his weakness by great care, especially by moderation in bathing. For as a rule he was anointed or took a sweat by the fire, after which he was doused with water either lukewarm or tepid from long exposure to the sun. When, however, he had to use hot salt water and sulphur baths for rheumatism, he contented himself with sitting on a wooden bath-seat and plunging his hands and feet in the water one after the other . . .

In winter he protected himself with four tunics and a heavy toga, besides an undershirt, a woollen chest-protector and wraps for his thighs and shins . . . He could not endure the sun even in winter, and never walked in the open air without wearing a broad-brimmed hat, even at home . . .[18]

And those privileged to be the spectators of his daily walks would be able to see him conclude them with a burst of jogging – after he had wrapped himself round with a cloak or a blanket.

Such, curiously enough, was the man who over a period of nearly half a century totally reconstituted the Roman world as he wished it to be; and such the man whom, although he had already suffered from a serious illness which made him miss a critical battle, Julius Caesar had nevertheless deliberately chosen out from all the Romans as his principal personal heir.

Missing battles owing to bad health became, for Augustus, a recurrent pattern, which raises difficult questions about the possibly psychosomatic origins of certain of his illnesses. Why, for example, when he and Antony were confronting Brutus and Cassius at Philippi (42 BC), was he not present at the first battle at all? His own explanation was that he decided to withdraw before the fighting started because his medical adviser had dreamt an ill-omened dream; according to another account, the dream had urged him to get up from his sick-bed and make a quick getaway before the victorious enemy sacked his camp. In any case, even his friends did not deny that he went and hid in a marsh. Furthermore, he was ill on the occasion of the Second Battle of Philippi as well. When both battles were finished and won, it was scarcely surprising to find that Antony, in the subsequent division of the Roman empire, emerged as very much the senior partner.

Moreover, the curious health pattern repeated itself at the decisive naval engagement of Naulochus against Sextus Pompeius in 36 BC, during which the future Augustus was said to have lain on his back in a stupor, not getting up until Agrippa had fought and defeated the enemy fleet. This was Antony's story, and one can imagine the extrovert Antony, who had a lot of tricky behaviour to put up with from his fellow triumvir, indulging in scornful laughter. It must have looked as if the young man was a physical coward. But the mere suggestion of such a thing was the gravest of handicaps to an upper-class Roman, and most of all to the personage who aspired to rule the Roman world.

In order to dispel the smear he drove himself into two series of campaigns, first in Dalmatia (35–3) and then in Spain (27–5). In the first of these two wars he was wounded, and in the second he was injured; then he had to abandon the Spanish operations altogether because he had fallen ill once more. It was from that time onwards that he never took the field again for the remaining thirty-nine years of his life. This decision may partly have been motivated by his consciousness that he was not a good enough soldier. For, after all, it was no good Augustus implying criticisms of Caesar's undesirable autocracy if at the same time he invited totally unfavourable comparisons with his predecessor's military talents – much better to keep away from that area of activity altogether. And so the great wars of expansion and annexation which brought the northern frontier to the Danube, and temporarily to the Elbe, were commanded by others on his behalf.

Yet, even without leading his legions in person, the amount of work that Augustus had set himself to do would have shattered men of far sounder health than himself. For this reason, it was more than ever essential that he should have reliable helpers.

In the first place, he would not have been able to do his work at all, indeed to judge from the fate of Caesar he would not even have survived, without the cooperation of the senate, whose members were the only men in the state possessing the necessary qualifications, experience and prestige to help him bear the load. So Augustus continually did everything within his power to enlist the cooperation of its members. It used to be said, by Theodor Mommsen, that his empire was ruled by a 'dyarchy', a dual control system of ruler and senate. In fact, it was the emperor who remained in charge. But the high degree of his reliance on the senate's collaboration is shown by the sort of message he sent out to the governors of provinces:

The Imperator Caesar Augustus, chief priest, holding the tribunician power for the nineteenth year declares:
A decree of the senate was passed in the consulship of Gaius Calvisius and Lucius Passienus, with me as one of those present at the writing. Since it affects the welfare of the allies of the Roman people, I have decided to send it into the provinces, appended to this my prefatory edict, so that it may be known to all who are under our care. From this it will be evident to all the inhabitants of the provinces how much both I and the senate are concerned that none of our subjects should suffer any improper treatment or any extortion.[19]

Here the ruler is deliberately citing the senate as a valuable, essential collaborative organ of his restored Republic and of his government.

If, however, it was to fulfil these roles, it had to be rehabilitated and made worthy of this trust. On three occasions, therefore, Augustus was granted powers which enabled him to revise the senatorial roll (later in his reign, this task was undertaken once more, by a special commission), until undesirable and disloyal elements had been weeded out. The first time, when Agrippa was his colleague, fifty or sixty senators were induced to resign, and 140 others were expelled. It was scarcely likely to be a popular operation.

He was thought to be wearing a coat of mail under his tunic as he presided, and a sword by his side, while ten of the most robust of his friends among the senators stood by his chair. The historian Cremutius Cordus writes that even then the senators were not allowed to approach except one by one, and after the folds of their robes had been carefully searched.[20]

By these revisions the total membership of the senate was gradually reduced from a thousand to six hundred. But there were more retirements than those figures imply, since the new total included numerous new senators whom Augustus had brought in. Many of them were his political supporters from municipalities throughout the length and breadth of Italy: 'A formidable collection', concludes Donald Earl, 'of hard-faced, tough-minded men enriched by civil war and revolution.'

Augustus himself attended the senate punctiliously until his advancing years made this difficult. But it was too large a body to consult all the time, and for this purpose he needed a smaller body of senators with whom to discuss business. Like Republican leaders of the past, he could gather his personal friends round him unofficially; but now the process gradually became more formal, and recognized 'friends of the emperor' emerged. From among these 'friends' and others he also appointed an inner council of senators as his official advisers, to act as intermediaries between himself and the senate, and to help him draw up its agenda. This council comprised the two consuls of the time, one holder of each of the other offices, and fifteen senators who were chosen by lot and were changed every six months.

But Augustus' real administrative breakthrough was to make the second element in the social and financial hierarchy, the knights, into salaried employees of the state, both in civil jobs and in the army. These men had already, over a long passage of time, been showing their talent for business and administration. But apart from their employment as judges (strongly contested by the senators), they had never before been systematically mobilized to occupy official posts. The knights broadened

73

the cadre of Augustus' helpers in a particularly valuable way because they represented a whole class of new men, in the towns of Italy and the provinces, who felt, on the whole, unattached to the ideals of the traditional Republican leadership, and were correspondingly susceptible to the appeal of the new regime. Their incorporation, which must have been peculiarly welcome to a man of his Italian background, meant the victory of the non-political classes, and the end of a purely Roman oligarchy. Moreover, below the knights, even the comparatively despised class of ex-slaves, known as freedmen, began to benefit from a degree of recognition and definition which, although still excluding them from the full Roman franchise and the official career, paved the way for the future when they would rise to significant heights. Meanwhile freedmen already played a busy subordinate role in Augustus' household, where they gave him unostentatious help in the conduct of his affairs.

Towards the bulk of the citizen population at Rome, his attitude seems to have been somewhat cynical – or perhaps he was merely realistic in his low appreciation of its practical role. As before, the Assembly of the Roman People remained, in theory, the sovereign body, and still conducted the annual elections of officers of the state. But it had never, even in Republican times, conducted those elections as an entirely free agent without impulsion and coercion by powerful personages, and it certainly did not do so now. Augustus refrained, it is true, from any systematic interference with the electoral processes. Such interference was unnecessary, since he already disposed of a vast variety of suitable underground means for ensuring that men he did not like were not elected. Formal nomination and commendation, such as subsequent emperors chose to employ, were rarely required. But, as Dio Cassius observed, he 'took care that none should be appointed who were unfit, or as the result of partisan cliques or bribery'. And when he chose to divulge his wishes about a candidate for election, the man he favoured duly found himself elected. Indeed, in Republican fashion, Augustus canvassed openly for his candidates in person, and went on doing so until AD 8, near the very end of his reign. Three years earlier a new law had devised an elaborate process which virtually compelled the voters to elect a given list – though still without actually destroying their right to conduct the election. An examination of the personages who proved successful in securing consulships reveals that a careful balance was struck between the traditional nobility and the new political supporters of Augustus. The latter class rises more rapidly from about 5 BC, when the practice began of usually appointing, in each year, at least two successive pairs of consuls who held office for only a part of the year, so as to make room for more partisans of the regime.

Augustus, then, did not suffer from the delusion that any measure of democracy could be introduced into the state. After all, it had never existed previously, and his own army-controlled discreet autocracy left, if possible, even less room for it than before. The imperial method employed for controlling the urban crowds, 'bread and circuses', was already nothing new in Augustus' time, but it was he who developed its application systematically. No less than 320,000 members of the city populace received money gifts from him in 5 BC, and the number of recipients was 200,000 three years later. Moreover, his public shows surpassed anything that had ever been seen before in their frequency, variety and magnificence. The people were kept happy, and Augustus showed his successors how this could be done.

Like all conscientious Roman rulers, he spent an immense amount of his time dispensing justice. In addition to the traditional law-courts, which remained active, his reign witnessed, by stages, the institution both of a senatorial court, presided over by the consuls, and an imperial court, in which he himself was the judge. Each of these institutions was based, to some extent, on Republican precedents, but each also represented something substantially new. Augustus took his duties as president of his court very seriously; there are contradictory accounts of whether he was lenient or not. From his or the senate's primary jurisdiction, there was no right of appeal, but another new innovation provided that appeals from other courts could now be heard either by the senate or, far more frequently, by himself.

In spite of his own vulnerable morals, he wished to be seen as a guardian of sound private, sexual, morality, which he sought to revive by an extraordinary range of enactments. The sort of laxity which Augustus sought to check was depicted with gloomy gusto by Horace, who wrote of the deplorable behaviour to which even a Roman matron might sink:

> Yes, she will rise quite openly from the table
> Watched by her husband, leaving to meet a huckster
> Or some insistent cargo-shipper
> Rich with the price of her degradation.[21]

Both Horace and Augustus were victims of the widespread ancient fallacy that legislation could cure such ills. It failed, as later emperors, in spite of their loyalty to their founder's memory, were obliged to admit.

Although Augustus' entire programme, political, military, social and moral, was so ingeniously designed and presented that he carried most of the ruling class with him – heavily infiltrated as this was by his own political supporters – those substantial remnants of the Republican nobility who regarded his constitution as a sham remained adamantly disloyal. The story of the whole reign could be told as a long list of Augustus' almost unremitting suspicions and fears, fed by repeated unpleasant incidents which even the continual presence of his highly paid praetorian guardsmen was never able to bring to an end. He did not need the alleged advice of Maecenas to 'employ persons who are to keep their eyes and ears open to anything which affects his supremacy'.

Maecenas was one of the confidential advisers whom a man of Augustus' dizzy eminence was compelled to call in to assist him. The Roman nobles who served as his councillors, even when their trustworthiness was beyond reproach, could not be asked to perform this indispensable function, and, in spite of elaborate marriage alliances, they remained curiously absent from the inner entourage he constructed around him. The members of this inmost group received a great deal of honour from Augustus, who clung to them with energetic persistence, since he did not form new friendships with any ease. Nevertheless he exploited them quite ruthlessly, expecting from them the same dedication in their duties as he was prepared to display himself and revealing an uncanny talent for turning them to his own purposes.

Maecenas, who came from a royal and rich Etruscan family, was not a senator, but a knight, and content to remain one. For many years he performed vital political and diplomatic functions for Augustus, acting for him at Rome during his absences, suppressing conspiracies on his behalf, exercising a moderating influence over his decisions, and encouraging Virgil and Horace to express the admiration they felt for the Augustan Peace. Yet Maecenas, effeminate, extravagant, homosexual, must have seemed the very reverse of everything admired by Augustus – who mocked at his love of precious stones and his 'curled and unguent-dripping' literary style, but made use of him in a thousand different ways.

These luxurious characteristics of Maecenas, and his liking for eating the flesh of young donkeys, were deplored by Augustus' even more influential helper Marcus Agrippa. The existence of Agrippa was a blessing for Augustus, who could never have gained the mastery of the Roman world without his talents as general and admiral. Nevertheless Agrippa was an utterly loyal subordinate – but willing to be the subordinate of Augustus and no one else. The *princeps*, in response, continued to trust him implicitly, and exploited him endlessly. Unaristocratic and puritan, dour, 'a man closer to rusticity than to sophistication', Agrippa was quite out of sympathy with the subtle new language of Virgil and Horace, but at home in such practical matters as the construction of aqueducts and public edifices (including the Pantheon), to supplement the enormous building programme of Augustus.

Agrippa wrote a memorandum advocating that privately owned art treasures should be confiscated by the government for the benefit of the whole population. The people loved him, but he was detested by the nobles, who carried their hatred beyond the grave by refusing even to come to his funeral Games. As a successor to the throne, they would never have endured him.

This was a thought which must have worried Augustus deeply when he himself was struck down by what seemed to be a fatal illness in 23 BC. Nevertheless, it was to Agrippa, in this crisis, that he handed his signet-ring. Agrippa, as he must have known, would never have been tolerated in his place. Yet, if he himself had died, someone would have had to carry on the government. It was true that 'succession' to his elusive status was, constitutionally speaking, impossible. But it was already obvious to most people that he would have a successor all the same, and there were signs that the nineteen-year-old Marcellus, whom he had married to his daughter Julia, was being groomed for the role. Presumably Augustus hoped, in 23, that if he died Agrippa would pave the way for Marcellus' eventual succession – though it was widely believed that in such circumstances Agrippa would have got rid of the young man altogether. The desperate issue was never put to the test, because Augustus recovered. Instead it was Marcellus who met his death, from natural causes, later in the very same year – whereupon Julia, aged sixteen, was married off to the forty-year-old Agrippa, who had to divorce Augustus' niece in order to become her husband. Even now, however, the attitude of the senatorial class still made it impossible to envisage Agrippa as successor, and instead plans were made to prepare the two sons Julia bore him soon afterwards, Gaius and Lucius, for this imperial destiny.

In 12 BC, while they were still young boys, their father Agrippa, shattered by a strenuous campaign on the frontiers, fell ill and died. Four years later the death of Maecenas too occurred, after a fifteen-year period of semi-retirement which may have begun when he indiscreetly communicated a political secret to his wife. Augustus' younger stepson Drusus, who had distinguished himself as a general in Germany, was also dead; and the man of the moment was now Drusus' elder brother Tiberius, who, after a period of withdrawal to Rhodes was formally adopted by Augustus in AD 4, after the premature deaths of Gaius and Lucius. From now on Tiberius' succession, although still legally unmentionable, was certain.

Yet Augustus' last years were disastrous. His family troubles deeply depressed him. His daughter Julia, whose third, unwilling husband had been Tiberius, was exiled; and so, later on, were her daughter Julia and her surviving son Agrippa Postumus. The women were accused of immorality – and one cannot help feeling at least a certain sympathy with the elder Julia,* matrimonially exploited beyond even the Roman norm – but the real fear was directed against their lovers, who were regarded as possible instigators of sedition.

Meanwhile the Illyrian revolt of AD 6 also upset Augustus very greatly. A senior Roman officer of the time, Velleius Paterculus, described the disastrous situation:

Roman citizens were overpowered, traders were massacred, a considerable detachment of discharged soldiers, stationed in the region which was most remote from the commander, was exterminated to a man, Macedonia was seized by armed forces, everywhere was wholesale devastation by fire and sword. Moreover, such a panic did this war inspire that even the courage of Caesar Augustus, rendered steady and firm by experience in so many wars, was shaken with fear.

Accordingly levies were held, from every quarter all the veterans were

* When surprise was expressed that her children looked like their legitimate father, she replied, 'I never take on a steersman unless the ship is full', i.e. only had lovers when she was pregnant.

recalled to the standards, and men and women were compelled, in proportion to their income, to furnish freedmen as soldiers.

Men heard Augustus say in the senate that, unless precautions were taken, the enemy might appear in sight of Rome within ten days.[22]

Then, in AD 9, came another and even heavier blow, the destruction of Varus and his three legions by Arminius in the Teutoburg Forest near Minden. This grave event directly resulted from Augustus' failure to have followed up the invasion of the lands between Rhine and Elbe by adequate occupation or organization: and these lands now had to be abandoned.

An army unexcelled in bravery, the first of Roman armies in discipline, in energy, and the unkindness of fortune, was surrounded, nor was as much opportunity as they had wished given to the soldiers either of fighting or of extricating themselves, except against heavy odds; indeed some had to pay a grave penalty for using the arms and showing the spirit of Romans.

Hemmed in by forests and marshes and ambuscades, the column was exterminated almost to a man by the very enemy whom it had always slaughtered like cattle, whose life or death had depended solely upon the wrath or the pity of the Romans. The general had more courage to die than to fight, for, following the example of his father and grandfather, he ran himself through with his sword.[23]

On hearing this news, Augustus, now aged seventy-one, seems to have succumbed to a temporary nervous breakdown. 'In fact, they say that he was so greatly affected that for several months in succession he cut neither his beard nor his hair, and sometimes he would dash his head against a door, crying: 'Quinctilius Varus, give me back my legions.'' '[24]

In the same unhappy years the government began to show an increased sensitiveness to criticisms and libels, which became the targets of treason charges; less tolerance was now shown towards differences of opinion. However, all the necessary steps were efficiently taken to mend the series of recent misfortunes, and the government of the empire did not fail.

In August AD 14 Augustus caught a chill on a night journey by ship, and on the nineteenth, at Nola in Campania, he died.

Ever since 2 BC, when the elder Julia was exiled, or at the latest from AD 6 and 9 when there were catastrophes in the field, Augustus had shown signs of losing his grip. Throughout his life he had suffered from deplorable health. He had overworked himself consistently. He had lived in constant fear of sedition and conspiracy. And now he was old. When things, in the end, turned out badly he was too worn out to cope with the emergencies by himself.

But the reason why his regime did not collapse was because he had arranged to have the support of Tiberius, who was elevated, finally, to the virtual position of his colleague. Not the least of all Augustus' achievements was the foresight he had exercised in buoying up his declining years and fortunes in this way. It was a commonplace of antiquity that he had been cruel in his earlier years, and mild in his later ones – or 'weary of his cruelty' as was sometimes said. But it would be also appropriate to add a third, final, phase in which he was scarcely any longer the master of his difficult position at all, and was saved by Tiberius.

Part II

The Julio–Claudian Emperors

3

Tiberius

Tiberius Claudius Nero was born in 42 BC, to highly aristocratic parents. When he was four, his mother Livia divorced her husband to marry Octavian, the future Augustus. During his stepfather's subsequent reign Tiberius spent twenty-two years commanding armies with great distinction, especially in Illyricum and Pannonia – the modern Yugoslavia and Hungary (12–9 BC, AD 6–9) – and in Germany (9–7 BC, AD 4–6).

After Agrippa's death in 12 BC Augustus compelled Tiberius to divorce his wife in order to marry the dead man's widow, the ruler's daughter Julia, with whom he lived unhappily until his withdrawal to Rhodes in 6 BC. But the deaths of the emperor's grandsons and destined heirs Gaius and Lucius caused Augustus to adopt Tiberius as his son (AD 4) – and as the obvious heir to his throne. During the difficult last decade of Augustus' life, as we have seen, Tiberius played an immensely prominent part at his side, and his position received still further official recognition in AD 13.

In the following year Augustus died, and Tiberius' accession was automatic. In the years immediately ahead he employed his adoptive son Germanicus and his own son Drusus the younger as his helpers, notably in the suppression of mutinies which at once broke out in Germany and southern Pannonia (north Yugoslavia) respectively. Germanicus, who was very popular, subsequently fought three imposing but unproductive campaigns beyond the German frontier (14–16). Then in the company of his wife Agrippina the elder (the daughter of Agrippa), he was

83

transferred to a major appointment in the east. This terminated in his death (19), which provoked widespread grief and resulted in the recall to Rome of Piso, governor of Syria, who was charged with his murder and committed suicide.

The obvious heir was now Tiberius' son Drusus the younger. But four years later he also died, and preferment next went to Nero Caesar and Drusus Caesar, the young sons of the late Germanicus and of Agrippina.

Meanwhile a powerful position was being gradually built up by Lucius Aelius Sejanus, the praetorian prefect. In 23 he concentrated the praetorian guard – previously dispersed round central Italian towns – in a single barracks at Rome itself.

There was continual fear of conspiracies and supposed conspiracies, which treason laws were employed to suppress. Sejanus took the lead in initiating such accusations, and became more powerful still after Tiberius had retired from Rome to the island of Capreae (Capri) in 26, never to return to the city again.

The combined suspicions of emperor and prefect now fell on Agrippina and her sons Nero Caesar and Drusus Caesar, who were arrested (in 29–30) and executed or forced to kill themselves in the years that followed. Meanwhile Sejanus was promised a marriage connexion with the emperor, and, although he had started his career as a mere knight, he gained the consulship in 31 as Tiberius' own colleague. But his downfall promptly followed. Warned that Sejanus was plotting against him, Tiberius secretly transferred the praetorian command to Macro, who succeeded in arranging for Sejanus to be arrested during a meeting of the senate: its members immediately ordered his execution.

Although the well-ruled empire as a whole scarcely felt these metropolitan tremors, the years that lay adead were perilous and destructive for the dead man's eminent friends. On 16 March AD 37, at the age of seventy-nine, Tiberius died at Misenum beside the Bay of Naples, and Caligula (Gaius), Germanicus' third and surviving son whom he had taken to live with him in Capreae, became his successor.

When Tiberius was two, his father, after whom he had been named, was on the run from the triumvirs because of his strongly Republican convictions. And so the infant 'passed his earliest years amid hardship and tribulation, since he was everywhere the companion of his parents on their flight'; and there were many perilous incidents, which may well have left their mark on his character.

Moreover, when he was not yet four years old, he saw his mother

Livia snatched away by Octavian, the very man who had made her and her husband into refugees and outcasts. Yet when Tiberius grew up, he served his stepfather in the field with incomparable loyalty and industry, and no other Roman of the age spent so many years commanding great armies in battle. The praises of Horace were more than justified.

> Tiberius next moved into deadly action:
>   Doomed by the Emperor's star,
> The uncouth Raetians fled; Nero pursued,
> A marvel and a prodigy in battle,
> Carving vast havoc among hearts devoted
>   To freedom and to death.
> As tireless and determined as the wave-
> Harrying south wind when the dancing Pleiads
> Glimmer through ragged cloud, he shocked the enemy's
>   Massed regiments, he spurred
> His neighing charger through the holocaust.[1]

But Augustus asked more terrible things of Tiberius than warfare. For' after Agrippa's death in 12 BC, he was compelled to divorce his beloved and pregnant wife, Vipsania, in order to marry Agrippa's widow Julia, the daughter of the emperor. The new marriage turned sour, and in 2 BC Augustus terminated it without even bothering to ask the husband's consent. For Tiberius was far away: four years earlier he had retired to Rhodes, because he did not want to seem to be standing in the way of Gaius and Lucius, the older sons of Agrippa and Julia, who were being speedily promoted; and probably, after all his services, he found their elevation too humiliating to endure.

When they died and Tiberius himself was adopted and clearly destined for the throne, Augustus ordered him, in his turn, to adopt his own eighteen-year-old nephew Germanicus, the son of his late brother Drusus the elder: although this implicit designation of Germanicus as successor presumptive must have seemed somewhat insulting to Tiberius, himself the father of a son (Drusus the younger) who was only about two years younger than Germanicus. The order seemed to show that Augustus still retained certain reservations about Tiberius in his mind. Indeed, on the occasion of his adoption of Tiberius, he declared 'I do this for the sake of the state'; and it appeared to some that he was deliberately expressing reluctance because he did not feel that Tiberius had the right sort of character for the job. Nor did he attempt to dissemble sorrow that his grandsons Gaius and Lucius were no longer there to succeed him.

However their loss meant that there was now no alternative to Tiberius, and so Augustus made the best of the situation, bringing Tiberius' name and portrait onto the coinage and writing him the most cordial letters as his stepson continued to fight the empire's wars:

Goodbye, my very dear Tiberius, and the best of luck go with you in your battles on my behalf – as well as on behalf of the Muses. Goodbye, dearest and bravest of men and the most conscientious general alive. If anything goes wrong with you, I shall never smile again . . . Your summer campaigns, dear Tiberius, deserve my heartiest praise; I am sure that no other man alive could have conducted them more capably than yourself in the face of so many difficulties and the warweariness of the troops.

If any business comes up that demands unusually careful thought, or that annoys me, I swear by the God of Truth that I miss my dear Tiberius more than I can say . . . When people tell me, or I read, that constant campaigning is wearing you out, I'm damned if I don't get gooseflesh in sympathy. I beg you to take things easy, because if you were to fall ill the news would kill your mother and me, and the whole country would be endangered by doubts about the rulership.[2]

And indeed, as Augustus grew old and disasters multiplied, it was to Tiberius that the stabilization of the damaged imperial system was probably due. It was he, too, who kept the administration going, and even improved it by useful but unobtrusive reforms – though in these difficult times a tightening of the treason laws, which became characteristic of the years that followed, had also become perceptible. Friends of Tiberius were substituted for friends of Augustus in important positions, and the military powers over the provinces and armies granted to the heir apparent in AD 13 were equal to those of Augustus himself.

When, therefore, Augustus died in the following year, the transition went smoothly enough. Possessing, as he already did, equal powers of command to the late ruler, Tiberius duly gave the watchword to the praetorian guard as its supreme commander. He also administered an immediate oath of allegiance to the people in general – the same sort of oath which his predecessor, too, had administered to the population of the west in 32 BC. The first to swear this allegiance to Tiberius were the consuls, and then, in their presence, the praetorian prefect Lucius Seius Strabo and the prefect of the grain supply; next the senate and the soldiers, and after them the public as a whole.

The first senatorial business of the new reign confirmed Augustus' bequests to the soldiers, without whose support the imperial regime could not continue. However there was general agreement – and this remained a cardinal principle for more than two centuries to come – that it was not for the troops but for the senate to set in motion the formal investiture of Tiberius with that uninheritable collection of powers which constituted the principate. For although, before his adoptive father's death, he had been granted almost all the individual powers already, he had not, of course, been in possession of the actual supremacy itself – the status of emperor, as it was now coming to be regarded.

Tacitus stresses the embarrassment that this unprecedented situation infused into the first senate debates after Augustus' death. But the essential point (to which he does not refer) is that the supreme position was formally decreed to Tiberius by the senate, on the motion of the consuls.

Throughout these discussions the new ruler had seemed reluctant to accept his elevation. Since none of the nobles stood a chance of competing with him, and since the army was unprepared to tolerate a revived Republic, Tiberius' apparent reluctance was widely interpreted as hypocritical – as it became when repeated, for form's sake, by a whole succession of subsequent emperors. And it could, indeed, be regarded, if not as hypocritical, at least as quite pointless, since he was merely resisting the inevitable.

But what he wanted to point out was the appalling burden of work he was taking on. The senators ought to understand, he felt, what a 'miserable and burdensome slavery' it was – a deliberate variation on the 'glorious slavery' of monarchy in Greek philosophical theory. He had already been working intensely hard, in positions of the utmost responsibility, for decade after decade – and fighting, too, since, as he remarked to Germanicus, Augustus had sent him to Germany alone, not to speak of other countries, no less than nine times.

But Augustus had done much worse than that. He had advanced the juvenile Gaius and Lucius at Tiberius' expense. And he had ruined his private life by forcing him to divorce a beloved wife for one whom he soon came to hate. Tiberius was deeply embittered by these cold-blooded, tyrannical marriage combinations, as by so much else. 'For him', remarks Sir Ronald Syme, 'the splendid prize was spoiled and tarnished.' And now, after all his years of hard labour and sadness, Augustus had left him a heritage which, as the heir knew very well, would be tougher than all that had gone before.

After his funeral, Augustus was consecrated a god of the Roman state, like Caesar before him.

But there was an unconscious irony in the new emperor's declaration that all his policies would conform utterly to the policies of the dead man: 'I treat all his actions and words as if they had the force of law.'* This was paradoxical not only because of all his past exploitation by Augustus, but because the future troubles and discords of his reign were directly due to his Augustan inheritance. For although well aware that it was too late for the machinery to be reversed, at heart Tiberius was a Republican like his forebears – fundamentally unsympathetic to Augustus' cunning elimination of the Republic, and to the emotional propaganda in which this process had been swathed.

Unlike Augustus' middle-class Octavian family, the Claudii from whom Tiberius came were of supremely ancient lineage, with the whole history of the Republic behind them. True, they had acquired, over the centuries, a reputation as self-seeking and opportunistic. But Tiberius did not share these traits. On the contrary, his consciousness of great family made him into a conservative – and a conservative lacking in enthusiasm for the subtle but sweeping Augustan innovations to which his duty, as he conceived it, obliged him to remain loyal.

Now Tiberius was incapable of displaying this reluctant loyalty with a good grace. Indeed he could do nothing with a good grace. For one thing he was too honest a man. Americans used to contrast their presidents William McKinley and Benjamin Harrison by saying that McKinley could make a friend by the way he said no, whereas Harrison could make an enemy by the way he said yes. Augustus was McKinley, and Tiberius was Harrison.

Moreover, despite the best intentions, he had an unhappy knack of getting himself into embarrassing situations, which were not necessarily

* Augustus had also perpetuated his memory by 'adopting' in his will his wife Livia, henceforward known as Julia Augusta.

his own fault but might have been avoided, all the same, by other and more agile men. When, for example, he was at Rhodes:

It happened once that, in arranging the next day's programme, he had expressed the wish to visit the local sick. His staff misunderstood him. Orders went out that all the patients in town should be carried to a public colonnade and there arranged in separate groups according to their ailments. Tiberius was shocked. For a while he stood at a loss, but at last went round each of the patients, apologizing even to the humblest and least important for the inconvenience he had caused them.[3]

After Tiberius became emperor, similar incidents continued to occur. During the initial debates one senator, Quintus Haterius, called out: 'How long, Caesar, will you allow the state to be without a head?' Tiberius was so manifestly annoyed at this rebuke that Haterius called on him afterwards to try to make matters right: 'He went into the palace to apologize, and, as Tiberius walked by, grovelled at his feet. Thereupon the emperor crashed to the ground, either by accident or because he was brought down by the grip of Haterius – who was then all but killed by the guards.'[4]

Because his personal encounters so often went awry in this sort of fashion, Tiberius found it a painful effort to make himself accessible – which Augustus had succeeded in doing so well. For he was totally lacking – and this was a grave handicap for a ruler of Rome – in Augustus' fluent capacity for communication. Tiberius was an excellent speaker, and had a fine gift for language, as befitted a man who loved Greek literature and culture and enjoyed the company of scholars and writers. But the words which he weighed out in so masterly a fashion, though forceful and imposing, were not only couched in an obsolete and pedantic vocabulary (which incurred the mockery of Augustus), but became famous for their obscurity and ambiguity. Cautious and secretive, slow to come to a decision, Tiberius had learnt during his hard life to hide his feelings and his thoughts; and he became obsessively averse to the open disclosure of his intentions.

As Dio Cassius observed,

He possessed a most peculiar nature. He never let what he desired appear in his conversation, and what he said he wanted he usually did not desire at all. On the contrary, his words indicated the exact opposite of his real purpose; he denied all interest in what he longed for, and urged the claims of what he hated. He would exhibit anger over matters that were very far from arousing his wrath, and make a show of affability where he was most vexed. He would pretend to pity those whom he severely punished, and would retain a grudge against those whom he pardoned. Sometimes he would regard his bitterest foe as if he were his most intimate companion, and again he would treat his dearest friend like a complete stranger.

In short, he thought it bad policy for the sovereign to reveal his thoughts; this was often the cause, he said, of great failures, whereas by the opposite course far more and greater successes were attained.[5]

Such was Tiberius' famous 'hypocrisy'; and it is easy to see how the term came to be applied to him, despite the basic honesty of his intentions. This conflict between what he said and what he thought, this unintelligibility he could not bring himself to avoid, caused a great deal of trouble. For he expected people to understand his guarded equivocations, and to deduce from them what he really wanted done. Not unnaturally, therefore, as Dio went on to observe, 'people often came to grief by approving what he said instead of what he wished'.

And what made matters worse was the manner in which he spoke, since this was severe, sarcastic and annihilating. Tiberius was a grim man – the grimmest alive, according to Pliny the elder. Moreover, despite all his iron reserve and self-concealment, he was liable to violent outbursts of anger. Augustus had complained to Livia of her son's unendurable sourness, and had been accustomed to break off his own freer and lighter conversation when he saw his stepson entering the room: he commiserated, it was said, with the Roman people, who were destined to suffer mastication by his successor's slow jaws.

Whether from preference or because he could not do otherwise, Tiberius failed to cultivate amiability. For example, he ostentatiously failed to share the popular taste for Games. 'Let them hate provided they approve', he was quoted as declaring, with aristocratic contempt for flattery and the crowd. He was ready, he added, to face resentment, however bitter or unjust, if the interests of the nation so required.

And yet, although that was the ideal he set before himself, his temperament made him incapable of living up to it. For when people misjudged him he became deeply disturbed, and would go to enormous lengths to justify himself. Basically humane though he was, this vigorous reaction to criticism sometimes gave him the appearance of being morbidly and callously self-centred: which, in turn, could make him cruel. And this happened all the more easily because his character showed a marked inclination towards suspicion and fright. For such tendencies no emperor, faced with all the perils of his station, can altogether be blamed, least of all Tiberius who inherited such a back-breaking assignment – which his character scarcely equipped him to fulfil.

The official artists who portrayed his features, though they did not wholly refrain from the idealization which had characterized the portraiture of Augustus, allowed themselves to express a hint, also, of his individual gloominess.

His looks were described in detail by Suetonius:

Corpulent he was, big-set, and strong, of stature above the ordinary, broad between the shoulders and large-breasted; in all other parts also of the body (from the crown of his head to the very sole of his foot) of equal making and congruent proportion. But his left hand was more nimble and stronger than the right; and his joints so firm that with his finger he was able to bore through a green and sound apple, with a fillip also to break the head of a boy, yea of a good stripling and big youth.

Of colour and complexion he was clear and white, wearing the hair of his head long behind, insomuch as it covered his very neck; which was thought in him to be a fashion appropriate to his lineage and family. He had an ingenuous and well-favoured face, wherein notwithstanding appeared many small tumours or risings, and a pair of very great goggle eyes in his head, such as (whereat a man would marvel) could see even by night and in the dark. But that was only for a little while and when they opened first after sleep, for in the end they waxed dim again. His gait was with his neck stiff and shooting forward, with countenance bent and composed lightly to severity.

For the most he was silent. Seldom or never should you have him talk with those next about him, and if he did, his speech was exceedingly slow, not without a certain wanton gesticulation and fumbling with his fingers.[6]

In his later years, according to Tacitus, 'the emperor became sensitive about his appearance. Tall and abnormally thin, bent and bald, he had a face covered with sores and plaster.' Otherwise, however, in spite of a tendency to take too much drink, he retained excellent health, and habitually rejected the services of doctors.

At the very outset of his reign, indeed while the initial deliberations of the senate were still going on, the armies in Pannonia and on the Rhine began to mutiny, because their terms of service and demobilization benefits had fallen short of what Augustus had promised them. Tiberius' son Drusus the younger dealt effectively with the Pannonian troubles; while Drusus' cousin and adoptive brother Germanicus proved less effective in his handling of the German disturbance, since he made extensive concessions, which Tiberius was subsequently obliged to withdraw.

Germanicus, handsome though spindle-legged (he tried to cure this by constant riding after meals), is one of Tacitus' heroes. Yet even in his account there are ambiguities and silences, and it seems today that his brilliance displayed a certain superficial flashiness. However his cheerful, open, affable manners gained him great popularity, since they presented such a contrast to the emperor's own awkwardness.

After the mutinies had been suppressed, Germanicus plunged into three campaigns designed to reconquer the lands between Rhine and Elbe that had been evacuated after Varus lost his life and his legions in AD 9. In spite of spectacular expeditions Germanicus failed to achieve this purpose, though he subsequently gained the award of a Triumph. Tiberius was accused of jealousy because he terminated these operations, but even if they had continued no positive or permanent result would have been achieved. Nevertheless, when Germanicus returned to Rome he received a tremendously enthusiastic reception, and this cannot greatly have commended him to his uncle.

Emperors liked to have two possible successors available at one and the same time. Augustus had promoted both Gaius and Lucius, and Tiberius elevated Germanicus (in accordance with Augustus' proposal) and at the same time advanced his own son Drusus the younger, without declaring openly between the two men. This may have been, on the part of each ruler, a policy of reinsurance, in case one or the other heir presumptive died before him (and in fact not one but both candidates predeceased their respective emperor, on both occasions). But Augustus and Tiberius were surrounded by people who were only too willing to encourage their suspicions, and if a group looking to the future collected round a young prince, as must inevitably happen, then it no doubt seemed to them only prudent to counterbalance this potentially hazardous faction by promoting a second prince and a rival party. And cliques of this kind duly collected round Germanicus and Drusus, although the princes themselves apparently remained on good terms with one another.

Drusus was now given an important Danubian command, and Germanicus was allocated a similar post in the east. He never returned from it, but died there in 19. His death followed an unedifying and violent dispute with Tiberius' governor of Syria, Cnaeus Calpurnius Piso. When Germanicus' wife, the violent and headstrong Agrippina, had sailed home with her husband's ashes, and the senior officials in the east had appointed one of their number to relieve Piso, he refused to depart, and even attempted, unsuccessfully, to expel his successor by force. Then, returning to Rome, he was accused in the senate of poisoning Germanicus. Without awaiting the verdict, he killed himself.

Germanicus had apparently died a natural death, and Tiberius never asserted that Piso had murdered him, though he could not forgive the governor for starting a private war. But it was widely believed that Piso had been requested secretly by Tiberius, before Germanicus' arrival in the east, to prevent the young man from doing anything stupid; and this, it seemed, was what he had been trying to achieve – with all the tactlessness of a Republican of the old school. The existence of such purely informal instructions from Tiberius is by no means improbable, though Piso refrained from claiming their existence, because any such public claim would have alienated Tiberius, thus leaving Piso's own prospects no better than they had been before.

The death of Germanicus meant that the emperor's son Drusus the younger now became the undisputed heir. Four years later, however, he died as well. Tiberius was proving no more fortunate than Augustus in his attempts to bring forward a successor.

Drusus was survived by two sons, but they were still only babies; and the obvious heirs were now the sons of Germanicus and Agrippina, Nero Caesar and Drusus Caesar, aged seventeen and sixteen respectively. And so the sixty-five-year-old emperor commended these youths to the parental protection of the senate.

But his relations with that body were by no means satisfactory. True, he showed almost painful eagerness to preserve the traditional dignity of the senior senators and holders of official posts. For example, if he saw one of the consuls approaching, he would rise to his feet, and if they came to the palace as dinner-guests, he meticulously received them at the door, and showed them out when they left. Moreover he was very careful to ensure that his methods for influencing the elections remained discreetly indirect. He also abandoned Augustus' advisory council of senators in favour of a larger collection of friends and leading men; this was a less formal body than hitherto, so that Tiberius was, in fact, flatteringly suggesting that there could only be one formal advisory body – namely the senate itself. He took care to attend its meetings assiduously, referring for its consideration all matters of public policy, great and small, intervening only when abuses made intervention necessary, and indeed generally going even beyond the precedent of his model Augustus in enhancing the senators' authority.

He assured them that this was his policy, in highly respectful terms:

'I say now and have often said before, Fathers of the Senate, that a well-disposed and helpful prince, to whom you have given such great and un-restrained power, ought to be the servant of the senate, often of the citizens as a whole, and sometimes even of individuals. I have no hesitation in telling you that I have looked upon you as kind, just, and indulgent masters, and still so regard you.'

And so he introduced a semblance of free government, by maintaining the ancient dignity and powers of the senate and the officials.[7]

But a semblance was all that it could be. Admittedly Tiberius, a Republican by ancestry and conviction alike, not only deprecated excessive adulation directed towards himself, but tried very strenuously and sincerely to make the senate a serious partner, and force it to assume its responsibilities. Yet his attempt inevitably proved unsuccessful, because it came at too late a historical stage. After half a century of Augustus' rule the senators had become incapable of initiating policy on their own account, and could not even cooperate, to any meaningful extent, in its initiation by the emperor.

The situation was perfectly summed up in AD 15, when the senator Marcus Granius Marcellus found himself accused of treasonable actions: offensive remarks about Tiberius' character, the setting-up of his own statue above those of the Caesars, and the removal of the head from a statue of the divine Augustus so that a head of Tiberius could be put in its place.

The charges were damning ... The emperor lost his temper and, voluble for once, exclaimed that he personally would vote, openly and on oath. This would have compelled the other senators to do the same. But, since there still remained some traces of declining freedom, Cnaeus Calpurnius Piso asked a question: 'Caesar, will you vote first or last? If first, I shall have your lead to follow; if last, I am afraid of inadvertently voting against you.'[8]

This struck home, added Tacitus, and well it might, since Piso had gone to the root of the imperial problem. Although the senators were still, within limits, able to speak up with impunity, even Tiberius' most tactful interferences (of which this does not seem to have been one) inevitably paralysed their free expression – just as his frequent appearances as an assessor in the public law-courts paralysed the initiative of the judges. For he was demanding from these dignitaries, with complete sincerity, a degree of independence which it was impossible for them to display. It was impossible because of the very nature of the Augustan principate; as the obsequious poet Ovid declared: 'The state *is* Caesar.' The consequent frustration of the senators, requested to act on their own account when they dared and could not, was ill-concealed by their offensively sycophantic proposals. No wonder that when he left senate meetings, Tiberius was heard to exclaim in Greek, 'Men fit to be slaves!'

Tacitus makes enormous play with the number of treason trials which disfigured his reign. The men involved were mostly senators, and the trials were habitually conducted by the senatorial court itself. Treason, *maiestas*, was ill-defined, and the recent invention of an imperial person, and creation of an imperial house,* increased the indeterminacies. The result was that the concept could now be stretched from actual conspiracy or alleged conspiracy to cover even the vaguest indications of hostility and disrespect towards the emperor's family. Tiberius himself often declared that a free country should have room for free speech and free thought; and he often stepped in to redirect the senatorial court in the interests of moderation – a quality, as his coins inscribed MODERATIONI confirm, of which he was particularly proud.

Indeed, at first, he would not even recognize slanderous utterances against himself as treasonable at all. But this was an attitude which, like Augustus in his last years, he failed to maintain. For the treason law, as he himself openly conceded, had to exist and had to be enforced;

---

* Pliny the younger pointed out that insults directed against the divine Augustus (e.g. that alleged against Granius Marcellus) presented a new opportunity for treason charges.

otherwise each successive ruler would be destroyed. Yet the existence of the law, in a country where no state prosecutors existed, meant that informers, those traditional, uncomfortable features of the Roman community, had to be tolerated as well. And that is what Tiberius himself, although he often tired of them and dispensed with their services, was obliged to conclude. 'Better cancel the laws', he asserted, 'than remove their guardians'. Besides, the existence of informers possessed a further special advantage, because the blame for such repressive measures as might prove desirable could be shifted from his shoulders on to theirs.

After he had been on the throne for a decade, treason procedures became perceptibly tougher.* This was partly because of his own ex-treme sensitiveness to personal insult. Had he been less sensitive, or had he been stronger, the tendency towards severity might have been checked. As it was, according to Seneca, who reached adult years just when the reign began, the traditional governing class suffered badly:

Under Tiberius [he wrote] there grew up a frenzied passion for bringing accusations, which increased till it became almost universal, and proved more destructive to citizens than any civil war. Words spoken by men when drunk and the most harmless pleasantries were denounced. There was safety nowhere; any pretext was good enough to serve for an information. Nor, after a time, did the accused think it worth while to await the result of their trials, for this was always the same.[9]

Was Seneca exaggerating? The surviving literary sources enable us to identify just over a hundred persons mentioned in judicial proceed-ings under Tiberius. Approximately eighteen of the cases were un-connected with treason, but most of the others were. Nineteen of the defendants were acquitted, twelve were allowed to go free without trial, four had their sentences cancelled or lightened; on eleven known occasions Tiberius used his influence in favour of mitigating sentences. But that still leaves a substantial margin of men executed or driven to suicide. Perhaps this was an inevitable by-product of the force-based system of Augustus. But in spite of Tiberius' humane interventions, his peculiar personal character contributed to the abuse.

Even so, the pervasiveness of this evil must not be exaggerated. It was

---

* The death sentences exacted in his later years seemed to have been imposed arbitrarily by the senatorial court, as an extension of the penalty of exile provided by the law.

only the inmost circles of the government that were affected at all: and even there the casualties were trifling, compared to modern holocausts. The vast territories of the empire, under the emperor's close and unremitting personal direction, were governed extremely ably and conscientiously, though with a certain bias towards immobility, since he kept the governors of the military provinces in office for lengthy durations, and once a question had been decided he did not like it to be reopened. He was careful about money, refraining from expensive building programmes, and departing from the Augustan policy of 'bread and circuses' by his insistence on a much diminished expenditure upon public entertainments. At his death, therefore, the treasury was full.

Yet his advice to his governors had been: 'You should shear my sheep, not flay them!' In contrast to the hostile interpretations of Tacitus, a contemporary Alexandrian Jew, Philo, declared that he 'gave peace and the blessing of peace to the end of his life with ungrudging bounty of hand and heart'. Later on Trajan was to become famous as 'the best of emperors'. Yet this superlative had already been applied to Tiberius first. And if one looks at him through the eyes not of a few hundred senators but of the remaining millions of inhabitants of the empire, the assessment is not wholly without justification.

But the greatest drama and tragedy of his life came from his selection of Augustus, during the earlier part of his reign, had relied heavily on Agrippa and Maecenas (d. 12 and 8 BC), and the latter was virtually succeeded by the wealthy Gaius Sallustius Crispus, who stayed on under Tiberius, and did not die until AD 20.* But thereafter a new development occurred.

Throughout all this period the prefecture of the praetorian guard, first instituted in 2 BC and reserved not for senators but for knights, had been growing gradually and unobtrusively in importance. It was the holder of this office whom Tiberius now decided to make into his principal adviser. Augustus had arranged for the guard to be commanded by a pair of joint prefects, but at his death there was a single commander, Lucius Seius Strabo. Immediately afterwards his son Lucius Aelius Sejanus was elevated to serve as his colleague, and then in

---

*In AD 14, on the orders either of Augustus or Tiberius, he had arranged the execution of Augustus' surviving grandchild, the exiled Agrippa Postumus.

the following year Strabo retired and Sejanus remained as sole prefect. This was the man on whom, henceforward, the emperor increasingly relied.

Sejanus found himself admirably placed to exploit his political influence – and to make use of his social standing as well. This was by no means as humble as Tacitus, with his snobbish senatorial contempt for knights, chose to suggest, since Sejanus, through his mother, was linked with some of the greatest families in Rome, and through his father he was related to the wife of Maecenas. He enjoyed a great success with women, being known as an efficient seducer of the wives of distinguished men; and he is described as a jolly sort of individual.

In about AD 23 Sejanus prevailed upon the emperor to take a step which made his own position a great deal more powerful. At first only three of the nine praetorian cohorts had been stationed in Rome, the other six being posted in various Italian towns. More recently all these units had been brought together in the capital, and now Sejanus obtained permission to concentrate them in a single new barracks constructed just outside the city boundaries on the Viminal hill, where its towering walls can still be seen today.

The prefect did not get on well with Tiberius' son Drusus the younger, who resented the growth of his influence. But Drusus' death, which took place a short time after the creation of the new praetorian camp, raised Sejanus to a considerably greater eminence than he had enjoyed before. The emperor had no confidants in his own family any longer, since the heirs apparent, Nero Caesar and Drusus Caesar, the sons of Germanicus, were still only in their teens. And so it was not they, but Sejanus, who now achieved the exceptionally rare feat of becoming Tiberius' intimate friend. 'My Sejanus', he called him, and in addressing the senate and the Assembly pronounced him the 'Partner of his Labours'. To the emperor, carrying his massive burden of work, Sejanus seemed like a new Agrippa, and these years may have witnessed the inauguration of a huge series of copper coins which directly recalled the memory of Agrippa by displaying his portrait and name.

It was now that the trials for treason showed signs of becoming more numerous and severe. For Sejanus played upon Tiberius' gnawing suspicion of conspiracies and revolts, a suspicion which the prefect himself no doubt fully shared. Moreover, he used the treason laws to eliminate his own political opponents. In AD 25, for example, the historian

PLAN OF ROME

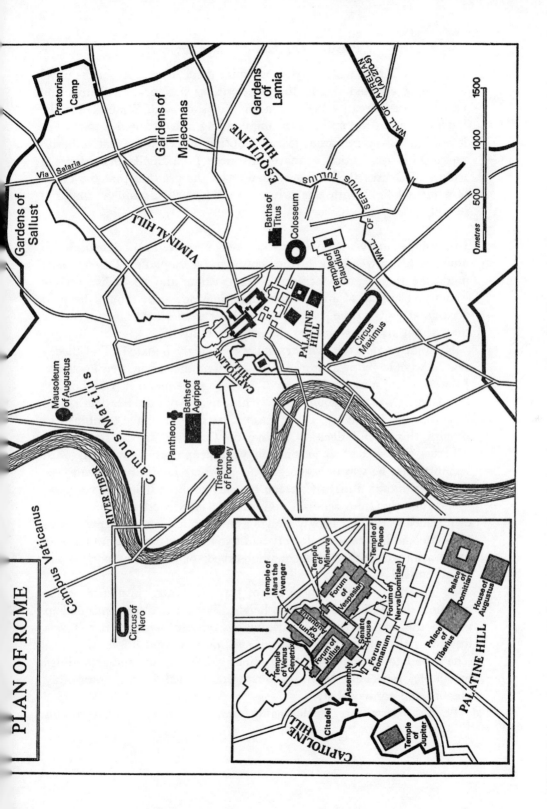

Praetorian Camp

Gardens of Sallust

Via Salaria

Gardens of Maecenas

Gardens of Lamia

ESQUILINE HILL

SERVIUS TULLIUS

WALL OF AURELIAN (A.D. 270-5)

VIMINAL HILL

Baths of Titus

Colosseum

Temple of Claudius

WALL OF SERVIUS TULLIUS

PALATINE HILL

Circus Maximus

CAPITOLINE HILL

Campus Martius

Mausoleum of Augustus

Pantheon

Baths of Agrippa

Theatre of Pompey

RIVER TIBER

Campus Vaticanus

Circus of Nero

0 metres   500   1000   1500

CAPITOLINE HILL

Temple of Venus Genetrix

Temple of Mars the Avenger

Temple of Minerva

Temple of Peace

Forum of Augustus

Forum of Julius

Forum of Vespasian

Forum of Nerva (Domitian)

Senate House

Assembly

Forum Romanum

Citadel

Temple of Jupiter

Palace of Tiberius

Palace of Domitian

House of Augustus

PALATINE HILL

Cremutius Cordus was forced to commit suicide, ostensibly for the novel and unprecedented reason that his writings had praised Brutus and Cassius, but in reality because he had clashed with Sejanus. Yet the latter's position was still not as commanding as he wanted it to be. For it was in this very same year, according to Tacitus, that Tiberius rejected his application to marry his niece Julia Livilla the elder, the widow of Drusus the younger, mainly on the grounds that the union of a mere knight with this princess would cause too much senatorial ill-will.

In the following year, however, the prefect received an opportunity to advance his power by a further considerable step. For Tiberius now made the remarkable decision to leave Rome and go to live on the island of Capreae (Capri). From that time onwards, though he paid occasional visits to the mainland, he never even set foot in the capital throughout all the remaining eleven years of his life.

His motives for this withdrawal were widely debated. The theory that he went to get away from his masterful mother Livia, now known as Julia Augusta, may be discounted. She was tiresome, it it true, but her tiresomeness was not enough to drive him away – nor did her death in 29 bring him back. But two other reasons are likely to have combined to prompt this fateful decision to live on Capreae. In the first place, Tiberius was so bad at getting on with people, and especially with senators, that he was only too glad to go where he did not have to see them any more: and to Capreae he only took with him a very few friends, mostly Greek scholars and astrologers. Secondly, terrors for his own safety were increasingly preying on his mind – and Capreae was very safe and inaccessible. It only had two landing-places. And no boat could approach either of them unobserved, or any other part of the island either.

So Tiberius settled in the Villa of Jupiter, located in a spectacular situation on the island's eastern height. From there he continued to govern the empire with his customary conscientiousness. But it was disastrous that, from now onwards, all his communications with the senate had to be made by letter, since this made misunderstandings inevitable, especially as the letters were framed in his notoriously obscure and equivocal style.

Besides, every sort of damaging rumour was stimulated by his solitary existence. Many of these stories related to his alleged sexual practices. He was said, among other things, to enjoy bathing with little boys who swam between his legs and nibbled at his private parts under water. This indeed would have been a considerable athletic feat, not only for Tiberius, who was approaching his seventieth year, but for the boys as well. However such tales may, in all likelihood, be dismissed, not for a modern editor's innocent reason that since Tiberius is known to have enjoyed good health he cannot have engaged in orgies, but because Seneca, who says everything he can find to say against Tiberius, does not mention any such aberrations at all. The anecdotes are historically significant, not because of any light they throw on the character of Tiberius, but because they show what sort of a reputation a permanently invisible ruler of Rome must inevitably earn.

But the outstanding result of the retirement to Capreae was yet another increase in Sejanus' power. He controlled access to Tiberius' person; and his guardsmen were responsible for the transmission of the imperial correspondence. Sejanus had probably prompted Tiberius' withdrawal in the first place, by accentuating his fears for his personal security; and when the emperor was installed on his island, he continued to play upon these fears.

The principal dangers that threatened him, Tiberius became convinced – and here his prefect's prompting can clearly be discerned – were presented by Agrippina the elder, and by her sons Nero Caesar and Drusus Caesar, the heirs apparent: they and their mother had all the prestige of the house of Germanicus behind them. In 26 Agrippina asked Tiberius if she could marry again, a prospect which so appalled him, owing to the peril which a new husband of Augustus' granddaughter would present, that he walked out of the room without answering a word. Three years later she and her sons were denounced, first by Sejanus and then by the emperor himself, and legal proceedings were instituted against them. The initial moves against Nero Caesar (for sexual perversion) and Agrippina (for seditious designs) provoked public demonstrations in their favour, which may conceivably have been instigated behind the scenes by Sejanus in order to frighten the emperor still further. Both the defendants were arrested and banished to islands, and Drusus Caesar, too, was imprisoned at Rome. Four years later, not one of the three was alive. Whether they had been guilty of plotting is uncertain. But this cannot be excluded, since the popularity of their family with the army may have tempted them to desperate measures.

Meanwhile, in AD 31, Sejanus became consul, as colleague of Tiberius. Since the emperor was permanently absent, this meant that the prefect was virtually sole consul; and other honours, too, were showered upon him, from all parts of the empire. When he and the emperor resigned their consulships in May, Sejanus was probably granted the superior military powers which Tiberius had received from Augustus. And the emperor at last authorized his engagement to his son's widow Julia Livilla.

But now came the utterly surprising move that destroyed Sejanus. In all probability a party of senators and provincial governors, profoundly resenting the indignity of having to queue for the privilege of an audience with a mere former knight, had gradually undermined his influence with the emperor – with the assistance of Antonia, the mother of Julia Livilla, who did not approve of his proposed marriage to her daughter. And the extraordinary thing was that Tiberius, too, somehow eventually came to believe that his trusted partner was not only unworthy of the confidence that had been placed in him, but must be totally eliminated.

The task of removing him, however, could not be entrusted, as would have been normal, to the praetorian guard, since this was under Sejanus' own command. So the emperor secretly summoned to Capreae a man he could rely upon, Quintus Naevius Cordus Sutorius Macro; and then, after giving Macro secret instructions, he sent him to Rome. His envoy secretly won over the prefect of the watch (a fire-brigade, with some police duties, instituted by Augustus). He also took one of the consuls into his confidence, and handed him a dispatch from Tiberius for communication to the senate. When this letter was read out at the senate meeting, Sejanus, who was present, confidently expected it was going to announce his elevation to the tribunician power, which was all he needed to make him virtually co-emperor. But instead, as the recitation of Tiberius' lengthy, involved message pursued its course, it astoundingly became clear that the emperor was not honouring the prefect at all, but denouncing him. Taken wholly by surprise, with no hand raised to help him even from those senators who had been his personal supporters, Sejanus was arrested on the spot. Then, on the very same evening, once the praetorians, too, were seen to have no intention of trying to rescue him, his senatorial captors, without waiting for any specific orders from Tiberius, handed him over to the executioner and he was strangled.

These events went down to history as one of the most spectacular downfalls of all time. Ben Jonson wrote *Sejanus His Fall* in 1603. But already in ancient times the whole melodramatic crisis had seemed to provide ample fuel for moralizing thought. The relevant sections of Tacitus' *Annals* are unfortunately lost. But his contemporary Juvenal had something to say about the total damnation of Sejanus' memory that immediately followed, including the pronouncement, to which inscriptions bear witness, that he was 'a most ruinous enemy of the Roman people', and the destruction of all the monuments that had been so respectfully dedicated to him:

> Down came the statues, following the rope,
> And next the crashing axe breaks up the chariot wheels,
> Fracturing the legs of the poor undeserving horses.
> Now the bonfires roar, now under bellows and blasts
> Glows the head once adored by the public, and crackles the mighty
> Sejanus: out of the face once second in all the world
> Are moulded jugs and basins, pans and chamber-pots.[10]

But *why* had the emperor completely changed his mind about Sejanus? Tiberius was not the man just to be overborne by a group of senators, unless he himself had become personally convinced that his previous estimate of his adviser's merits was totally and disastrously misplaced. Juvenal was well aware of the mystery.

> But what were the charges against him?
> Who were the witnesses, the informant? How did they prove it?
> Nothing like that at all; the only thing was a letter,
> Rather wordy and long; it came from Capri.[11]

Tiberius himself publicly explained that he had eliminated Sejanus because he found him 'venting his hatred against the sons of Germanicus'. Yet this cannot entirely be taken at face value. For, although it was too late to rehabilitate Nero Caesar, who was already dead, Drusus Caesar could have been restored to favour once Sejanus had fallen: but he was not. On the contrary, his captors went on brutally ill-treating him, and he was shortly afterwards starved to death.

Following the disappearance of these two brothers, however, there was still a third brother to reckon with. This was Gaius (Caligula), who at the time of the execution of Sejanus was just nineteen. *He* was the son of Germanicus whom Tiberius, although his utterance is characteristically obscure, had suspected Sejanus of intending to kill. And his suspicion was probably accurate, since if Caligula, who could already be seen to be a forcible personality, were to come to the throne, the position of Sejanus, the man who had helped to do away with Caligula's brothers, would become exceedingly insecure.

Sejanus did not probably harbour any intention of gaining the empire for himself, either by causing Tiberius' death (as some thought he proposed to do) or by just waiting for it, after the removal of Caligula. For in a highly hierarchical society like Rome's a man such as Sejanus, who until recently had not even been a senator at all, could have no hope of asserting any such claim to the throne with success. What he hoped for instead, it seems, was to become regent, after Tiberius' death, for a younger and more malleable emperor than Caligula. And such a candidate would have been forthcoming in the person of Gemellus, the twelve-year-old child of Tiberius' late son Drusus junior.

Yet now Caligula and Gemellus were still there; but Sejanus and his plans had been utterly destroyed.

There followed the destruction of his family as well. His widow, Apicata, was one of those who committed suicide. Before dying, however, she wrote to Tiberius declaring that his son Drusus the younger, when he died eight years earlier, had been murdered by Sejanus, acting in collusion with the dead man's wife Julia Livilla, of whom he was already, at that time, the lover. The charge may well have been false. But Tiberius believed it, and Livilla, too, now met her end.

Under the supervision of Macro, who had become praetorian prefect, the number of treason trials increased, and reached its highest point. The leading figures in Roman society and government found the last six years of Tiberius' reign terrifyingly perilous.

As his life drew to its melancholy close, he composed a will, instituting Caligula and Gemellus as his joint heirs. But he felt a certain distaste for Gemellus, upon whose paternity Apicata's revelations had cast a doubt; and it was made clear enough that Caligula would be his successor.

In March 37, on one of his periodical excursions to the mainland,

Tiberius was at the Villa of Lucullus at Misenum; and there, in his seventy-eighth year, he died, apparently from natural causes.

Tacitus was obsessed by the figure of Tiberius, and noted a series of progressive deteriorations in the quality of his rule. In this he was perfectly correct – although the deterioration was more noticeable to the leading circles of Rome than elsewhere.

But Tacitus, like so many ancient writers, believed that man's personality remained immutably the same from birth to death, and that if his actions did not always exhibit that personality this was only because he was sometimes able to conceal it. This interpretation, that 'the child is father to the man', he applied to Tiberius, regarding him as wholly bad. To some extent this picture reflects his own unhappy experiences of Domitian, of whom Tiberius is made into a sort of mirror image. The many good actions which Tacitus is obliged to ascribe to Tiberius are therefore interpreted as mere signs of the emperor's persistent, fiendish dissimulation.

His behaviour had its different stages. While he was a private citizen or holding commands under Augustus, his life was blameless; and so was his reputation. While Germanicus and Drusus the younger still lived, he concealed his real self, cunningly affecting virtuous qualities. However, until his mother died there was good in Tiberius as well as evil. Again, as long as he favoured (or feared) Sejanus, the cruelty of Tiberius was detested, but his perversions unrevealed. Then fear vanished, and with it shame. Thereafter he expressed only his own personality – by unrestrained crime and infamy.[12]

Here, then, was a theory which seemed to account for Tiberius' deterioration while at the same time denying that his character had ever been anything but wholly bad. Suetonius and Dio Cassius, although taking a more favourable view of the earlier part of the reign, are aware of this theory that his badness was only concealed at first; and Suetonius at least, or the source he is quoting, is disposed to accept such a view.

His cruel and cold-blooded character was not completely hidden even in his boyhood ... All believed, and with good reason, that the cruelty of Tiberius, which soon burst forth, had been held in check through his respect and awe for Germanicus ... Having gained the licence of privacy he gave free rein at once to all the vices which he had for a long time ill concealed.[13]

Dio Cassius is not so sure. At one point he is so puzzled by Tiberius' conflicting qualities that he just feels tempted to list them on either side of the ledger, and leave it at that: 'He possessed a great many virtues and a great many vices, and followed each set in turn as if the other did not exist.' But another passage from the same writer, while suggesting, with dubious accuracy, that the death of Germanicus brought a sharp deterioration, supplements the Tacitean view by another which contradicts it:

After Germanicus' death Tiberius changed his course in many respects. Perhaps he had been at heart from the first what he later showed himself to be, and had been merely shamming while Germanicus was alive, because he saw his rival lying in wait for the sovereignty.

Or perhaps he was excellent by nature, but drifted into vice when deprived of his rival.[14]

The last sentence is a little vague. Is Dio really saying that Tiberius *changed*? If so, then he is quoting a view which goes right back to the time of Tiberius himself. For this opinion, although opposed to the theory of Tacitus and others, had nevertheless been honestly recorded in his *Annals*, where it was attributed to one of the greatest noblemen among Tiberius' own contemporaries, Lucius Arruntius. 'Tiberius,' Arruntius remarked, 'in spite of all his experience, *has been transformed and deranged by the force of absolute power.*'[15]

Arruntius was right, and Tacitus and the others who believed in immutable characters were wrong. People's characters do change, under pressure of circumstances, and the character of Tiberius, under the most terrible pressures that a man could endure, changed markedly. The burden of empire, predicted by himself on his accession to be crushing, proved even heavier than he had ever anticipated: and it was more than he could endure.

Justice Holmes described Franklin D. Roosevelt* as a 'second-rate intellect but a first-class temperament'. Tiberius was the opposite. Although his mental power and gigantic capacity for hard work were not inferior to the talents of Augustus, he lacked his predecessor's gift for getting on with people. That famous, necessary, Augustan humbug was something he could not achieve, and did not want to. And Suetonius is surely right to emphasize the terrible anxieties from which he suffered –

* Also perhaps a 'changed man': see above, Introduction.

anxieties from which he tried to escape by fleeing to Capreae, but which were subsequently redoubled after the greatest catastrophe and downward turning-point of his reign, the fall of Sejanus. Eight years earlier the emperor had prayed the gods, without much hope, to grant him peace of mind until the end of his life. His prayer was not granted, and his despairing cry to the senate after Sejanus' removal is one of the saddest sentences in historical literature: 'If I know what to write to you at this time, senators, or how to write it or what not to write, may heaven plunge me into a worse ruin than I feel overtaking me every day!'[16]

And yet, although some business was now likely to get delayed owing to the ageing Tiberius' continual preoccupation with the security of his own life, the empire was still very well governed. The proof that so little of this torment was apparent in the provinces is provided by Philo's extraordinarily ill-informed remark: 'What other king or emperor ever enjoyed a happier old age?' Tiberius had once declared: 'As long as I keep my senses, I shall always be consistent, and never change my ways.' But he did change his ways, because his senses almost abandoned him. Although his mind remained clear enough for most ordinary administrative purposes, his reason was almost unhinged by terror, self-pity and the desire to avenge himself on those he believed were trying to break him.

The delicately balanced imperial task set him by Augustus would have been too much for almost any man. It was certainly too much for Tiberius, in spite of his outstanding ability.

4

Caligula

Gaius, the third son of Germanicus and Agrippina the elder, was born at Antium (Anzio in south-western Italy) in AD 12. While he was an infant with his parents in Germany, the miniature military boots he was given to wear caused the soldiers to address him by the nickname Caligula, Little Boots. When he was seven, his father died in mysterious circumstances, and during his eighteenth and nineteenth years his mother and two elder brothers were arrested, to meet their subsequent deaths.

In the midst of these events, after spending some time in the houses of Livia and his grandmother Antonia, Caligula was taken to live with Tiberius on the island of Capreae, and it was understood that he would succeed to the throne, although the emperor appointed his own eighteen-year-old grandson Gemellus (son of the late Drusus junior) to share the inheritance of his personal property.

On Tiberius' death in 37 Caligula, with the support of the praetorian prefect Macro, was acclaimed emperor. His predecessor's will was declared invalid by the senate in order to deprive Gemellus of his share, although Caligula formally adopted the young man as his son. In the first period of his reign he emphatically revered the memories of his relatives who had died or been killed under Tiberius, in addition to paying special honour to his three living sisters.

In October 37 Caligula suffered from a serious illness. Early in the following year he compelled both Gemellus and Macro to kill themselves. But the real turning-point in his reign came in January AD 39, when he formed a violent *aversion to the senate. In September he proceeded hastily to Upper Germany to forestall a plot against his life by the governor Gaetulicus, an event which caused a further sharpening of his anti-senatorial attitude. Those executed on this occasion included not only Gaetulicus but Caligula's brother-in-law and heir-apparent Marcus Lepidus; and on suspicion of complicity his two surviving sisters, Agrippina the younger and Julia Livilla the younger, were disgraced and sent into exile.*

Abandoning proposed German and British expeditions, Caligula returned to Rome in August 40, and set in motion far-reaching plans to convert the Augustan principate into a thoroughgoing autocratic system. Although extravagant honours were showered on the emperor, plots and threats of plots abounded, and security precautions were correspondingly intensified. Before long, however, Caligula became estranged from the command of the praetorian guard, and on 24 January 41 a group of its officers assassinated him. His wife, Caesonia, and their infant daughter – his only child – were also put to death.

Caligula, who came to the throne in his twenty-fifth year, had spent a truly disastrous youth, likely to affect his development in the worst possible way. At the time of the harrowing downfalls of his mother and brothers he was summoned to Capreae to pass his time in the company of the man who, whether justly or not, had brought these tragedies about, his dreary old great-uncle Tiberius. Caligula's life on the island, as described by Suetonius, cannot have been easy since he was continually tempted by *agents provocateurs*:

Who would have drawn and forced him to quarrels, yet gave he never any occasion, having rased out and quite forgotten the fall and calamity of his mother, brethren and near friends, as if nothing had befallen to any of them; passing over all those abuses which himself had endured with incredible simulation so obsequious and double diligent besides to his grandfather and those about him that of him it was said and not without good cause:
A better servant and a worse master there never was.[1]

Nevertheless, according to the Jewish historian Josephus, Caligula very nearly ran into trouble owing to an indiscretion by his friend the Jewish prince Julius Agrippa. At a hearing on Capreae in September AD 36 a certain Eutychus, who was Agrippa's coachman and valet and had been charged with stealing some of his master's clothes, declared that while driving Caligula and Agrippa round the island he had overheard a treasonable conversation. 'Oh for that day', Agrippa had allegedly remarked to his companion, 'when the old boy dies and leaves you ruler of the entire habitable earth!'

Agrippa was placed under arrest by the praetorian prefect Macro, but Tiberius introduced no perceptible change into his relations with Caligula. On the other hand, apart from allowing him a priesthood in 31 and the minor state office of a quaestorship two years later, the emperor gave the youth no administrative experience to prepare him for the imperial destiny which would obviously be his.

When Tiberius died in 37, the rumours that Caligula poisoned, or starved, or strangled, or smothered him were probably not accurate. It is true that the testimony of the rhetorician Seneca the elder (father of the more famous author of the same name) that Tiberius died a natural death is of little value, because the elder Seneca was writing in Caligula's reign and could not have said otherwise. But Tiberius' death from natural causes was in any case imminent, and seems the most likely explanation.

And so Rome embarked on its first experience of government by a descendant of its second founder Augustus.

As soon as Caligula returned to the capital, the senate, which had declared him emperor on receiving the news that Tiberius was dead, appears to have proposed that the Assembly should vote him, in one single enactment, the totality of the imperial powers – a collective award such as is recorded on a famous inscription, the *lex de Imperio*.* In spite, however, of their apparent unanimity, the senators, at heart, were not very enthusiastic about the new ruler, since most of the supporters of Germanicus' house, who would have applauded his succession, were no longer there to perform that service, having been eliminated during the course of the previous reign.

But the army still loved the family of Germanicus, and it pleased them when Caligula emphatically rehabilitated the memories of its members who were dead, honouring them one after another on his coinage and proceeding in person, in wintry stormy weather, to the islands where his mother and eldest brother Nero Caesar had perished, in order to fetch their ashes, which were then given magnificent funerals at Rome. First, however, he had celebrated the funeral of Tiberius.

* This relates to the accession of Vespasian. Some of the detailed provisions may post-date Caligula.

But since neither senate nor people regretted the late emperor's death, Caligula quietly dropped his initial request that he should be deified: and before long he was abusing his predecessor's memory and allowing others to do so as well.

Caligula's appearance seems to have been disconcerting.

He was very tall and extremely pale, with an unshapely body, but very thin neck and legs. His eyes and temples were hollow, his forehead broad and grim, his hair thin and entirely gone on the top of his head, though his body was hairy. Because of this to look upon him from a higher place as he passed by, or for any reason whatever to mention a goat, was treated as a capital offence. While his face was naturally forbidding and ugly, he purposely made it even more savage, practising all kinds of terrible and fearsome expressions before a mirror. . . .

He was sound neither of body nor mind. As a boy he was troubled with the falling sickness, and while in his youth he had some endurance, yet at times because of sudden faintness he was hardly able to walk, to stand up, to collect his thoughts, or to hold up his head. He himself realised his mental infirmity, and thought at times of going into retirement and clearing his brain.[2]

Suetonius also reported that what had unhinged Caligula was an excessively strong aphrodisiac given him by his wife Caesonia. Philo, on the other hand, suggested that the illness from which he suffered in the early part of his reign was a breakdown due to over-indulgence.* Caligula was a very poor sleeper, only able to sleep for about three hours every night; and he suffered from unpleasant dreams, which he used to escape by wandering about the palace during the nocturnal hours. He has been variously labelled epileptic, schizoid, schizophrenic, or just chronically alcoholic. Tacitus described his mind as disordered and upset, but Caligula was probably not mad in any accepted sense of the term; though diagnoses by modern psychologists or physicians are useless, because there is no adequate evidence to go on.

In any case, the new emperor possessed very considerable gifts, as even Josephus, who had every reason to detest him for his treatment of the Jews, is obliged to admit. His talent for oratory, for example, was unquestionable.

He was a first-rate speaker, deeply versed in the Greek and Latin languages. He knew how to reply impromptu to speeches which others had composed after long preparation, and to show himself instantly more persuasive on the

* The passage is quoted at the end of this chapter, p. 124.

subject than anyone else, even where the greatest matters were debated. All this resulted from a natural aptitude for such things, and from his adding to that aptitude the practice of taking elaborate pains to strengthen it.

For, being the grandson of the brother of Tiberius, whom he succeeded, he was under a great compulsion to apply himself to education, because Tiberius himself also had conspicuously succeeded in attaining the highest place in it. Caligula followed him in his attachment to such noble pursuits, yielding to the injunctions of a man who was both his kinsman and his commander-in-chief. Thus he came to stand highest among the citizens of his time.

For all that, the advantages obtained from education could not withstand the corruption wrought upon him by his rise to power; so hard to achieve, it seems, is the virtue of moderation for those who find it easy to take action for which they need account to no one.[3]

The contrast between Caligula's previous six years of perilous self-repression and his subsequent promotion to unlimited flattery and power would have gone to almost anyone's head, and certainly went to his. He was a megalomaniac, and an able one, with the prodigal extravagance of a true autocrat. He has been compared to the last German emperor Wilhelm ii, but also to the last Austro–Hungarian emperor, who was known as 'Karl the Sudden'. Caligula, too, was sudden, oscillating between extreme affability and frightening bleakness, between an enjoyment of vast throngs and a hankering for complete solitude.

He used to get very excited. Anger provoked him to violent outpourings of words, and he would fidget about nervously while continuing to shout at the top of his voice. He was a young man of frantic energy, but his powers of application failed to last. He could start all manner of things, but found it almost impossible to finish them.

Caligula's sharp tongue continually caused dismay. Very often this was precisely his intention, because he felt a vigorous hatred of the official shams which Augustus had so delicately concocted and Tiberius so glumly accepted. There was a savage, impudent lucidity about Caligula's numerous epigrams. For example, he openly expressed disrespect for the traditional gods, about whose acceptability he was evidently sceptical. So, no doubt, were many other emperors too, but they did not say so. Caligula did say so, very frankly and outspokenly.

Literary men, too, found him equally disconcerting. He had the nerve to remark that the only man who had ever treated Homer

properly was Plato because he had expelled the poet from his ideal
state! Virgil, too, the emperor was heard saying, had been a writer of no
talent and very little learning; and Livy was verbose and careless.
Caligula also expressed the view that his own contemporary Seneca (son
of the rhetorician), who was embarking on a highly fashionable oratorical and literary career at the time, wrote deplorable stuff – flashy
theatrical displays, mere sand without lime. But Caligula had to pay
dearly for these censorious words because Seneca, belying the emperor's
belief that he would die shortly of tuberculosis, was able to retaliate for
many years to come by depicting his imperial critic, once he was safely
dead, in the worst possible light.

Caligula had an irrepressible, bizarre, sense of the ridiculous,
deliberately designed to shock, but frequently taken by his alarmed subjects too seriously. Notoriously absurd traditions of the kind which
inspired Albert Camus' *Caligula* (1944) – such as the story that he
intended to give a consulship to his favourite horse Incitatus – no doubt
originated from his continual stream of jokes. Probably he remarked
that Incitatus would do the job as well as most of the recent incumbents;
and meanwhile he ordered silence in the entire neighbourhood, to
prevent the horse from being disturbed.

The anecdote of Aponius Saturninus displays his sense of humour in
another form. In order to raise money, Caligula used to have the
properties left over from public shows sold by auction. On one such
occasion Aponius began to nod his head sleepily. Seeing this, the emper-
or warned the auctioneer to take due note of the nods, and the bidding
was not stopped until thirteen gladiators had been knocked down to the
somnolent senator for a gigantic sum. A knight who made a noise while
Caligula's favourite actor Mnester was giving a performance received
imperial instructions to leave the country, and carry a sealed message to
King Ptolemy of distant Mauretania. When opened by the king, the
message only read: 'Do nothing at all to the bearer, either good or bad.'

An anxious Jewish deputation, too, found Caligula in mocking mood.
When they were brought to him, he was dashing round the buildings of
the Gardens of Maecenas and Lamia on a tour of inspection.

We were driven along and followed him upstairs and downstairs, while our
opponents mocked and railed at us just as in farces on the stage ... After
giving some of his instructions about the buildings, he asked us an important
and solemn question: 'Why do you not eat pork?' At this inquiry our

opponents again burst into such violent peals of laughter ... that one of the servants attending Caligula was annoyed at the scant respect being shown to the emperor, in whose presence it was not safe for people who were not his intimate friends even to smile quietly.[4]

At Lugdunum, now Lyon in France, he arranged a Greek and Latin oratory competition in which the unsuccessful candidates had to erase their compositions with their tongues, unless they preferred to be beaten with rods or thrown into the river. Sometimes, however, Caligula's wit assumed a more ominous form, for example when he kissed the necks of his wives or mistresses and murmured: 'Off comes this very attractive head whenever I choose to say the word'. This, like so many other alleged utterances of Caligula, was sadistic, and the psychologist Otto Kiefer plausibly concluded that sadism was the fundamental feature of Caligula's temperament. He himself was very sensitive to insult and pain; but he found their infliction highly enjoyable.

The rumours about his sex life were startlingly varied. For example, although he professed the utmost distaste for male whores, whom he expelled from the city and threatened to drown, the young nobleman Valerius Catullus declared that he had worn himself out sodomizing the emperor. Caligula was also thought to display excessive enthusiasm in the kisses he bestowed on the actor Mnester in public.

In spite of such interests, however, the emperor was said to live in habitual incest with all his three sisters, as well as prostituting them to his personal friends. In addition, during his short life of less than thirty years, he married no less than four wives in succession. The last of these marriages, to the tough Caesonia who was already a mother of three, proved extremely happy. He used to dress her up in military uniform, and exhibit her to his friends in the nude; and no doubt they had many a hearty laugh together when he expressed a keen inclination to have her tortured in order to find out from her why he loved her so devotedly.

All this, of course, was mere gossip. But the consistent tone of the stories suggests a kernel of truth.

On the other hand, there was also a good deal to be said in Caligula's favour, at least at the beginning of his reign. He was cooperative and courteous to the senate, greatly pleasing it by the abolition of the treason trials that had disfigured his predecessor's reign. He also gave satisfaction to the knights by promoting some of them to the senate, including (in tactful moderation) a number of men from the provinces: and their order secured its first reference on an imperial coin.

Philo reports the extraordinary personal tributes Caligula received when he fell ill not long after his accession.

The news of Caligula's illness spread widely, as the seas were still open – it was the early autumn, the time when seafarers make their own ports and havens, especially those who are trying to avoid wintering abroad.

People then gave up their lives of luxury and went about with long faces. Every house and every city became anxious and dejected. Their recent joy wavered, counterbalanced by a grief equally keen. All parts of the habitable world were ill with Caligula.

But they were suffering from a more serious illness than that which had seized him. For his illness was merely physical, whereas theirs was universal, affecting their mental health, their peace, their hopes, and their participation in many serious evils which anarchy breeds – famine, war, devastation, ravaging of fields, loss of property, arrests, and the desperate fear of slavery or death. This fear no doctor could cure, and the only remedy lay in the recovery of Caligula.[5]

These demonstrations of Caligula's popularity were not entirely unjustified. Unstable and unboundedly conceited though he was, there were initial indications that he was prepared to devote his undoubted ability to the service of the state.

For example, he maintained his predecessors' tradition of taking his judicial duties very seriously. Indeed he even extended these sanctions by initiating the practice of hearing cases on appeal from the senate. But his attentions to the courts were a little eccentric.

He often published refutations of speakers who had successfully pleaded a cause; or composed speeches for both the prosecution and the defence of important men who were on trial by the senate – the verdict depending entirely on the caprice of his pen – and would invite the knights by proclamation to attend and listen.[6]

Yet, however industrious Caligula may at first have intended to be, his good intentions soon showed signs of flagging. This was a far more serious matter than his sexual aberrations, since an emperor could not hold his own unless he worked extremely hard and continuously. And active though Caligula remained, it soon became clear that, after all, he was failing to concentrate this activity on affairs of state.

For he was also passionately devoted to the circus and the stage. He constantly dined and spent the night at the charioteers' stables, and was to be seen

watching dancers with wild excitement or occasionally joining in the dance himself, or roaring with laughter like a schoolboy at comedians who indulged in obscenities and ribaldry – instead of smiling at them in a dignified way – or carried away by the music of lyre-players or choirs, and sometimes even joining in songs.[7]

He was by no means always content with the role of a spectator of such entertainments. Nero is often regarded as the first emperor to have aspired to success as a charioteer and singer and dancer and wearer of drag. But Caligula anticipated him in all these tastes.

He often danced at night, and once, at the close of the second watch, summoned three senators of consular rank to the palace. Arriving half dead with fear, they were conducted to a stage upon which amid a tremendous racket of flutes and heel-taps, Caligula suddenly burst in, dressed in cloak and ankle-length tunic, performed a song and dance and disappeared as suddenly as he had entered.[8]

He also liked to put on armour and fight as a gladiator – employing real weapons.

Now all this meant that he had far less time available for governing the empire. Caligula, that is to say, became the first emperor to attempt this enormous task as a part-time job. It was an attempt that could only be unsuccessful.

For one thing it greatly increased the authority of the freedmen who were his courtiers; and this novel situation cast a long shadow over the future. The most prominent among them were Greeks from Alexandria who entertained a particular dislike for the Jews who were so numerous in that city, and contributed largely to the emperor's anti-Jewish policy, so that we hear a lot about them from Josephus who came to Rome with a Jewish deputation. The most powerful of these Alexandrians was the emperor's chamberlain Helicon.

For he played ball with his master, exercised with him, bathed with him, had meals with him, and was with him when he was going to the bed . . . with the result that he alone had the emperor's ear when he was at leisure or resting, released from external distractions and so able to listen to what he most wanted to hear.[9]

One of the reasons why Caligula liked Helicon was because they had the same sort of sardonic, malicious wit. Another of the emperor's companions, likewise anti-Jewish, was the eminent tragic actor Apelles of Ascalon (Ashkelon). He too had to be reckoned with as a significant personage, though later he fell from favour, and the emperor, while watching him being flogged, found it amusing to compliment him on the melodious tone of his shrieks.

For Caligula was said to be wholly unmindful of friendships, however close. This worried the freedman who was most important of all, probably the most important freedman whom Rome had ever seen, Callistus, who had thirty columns of oriental alabaster in his dining-room and anticipated the great imperial secretaries of the years that lay ahead. Indeed, a part was still reserved for Callistus in those future years, since he deserted the unpredictable Caligula in good time, and remained in favour during the following reign.

This greatly enhanced position of the imperial courtiers, to the obvious detriment of the power of the senate, was just one sign of what was now becoming apparent: that Caligula's concept of empire differed markedly from the ideas of Augustus and Tiberius. Each of those rulers had gone to considerable trouble to avoid displaying himself as an out-and-out autocrat. Caligula, on the other hand, impatient of such pretences, gradually revealed his clear intention of becoming and remaining just that.

His youthful residence at the home of his grandmother Antonia may have influenced his ways of thinking, since she had maintained a court frequented by eastern princes with absolutist ideas, including the Jewish potentate Julius Agrippa who became Caligula's close friend. Moreover, Antonia was the daughter of the phil-hellenic Mark Antony, who had adopted some of the attitudes of Ptolemaic monarchy from his partner Cleopatra. Now Caligula, who felt sympathetic towards the Greeks, was also proud of descent from Antony, the anniversaries of whose defeat at Actium temporarily ceased to be celebrated during his reign.

His coinage, too, shows certain Hellenistic trends. One of the most surprising coinages of the early empire consists of large brass pieces of Caligula which display and name his three sisters, Agrippina the younger, Drusilla and Julia Livilla the younger, who are seen standing with the attributes of goddesses. The incestuous relations with his sisters which rumour ascribed to Caligula had been traditional at the court of the Ptolemies, as was the exceptional importance which the emperor deliberately assigned them on these coins. When the sister of whom he was particularly fond, Drusilla, died in AD 38, she was officially deified, the very first Roman woman ever to receive this honour, which was not even accorded, until another three years had passed, to Augustus' revered widow Livia.

Caligula held the consulship himself during four out of the five years of his reign. Yet he rejected the offer of a perpetual series of consulships, to be conferred once and for all, since these traditional Roman trappings did not particularly interest him. His concept of his position was different. It involved a deliberate tearing away of the legal fictions so that he could become the undisguised master of the Roman state, in the tradition not of Augustus but of Julius Caesar, though without the need for Caesar's perpetual dictatorship since the powers he already possessed adequately took its place.

Although Caligula was in other matters inclined to fritter away his time and intentions, his theory of imperial power was fairly systematic and coherent. He himself significantly remarked that the feature in his character of which he felt most proud was his *inflexibility*. He used a Greek word employed by the Stoic philosophers, and although those who knew how changeable he was must have found it a somewhat strange choice of terms, it was an accurate enough label for his determination to sweep away the evasions and pretences of the Augustan order and set an unconcealed absolutism in its place.

This meant the end of the honeymoon with the senators.

They must already have been feeling alarmed in 38, when Gemellus and Caligula's own father-in-law Marcus Sitlanus, father of the emperor's first wife Junia Claudilla, were driven to suicide. But the decisive break came early in the following year. The emperor more or less openly proclaimed it when he declared at a meeting of the senate how Tiberius had once recommended to him that treason trials ought to be continued. This had been a very sensible recommendation, Caligula went on to say, and the trials, which had been in abeyance since his accession, would be reintroduced straightaway. What inspired this *volte face* is not known, but his intelligence service had presumably warned him of menacing discontents among the upper class.

After sitting through this oration in stunned silence, the senate felt too unnerved to conduct any further business at the time. On the following day, however, with depressing obsequiousness, they voted that annual sacrifices should be offered to the emperor's Clemency; and on the days when this was done, they hastened to add, his golden statue should be carried up to the Capitol, while hymns were sung in his honour by boys of the noblest birth.

This did not, however, appease Caligula, who was well aware that, as in the days of Julius Caesar, certain malicious senators liked to manoeuvre him into accepting extravagant honours in order to make him look ridiculous. So, in response, he went out of his way to humiliate the senate. Before long respected elderly personages were seen running for miles beside his carriage in their heavy togas.

The emperor now prepared a demonstration to symbolize his highly personal concept of his office. His idea was to ride in triumph over the sea. For this purpose a section of the Bay of Naples was bridged with a double line of ships, some two or three miles long, upon which was constructed a roadway to enable him to ride upon the waters. The weather for his parade was fortunately calm, so that he could jokingly observe that even the sea-god Neptune evidently acknowledged his master. Accompanied by cavalry and infantry, he passed from end to end of the bridge on horseback, wearing the breastplate of Alexander the Great which had been brought from the king's mausoleum at Alexandria. Then, two days later, he rode back in a chariot drawn by two famous racehorses; behind him came his friends, and distinguished foreign visitors, and the entire praetorian guard, which had been enlarged by his orders. Finally, at night, the whole bay blazed with flares lit round the coast. Caligula had already made the sea into land, and now, it was declared, he had transformed night into day as well.

But such splendid spectacles cost money. So did his abolition of a sales tax introduced by Augustus, a popular measure recorded on the coins from AD 39 onwards. But this subsequently proved to have been an excessively generous gesture, so that new taxes had to be introduced in compensation. They included levies on foodstuffs, lawsuits and the takings of porters, prostitutes and pimps.

The senators and governors, some of whom had grumbled even at the far more tactful regimes of Augustus and Tiberius, were not likely to tolerate Caligula's open displays of autocracy. Rumours of disloyalty were in the air: and some of them were amply justified. One concerned a recently retired governor of Pannonia, who was forced to commit suicide. And then Caligula learnt of a serious plot amongst the armies of Germany. He had been planning to revive the aggressive adventures of his father Germanicus across the Rhine, and he may also have intended to invade Britain, which in spite of Caesar's expeditions nearly a century earlier still remained unconquered. To launch these projects, Caligula was to proceed to the Rhine garrisons. But before he left Rome startling information reached his ears: when he reached Moguntiacum (Mainz), the very important and aristocratic army commander in Upper Germany, Cnaeus Cornelius Lentulus Gaetulicus, was going to have him assassinated. Probably Gaetulicus intended to give the throne to Marcus Aemilius Lepidus, the widower of the emperor's deified sister Drusilla and the lover of her sister Agrippina the younger. For he was widely regarded as Caligula's most likely successor.

So in September AD 39, on receiving this news, the emperor departed suddenly and prematurely for the north, with a substantial contingent of praetorian guardsmen. He was also accompanied by Lepidus, Agrippina and her sister Julia Livilla the younger. On the arrival of the party in Germany, Gaetulicus, as well as Lepidus, was arrested and executed. And so the first attempt, in the history of the Roman empire, to raise one of the great provincial garrisons against a ruler had failed abysmally. But it was a most upsetting experience for Caligula, whose natural tendency to become excitable, suspicious and frightened became alarmingly accentuated. Agrippina was forced by her brother to carry the ashes of her lover Lepidus back to Rome; and then she was sent into banishment on an island. Her sister Julia Livilla, who was likewise accused of improper relations with Lepidus but may only have been Agrippina's confidante, was exiled as well. Nor did Caligula forget to arrange that the two sisters' property, of which their treason had deprived them, should be sold up; and it was sent away to be auctioned at Lugdunum.

Then he spent the following winter in the Rhine camps and in Gaul. On the German frontier, where an expedition was being spoken about, nothing happened except large-scale military manoeuvres, which were intended to overawe the tribes and restore legionary discipline. In the following spring Caligula's projected British expedition likewise failed to materialize, and there were preposterous stories of his ordering the troops to pick up seashells on the Gallic shore. But the reason why he called the invasion off was probably because he wanted to get back to Rome, knowing how dangerously his executions of Gaetulicus and Lepidus had alienated the senatorial class.

Already, by letter, he had launched a number of prosecutions rising from their plot. Then, during the summer, when he returned to the neighbourhood of the capital, he deliberately insulted the senators by failing to inform them of his return. They, on the other hand, with ostensible servility, voted that he should be allowed to introduce a military bodyguard whenever he attended their meetings, and gave instructions that while he was in the senate house he should be seated on a high and inaccessible platform.

Very soon Caligula began to go farther than ever before, much farther than either of the two previous emperors, in authorizing his own deification – to take effect immediately, now while he was still alive. He ordered the Jews to set up his statue, in the guise of Zeus, in their Temple at Jerusalem. For his freedmen advisers, who were hostile to the Jews, easily persuaded him that they should follow the practice of the rest of the empire, and demonstrate their place in the pattern of universal loyalty, by revering his image in their holy place. This total miscalculation of the feelings of the Jews, who would have died rather than concur, must have led to a serious revolt if Caligula had not been persuaded, at the last moment, to change his mind.

Temples dedicated to ruling emperors were a well-known phenomenon in the Greek-speaking eastern provinces. But it was at Rome, where this idea was not familiar, that his policy of self-divinization had even more serious effects. It had already entertained him to dress up as a god or a goddess or even as Jupiter himself; though when a Gallic cobbler, asked what he thought of the emperor masquerading as the king of the gods, replied that it was just a load of nonsense, Caligula may have been amused, for the man was not punished. Although he himself did not believe in the gods, he firmly considered that his own deification, on the lines of the deification of Hellenistic kings, was a useful and natural corollary, even in the capital itself, of the openly absolute monarchy he intended to establish. And so what Caligula now arranged at Rome was something quite unprecedented, the establishment of two temples of his own godhead, one erected from his own resources and the other at state expense by decree of the senate.

By such measures he was emphasizing his unpalatable theory of the monarchy in so forthright a fashion that at least three further conspiracies were immediately launched against his life.

The emperor lashed out against a group of Romans whose philosophical, Stoic principles tolerated monarchy but not bad monarchy – and since they could not fail to regard Caligula's rule as bad, they were no doubt indiscreet or even seditious. But much more perilous, if justified, was his suspicion that the joint praetorian prefects themselves, Marcus Arrecinus Clemens and a colleague whose name is uncertain, were planning to murder him. True to his taste for unvarnished frankness, Caligula taxed them with this intention to their faces, telling them to go ahead and kill him if they really disliked him so much as all that. This advice they refrained from taking, but after such an uncomfortable interview they understandably felt that they themselves were no longer safe. And so it seems to have been Clemens, and perhaps his fellow-prefect as well, who took the initiative, in association with disgusted and frightened senators, in the successful plot which now followed. But the most active part in the scheme was played by another senior praetorian officer, the military tribune (or colonel) Cassius Chaerea. The emperor's propensity for jokes in bad taste had insulted Chaerea deeply. For although he was a tough, old-fashioned man of fairly advanced years, it used to amuse Caligula to taunt him for being a sexual invert. When Chaerea's turn came to ask for the watchword, the emperor always seemed to choose words like 'love' or 'Venus' or 'Priapus', the god with the large erect member; and this had made the tribune a laughing stock among his men. Moreover, when the emperor held out his hand for Chaerea to kiss, it amused him to arrange and move his fingers in a gesture of obscene significance.

In consequence Chaerea lent his services to the conspiracy, and on 24 January AD 41, in a covered passage beneath the palace, he and two fellow officers struck Caligula down – the first of many occasions when praetorians turned upon the emperor they were supposed to be protecting. Some of his German bodyguard ran up to help him, but they came too late. Then a praetorian stabbed his wife Caesonia to death. Next their baby daughter was seized. When she was born, she had been set upon the knees of Jupiter's statue and placed in the charge of Minerva to be suckled. But now one of the officers smashed her head against a wall.

When Caligula was waylaid, he had been on his way to the theatre, and as the information reached the large crowd that was assembled there Josephus describes its varied reactions.

There was consternation and incredulity. Some, who heartily welcomed his assassination and would have regarded it long since as a blessing to themselves, were incredulous from fear. There were others to whom the news was quite contrary to their hopes because they had no desire that any such thing should befall Caligula; and they did not credit it, because it seemed to them impossible for any human being to have the courage to kill him.

Among them were silly women, children, all the slaves, and some of the army. The last named were of this mind because they were mercenaries, and no less than partners in his tyranny – by playing the lackey to his insolence, they gained both honour and profit, for the noblest citizens were in terror of them. The womenfolk and the youths, after the fashion of the mob, were captivated by his shows and by the gladiatorial combats that he presented, as well as by the enjoyment of the meat distributions that he sponsored.[10]

Yet all these supporters had not availed to save Caligula, since he took the fatal step of alienating the upper class – the senators and the senior praetorian officers. As a result his reign, after starting well enough, had sunk into utter disaster.

Similar processes of decline, of a less spectacular nature, had been seen under previous emperors. The rule of Augustus, after decades of anxious efficiency, had shown signs of ending badly, but had been saved by the hard work of his deputy Tiberius. The subsequent regime of Tiberius, too, once again after a long period of effective administration, had terminated in misery. About Caligula's short reign we are comparatively ill-informed, since the relevant books of Tacitus are missing, and the tales in Suetonius and Dio Cassius caused Theodor Mommsen to comment sternly that 'what merited silence has been told, and what deserved telling has been passed over in silence'. Nevertheless, although the empire as a whole remained well enough governed, Caligula's behaviour and position manifestly began to deteriorate, at some point or other, with headlong speed.

Philo believed that the decisive moment came in October 37, when Caligula had fallen ill.

In the eighth month of his reign a serious illness attacked Caligula who had exchanged the more moderate, and therefore healthier, mode of life which he had followed hitherto, during Tiberius' lifetime, for a life of luxury. Heavy drinking and a taste for delicacies, an appetite insatiable even on a swollen stomach, hot baths at the wrong time, emetics followed immediately by further drinking and the gluttony which goes with it, indecent behaviour with boys and women, and all the vices which destroy soul and body and the bonds which unite them, attacked him simultaneously. The wages of self-control are health and strength, while those of a lack of self-control are weakness and an illness which may prove fatal.[11]

It was this illness, according to Philo, which caused Caligula's brain and reign to take such a decided turn for the worse. But this interpretation scarcely seems tenable, since he remained an effective ruler, without incurring serious opposition, until AD 39. Then, however, a number of adverse developments occurred. First, he began to disclose his unprecedented concept of imperial autocracy, which involved some excessively straight talking to the senate. Had he, one may ask, only formed these convictions recently, or had he always possessed them, but hitherto concealed their existence under a cloak of hypocrisy? Philo, being an adherent of the ancient belief that character is immutable from birth – the belief that was to bedevil Tacitus' assessment of Tiberius – adopts the latter view. And certainly, in this case, Caligula seems to have been imbued with this kind of doctrine, if not from his infancy, at least quite early on, since there is reason, as we have seen, to detect the absolutist influence of the Jewish and eastern princes whom he met as a youth at the household of his grandmother Antonia. Nevertheless it appears probable that he only became a really convinced absolutist gradually, as he became more and more conscious of the infinite possibilities of his imperial position, which presented such an extraordinary antithesis to the repressed existence he had been leading before.

The second critical development of AD 39 had been the inauguration of the serious plots against his life, some imaginary perhaps but others authentic. Above all, the conspiracy of Gaetulicus was the turning-point of Caligula's character and reign. Tyrannical tendencies had no doubt been evident even before this emergency. But after it they could not fail to be greatly enhanced.

Yet Caligula, in a sense, was doomed to failure at the start, for if even the able and hard-working Tiberius had found the Augustan inheritance intractable, then his young, inexperienced, impetuous, unindustrious successor could not be expected to grapple with its formidable problems with any likelihood of success whatsoever.

5

Claudius

Tiberius Claudius Nero Germanicus, the youngest son of Drusus the elder and Antonia, was born at Lugdunum (Lyon) in 10 BC. Handicapped by constant illness and an uncouthness approaching deformity, he obtained no government posts from Augustus or Tiberius, and instead devoted his time to important scholarly pursuits. His nephew Caligula gave him a consulship (37).

After Caligula's assassination in 41, Claudius was hailed emperor by the praetorian guard, of which the senior officers may have planned in advance that he should be the new emperor. The senate, however, which had discussed the restoration of the Republic after the murder of Caligula, included many members who sympathized with the rebellion which Scribonianus tried to launch in Dalmatia in the next year. Its suppression was followed by a fierce tightening of security measures – and a series of further seditious movements, real or suspected, followed by treason trials.

At the same time, however, the government of Claudius displayed imposing activity. Under the command of Aulus Plautius, southern and central England was overrun and annexed as the province of Britannia. Claudius himself came to the country for the decisive capture of Camulodunum (Colchester), leaving behind him, in control of Rome, his principal adviser Lucius Vitellius.

Moreover, the emperor displayed marked administrative gifts, and an unremitting absorption in his judicial duties. Caligula's employment of Greek or Hellenized freedmen as advisers and imperial secretaries was continued and extended. However at this stage Claudius still kept even his most powerful secretaries, Narcissus and Pallas, under control; and his young wife Messalina, who had borne him a daughter Octavia and a son Britannicus, was initially more interested in enjoying herself than in exerting power. In 48, however, the charge that she was planning to set one of her lovers, Gaius Silius, on the throne in Claudius's place seems to have been justified. Both were struck down, their suppression being directed by Narcissus.

But Narcissus's moment of power ended abruptly when Claudius, in the very next year, married his niece Agrippina the younger. During the five years that followed the ageing emperor, overworked, terrified of plots, and weakened by a bad medical record and by drink, seems to have partially lost his grip of the situation. The government was now in the hands of Agrippina, assisted by Pallas – who had supported her marriage to Claudius – and by a new praetorian prefect Burrus. Actively stamping out opposition, Agrippina arranged in 50 that Nero, her son by a former marriage, should be adopted by Claudius with the clear intention that he should succeed to the throne at the expense of Claudius's own son Britannicus. Four years later the emperor suddenly died – and it was believed that Agrippina had given him poisoned mushrooms. Nero was appointed in his place without incident.

After the murder of Caligula there was chaos, and the senators thought they saw an opportunity to seize the guidance of events for the first time in very many years. After moving the contents of the treasury to a safe place on the Capitol, they held a meeting at which the consuls proposed the restoration of the long since deceased Republic. The discussion however was inconclusive, and the proposal was in any case out of the question, since the army, which wanted a single supreme commander who could assure their pay, would never have tolerated such a move; even the folly of Caligula had not in the least deterred them from this attitude. Nor would the soldiers have been willing to consider a further proposition that was being canvassed, the transfer of the principate to another family. For they felt closely attached to the Julio–Claudian house.

The only surviving member of that family was the fifty-year-old Claudius, and it was he therefore whom the praetorian guardsmen, acting upon the direction of their joint prefects and entirely ignoring the senate, conducted to their camp and proclaimed emperor. 'While the senate deliberated,' remarked Edward Gibbon, 'the praetorian guards had resolved.' No doubt the prefects, of whom one at least had apparently been privy to Caligula's murder, were acting in accordance with a preconceived plan – of which the late emperor's chief freedman Callistus had also been cognisant. When the guardsmen went to look for Claudius, they may well, as Suetonius reports, have found him cowering behind a palace curtain. But where the biographer carries melodrama too far is to suggest that his elevation to the throne was the sudden bright idea of the ordinary soldier who found him there.

The senators gave way to the demand of the praetorians and granted Claudius all the imperial powers – although he never afterwards forgave them for their brief initial period of hesitation, any more than they forgave him for having taken the matter out of their hands. It was the first time that their right to name a new emperor had ever been bluntly ignored and contested, and the new ruler, with a frankness that finds no parallel under any of his successors, issued coinage declaring openly that he owed his throne to the imperial guard. He was also the first emperor to make the praetorians a substantial gift when they proclaimed his accession.

Claudius was particularly well placed to make a good start with the army, because Germanicus had been his brother. And he took very great care, with complete success, to retain this popularity among the soldiers. That was why he went all the way to Britain for a sixteen-day visit, to be present at the final victory himself. And for the same reason he allowed himself to be saluted as *imperator*, triumphant general, on no less than twenty-seven occasions, six more than the number of salutations received even by Augustus himself.

Yet at the same time, like his two immediate predecessors, he declined to copy Augustus' use of the title *imperator* as a special prefix which indicated that he himself was *the* general. For this would have seemed a ridiculous claim for Claudius, who during his fifty years had failed to gain any military experience. Seneca, writing after he had died, made sarcastic fun of his total inexperience in martial affairs.

> Rebellious Parthians he did defeat;
> Swift after the Persians his light shafts go:
> For he well knew how to fit arrow to bow.
> Swiftly the striped barbarians fled:
> With one little wound he shot them dead.[1]

Indeed the new emperor was not only quite ludicrously unmilitary in

appearance and character, but his bizarre figure could not by any
means inspire confidence at all. For there was something very wrong
with Claudius.

Right personable he was and carried a presence not without authority and
majesty, whether he stood or sat, but especially when he was laid and took his
repose; for of stature he was tall, and natheless his body not lank and slender.
His countenance lively, his grey hairs beautiful, which became him well, with
a good fat and round neck under them.

Howbeit, both as he went his hams, being feeble, failed him, and also
whiles he was doing aught, were it remissly or in earnest, many things
disgraced him: to wit, indecent laughter and unseemly anger, by reason that
he would froth and slaver at the mouth and had evermore his nose dropping;
besides, his tongue stuttered and stammered; his head likewise at all times,
but especially if he did anything, were it never so little, used to shake and
tremble very much.[2]

That was what Suetonius had heard, and the elder Pliny added
the curious detail that the corners of the new emperor's eyes had
a fleshy cover, streaked with tiny veins, which at times filled with
blood.

What was the matter with him? At this distance of time, with our
fragmentary information, we cannot tell. His ailment has been variously
diagnosed; and the suggestions have included meningitis, poliomyelitis,
pre-natal encephalitis, multiple sclerosis, alcoholism and congenital
cerebral paralysis. Evidently the trouble was paralysis of some sort or
other, and when he was young it caused him to suffer from a wide
variety of obstinate disorders. But in his later years he summoned up the
power to overcome his infirmities, so that throughout his entire reign
his health, surprisingly enough, was excellent – with the single exception
of recurrent attacks of stomach-ache or heartburn, which were so fierce,
he complained, that they almost drove him to suicide.

The youthful Claudius had greatly depressed his mother Antonia,
who described him as a monster, whom nature had begun but had
failed to complete. Augustus, too, was extremely worried about the
young man – and, while recognizing that he was not without excellent
qualities, deplored many things about him, including his choice of low
companions. Considering what a political embarrassment Claudius
must have been, Augustus confronted his problems with considerable
patience; but his conclusion, in a letter to Livia, was not encouraging.

I have talked with Tiberius, my dear Livia, as you requested, with regard to what is to be done with your grandson Claudius at the Games of Mars. Now we are both agreed that we must decide once for all what plan we are to adopt in his case.

For if he be sound and, so to say, complete, what reason have we for doubting that he ought to be advanced through the same grades and steps through which his brother has been advanced? But if we realize that he is wanting and defective in soundness of body and mind, we must not furnish the means of ridiculing both him and us to a public which is wont to scoff at and deride such things. Surely we shall always be in a stew, if we deliberate about each separate occasion and do not make up our minds in advance whether we think he can hold public offices or not.[8]

It was concluded that there was little to be done for the young Claudius, and in AD 12 Augustus and Tiberius decided to exclude him from public life. Twenty-five years later, once again, Tiberius was said to have ruled Claudius out as a possible successor to his throne, on the grounds that his good intentions were not matched by mental normality. His nephew Caligula, however, made him consul in his own accession year 37, with himself as his colleague. After that the only attentions he gave his uncle were some of his notorious practical jokes. Nevertheless, following the executions of Caligula's two brothers-in-law, it must have looked probable to a number of people, including the praetorian prefects, that if any accident befell the young emperor his successor would be Claudius. And so, by their management, it turned out.

What was novel about the new ruler, apart from his disconcerting appearance and manner, was his immense learning; the elder Pliny, who quotes him four times in his *Natural History*, ranked him among the hundred foremost scholarly writers of the day. Claudius had originally taken to scholarship as a substitute for the official career of which he had been deprived; and it was no less an authority than Livy, prompted, no doubt, by Augustus, who had recognized and stimulated his bent towards historical studies.

Claudius wrote a pamphlet in defence of Cicero, and got to work on a Roman history. He proposed to start it at the death of Julius Caesar, but when his mother Antonia and grandmother Octavia explained to him that the civil wars at the outset of this period were too embarrassing a theme, he abandoned the early part of the project, and began again with the inauguration of Augustus' new order in 27 BC, carrying on until his death in AD 14.

Claudius also composed twenty volumes of Etruscan history and eight of Carthaginian history, in Greek. All these books have vanished; the disappearance of the information they must have contained – especially the former work to which his first wife, of Etruscan blood, may have contributed original information – is one of the gravest of our losses in ancient historiography. Since, however, his profound admiration for the Greek language and its literature did not suffice, as we know from surviving pronouncements, to make his manner very easy or smooth, some sympathy may be felt for the citizens of Alexandria:

> For because of these works there was added to the old Museum at Alexandria a new one called after his name, and it was provided that in the one his Etruscan History should be read each year from beginning to end, and in the other his Carthaginian, by various readers in turn, in the manner of public recitations.[4]

Claudius was also the author of an eight-volume autobiography; a treatise on dicing, an occupation of which he was fond; and a historical study of the Roman alphabet, which he suggested should be augmented by the addition of three letters. After he had come to the throne, this suggestion was given effect, though the reform did not survive him.

While he was emperor, he still did not allow his learned and literary activities to flag, since he continued to write a great deal, employing a professional reader to give public readings from his works.

His scholarly activities, and the secluded years he had spent pondering on them, offer the key to many features of his principate that lay ahead. In his own single person he united both of the opposed qualities that characterized the historians of his epoch: he was at one and the same time an erudite antiquarian and a writer of modern history.

Each of these different tastes comes out clearly in his administrative achievements as emperor of Rome. On the one hand, he was determined that ancient traditions, the traditions of the great past in which his Claudian family had fulfilled so important a role, should be meticulously observed, and this insistence sometimes strayed into a deliberate revival of archaisms. But his researches had also taught him that life does not stand still. There were changes, he was convinced, which could and should be introduced, without affording conservatives any good reason to take offence.

Augustus, whom Claudius like so many other emperors explicitly admired, had managed to combine these two aims. But Claudius gave a new savour to the blend, because of the historian's relentless curiosity and learned precision which was his personal contribution to the process: although at the same time he partly cancelled out these excellent qualities by a further and very un-Augustan trait, the clumsiness of the man of learning who tries to become a man of action. The distinctive marks of his personality are detectable in all the major developments of his time. However his precise intellectual calibre remains hard to assess, and his biographer V. M. Scramuzza could only conclude that he presents one of the most perplexing problems in all Roman history. Although notoriously absent-minded – on the very day his wife Messalina had been executed he was said to have asked where she was – he earned Seneca's praise for his exceptionally tenacious memory. Even Augustus, who found Claudius so unpresentable, noted it as strange that a man who mumbled obscurely in ordinary conversation could declaim publicly with such complete lucidity, and Tacitus too, though not in the least disposed to pay him compliments, was willing to confirm that his oratory was graceful enough, provided that it had been prepared in advance.

Fortunately we can judge his style for ourselves, from a number of important statements that have survived on inscriptions and papyri. They show all the qualities, good and bad, that his scholarly background has led us to expect – and certain special peculiarities as well. Although, for instance, his mind was seething with good ideas, he evidently found it hard to coordinate them in a concisely expressed form. His opening sentences, in particular, display an involved structure which reflects some difficulty in getting going. Another striking phenomenon is a tendency to stop in mid-speech, and call himself to order, and bid himself return to the point. He also suffered from that characteristic professorial desire to inflict the more esoteric products of his learning upon the general public. On one occasion he published twenty edicts on a single day, and two of them were these: 'This year's vintage is unusually abundant, so everyone must pitch his wine-jars well,' and 'Yew-juice is sovereign against snake-bite.'

Claudius found it hard to get rest, since he was not able to sleep for very long at a time; after going to bed he was usually awake again before midnight. This meant that he often used to drop off in the day-time, and lawyers, when they noticed him asleep in court, formed the habit of tactfully raising their voices.

He was vulgar and garrulous, and poured out a constant stream of jokes, not so pointed as those of Caligula and indeed often very unfunny indeed. Many stories went the rounds about his compulsive appetite. When there was a debate in the senate about butchers and wine-merchants, he cried out: 'Now I ask you, who can do without a snack?' And he for one could not.

He was eager for food and drink at all times and in all places. Once when he was holding court in the Forum of Augustus and had caught the savour of a meal which was being prepared for the Salii in the Temple of Mars hard by, he left the tribunal, went up where the priests were, and took his place at their table.

He hardly ever left the dining-room until he was stuffed and soaked. Then he went to sleep at once, lying on his back with his mouth open, and a feather was put down his throat to relieve his stomach.[5]

In spite of this habitual post-prandial condition, Claudius was an immoderate and relentless womanizer. But he could not, all the same, be regarded as wholly 'normal'; since he possessed a nasty rancorous ill-temper which frequently crossed over the border into sadism, a quality which he shared with his nephew and predecessor. For example, he had people tortured in his presence, and liked watching horrible archaic forms of execution.

Much of his cruelty, however, arose directly from the timidity, suspicion and alarm which were perhaps his dominant characteristics. All emperors had very good reason to be afraid of plots, but reports of such activities, whether founded or unfounded, cast Claudius into a state of extreme fright which did much to cancel out his benevolent intentions, and made it all too easy for interested parties to work upon his panics. The security precautions which surrounded him were raised to fantastic dimensions. When he went out to dinner, for example, he would insist, rather insultingly, upon being waited on at table by his own guards-men; and before he visited the sick their pillows and bedclothes had to be searched and shaken out.

Many of the severest security measures were the consequences of an abortive revolt by the governor of Dalmatia, Marcus Furius Camillus Scribonianus, scarcely more than a year after Claudius's accession. Although the rebellion was suppressed before it started, its would-be leaders possessed links with extremely influential noblemen in Rome. This incident afflicted Claudius with the same permanent consternation into which an equally abortive act of defiance in Germany had plunged his predecessor Caligula. In both cases, nothing was ever the same for the terrified emperors again; and the attempted uprising made it harder than ever for Claudius to forget that, at first, the senators had not wanted to have him on the throne at all.

He did not, it was true, repeat Caligula's openly admitted breach with the senate. Yet since, even after the suppression of Scribonianus, he had to contend with at least six further alleged plots, the net result, in terms of average senatorial casualties per year, was scarcely better. After Claudius's death, Seneca accused him of having caused havoc in the ranks of the upper classes: for during his reign no less than thirty-five senators, and between two and three hundred knights, became his victims. His promise not to force the senate to condemn its own members to death proved little consolation – since he tried them himself instead.

And yet at the same time Claudius, ironically enough, as benefited such an ardent traditionalist, paid meticulous honours to the senators. In spite of his infirmity he maintained Augustus's practice of rising to his feet when they rose, or when a consul approached him. Moreover he was extremely eager that the senate in its corporate capacity should pull its weight and fulfil a genuinely responsible role. In a speech that has come down to us, he told its members this, with a delicately ironical allusion to the supine behaviour which he found so objectionable.

If these proposals are approved by you, show your assent at once plainly and sincerely. If, however, you do not approve them then find some other remedies but here in this temple now, or if you wish to take a longer time for consideration, take it, so long as you recollect that wherever you meet you should produce an opinion of your own.

For it is extremely unfitting, Conscript Fathers, to the high dignity of this order that at this meeting one man only, the consul designate, should make a speech (and that copied exactly from the proposal of the consuls), while the rest utter one word only 'Agreed', and then after leaving the House remark 'There, we've given our opinion.'[6]

But in spite of these praiseworthy aims, Claudius was naïve to ask the senators to display their former initiative and independence when they were being executed at an average rate of two or three a year. Besides, he himself frequently acted on his own in matters which might otherwise have fallen within the senate's sphere, so that business tended to become centralized in his own indefatigable hands. His governor of Asia, Paullus Fabius Persicus, declared that he had 'received the whole race of men into his personal care'. This was true, but it meant also that he ruled the provinces with such efficient thoroughness that the senate's traditional rights could scarcely fail to become infringed at some point or other. Moreover, he was heard to admit that he regarded senators who helped him as *his* officials rather than as functionaries of the state.

Meanwhile they in their turn, on occasion, ventured to treat him with polite sarcasm. But this had to be done with great caution, since Claudius, in addition to executing members of the senate, exerted more direct control over its composition than any previous emperor. Indeed he openly displayed that this was what he proposed to do, by a constitutional innovation. For whereas Augustus had assumed censorial power without office for this purpose, Claudius instead characteristically revived the antique Republican office of censor itself.

This tenure of the censorship in AD 47–8 enabled Claudius to replace the losses in the senate's ranks by men who were his own personal supporters. In this respect he was determinedly liberal, considering that his predecessors' practice of introducing senators from the Italian municipalities, as well as a few from citizen municipalities in southern Gaul, should now be extended to Roman citizens from other, less highly Romanized parts of Gaul. The speech was reproduced in edited form by Tacitus. But an inscription recording the original version reveals the full flavour of Claudius' highly individual blend of progressiveness and antiquarianism.

I myself deprecate that first thought of everyone, which I foresee will be my chief and first obstacle – you should not be alarmed, as if a novelty is being introduced, but rather think of all the many novelties which this city has undergone, and of the many shapes and forms which our commonwealth assumed right from the origin of our city.

At one time kings ruled the city, and yet they did not hand the kingship on to successors of their own house. Outsiders, and even foreigners, came in; Numa, who succeeded Romulus, came from the Sabines, a neighbour it is true, but in those days a foreigner, and Ancus Marcius was followed by Priscus Tarquinius . . .

Surely both my great-uncle, the deified Augustus, and my uncle, Tiberius Caesar, were following a new practice when they desired that all the flower of the colonies and the municipalities everywhere – that is, the better class and the wealthy men – should sit in this senate house. You ask me: Is not an Italian senator preferable to a provincial? . . . I think that not even provincials ought to be excluded, provided that they can add distinction to this house.[7]

Claudius' argument was that his proposal was *not* a departure from the traditional constitution but its fulfilment, a legitimate and normal adjustment to the changing times – and that if any novelty was involved it had already been anticipated by his predecessors. But any and every imperial senate, in spite of all its periodical injections of new blood, rapidly became as conservative as the senates of bygone days; and Claudius' suggestion, although it had to be accepted, aroused a storm of xenophobia. Amid wild reports of indiscriminate enrolments arose the trumpet-cry that Italy could still perfectly well take care of the empire by itself – without all these deplorable injections of outside blood. 'Do we have to import foreigners in hordes, like gangs of prisoners?' That had never, such objectors urged, been the policy of Augustus: Claudius, on the other hand, maintained that he was only harvesting where his great forerunner had sown. Yet, in any case, the whole dispute was exaggerated. The changes were not sensational. During the reign of Claudius and his successor scarcely a dozen consuls can be counted from the provinces of the west, and none at all from the east; and the first pair of provincial consuls did not emerge for forty years after Claudius' death.

Without him, however, even this reasonable degree of social mobility would have been delayed. And his policy for the extension of Roman citizenship was similar. At the end of Augustus' reign there had been nearly five million citizens, including wives and children. The number had increased, fairly slowly, since that time, and Claudius' census showed a figure of nearly six million. The increases mainly concerned the provinces, since the population of Italy had consisted, for the most part, of citizens already. Once again, then, the change was only gradual: Italy had still not lost its supremacy. Yet Claudius had also made it clear that he was not disposed to disregard the claims of the provinces. As Kenneth Wellesley observed, he saw Rome 'as a pebble thrown into the water of history whose waters were to move ever outwards'. Nevertheless this policy of moderate enfranchisement, like his policy for senatorial membership, was distorted into a wholly indiscriminate process of creating new Roman citizens. For example, Seneca makes Clotho, one of the Fates, remark as the emperor was about to die: 'Upon my word, I did want to give him another hour or two, until he should make Roman citizens of the half dozen who are still outsiders. He made up his mind, you know, to see the whole world in the toga, Greeks, Gauls, Spaniards, Britons and all.'[8] The joke accurately reflects the prejudices which had been encountered by Claudius, and which still make it peculiarly difficult to discover what really went on during his reign.

Undoubtedly he concentrated on his judicial duties more than any emperor ever had before. Whereas every ruler, or at least every conscientious ruler, felt that it was one of his principal duties to serve regularly as a judge, Caligula, when he ceased to pay very much attention to his duller imperial duties, had perhaps allowed this function partially to lapse. With Claudius, on the other hand, jurisdiction was a passion, and it occupied a good deal of his time nearly every day. He was assiduous in his attendance at the senatorial courts, but his own imperial court was what engaged most of his attention. Treason cases were only one of several categories of criminal trials which his forerunners might have remitted to the senate, but he preferred to conduct himself, with the help of assessors. Thus he extended imperial jurisdiction over a wide range of criminal activities with which it had not concerned itself before.

Naturally the senate resented his increased activity in this field, since it strengthened the imperial authority still further at the cost of their own. In consequence spiteful stories readily arose.

> O weep for the man! This world never saw
> One quicker a troublesome suit to decide,
> When only one part of the case had been tried –
> He could do it indeed and not hear either side.[9]

Suetonius, too, had heard that Claudius's behaviour in court was unpredictable and arbitrary, if not sometimes downright nonsensical.

One Greek lawyer lost his temper with him and shouted that he was a stupid old idiot. Moreover, a Roman knight, accused of unnatural behaviour towards women, was so annoyed by the emperor for admitting the evidence of prostitutes that he hurled his tablet and pen at him and badly gashed his cheek.

And old people I know [added the biographer] have told me that pleaders imposed so rudely on his good nature that they would not only call him back after he had closed the court but would catch at the hem of his gown, and even at his foot, in their efforts to detain him.[10]

Nevertheless, his patient reception of such treatment did at least contradict the rumours of his hasty behaviour by showing the endless trouble that Claudius was prepared to take; and despite the sourness of the ancient tradition a number of reports praising the quality of his judicial achievements have survived. He wanted to speed up proceedings. He was eager to protect the weak, and ensure that every man should receive his due. He took measures to increase the number of judges. He greatly shortened legal vacations. And he was boldly prepared to cast aside the letter of the law to preserve the spirit behind it. 'Of course I am aware,' he said, 'that dishonest accusers will never lack tricks. But I hope we shall find remedies against their evil arts.'

This conscientious search for remedies was typical of the man. Claudius, not without a good deal of complaint, overloaded himself with work. Even on days when he should have been celebrating the anniversaries of his accession and the birthdays of his family, he preferred to work on steadily as usual, from morning till night. Seneca, before the emperor's death enabled him to become more malicious, rightly stressed his watchfulness and unremitting labour. A new imperial virtue is commemorated on the coins of his reign, right from the very beginning: it is CONSTANTIA, perseverance. Those of his predecessors who had lacked this quality incurred Claudius's criticism. Although Tiberius could not have been accused of shirking his work, Claudius found it highly reprehensible that he had withdrawn permanently to Capreae – and spoke of his 'obstinate retirement'. Caligula's lack of *constantia* scarcely needed to be underlined, and although Claudius refrained from official condemnation of his memory, he was prepared to refer publicly to his predecessor's deplorable 'want of understanding'.

And yet, ironically enough, the empire's transformation into an absolute monarchy, to which Caligula had devoted himself, inexorably went on. In addition to the continuing process of insidious centralization, the aggrandisement of the emperor's revered person went on as well: there was no appreciable regression from the flattering language that had been lavished upon Caligula. It is true that Claudius went through ritual disclaimers of personal divinity, writing to the Alexandrians, for example, that he did not want temples or priests of his own cult. Nevertheless he allowed them to carry his statues in procession on days specially set apart for his veneration; and writers were permitted to speak of his Sacred Hands and Duties, and even to describe him as 'our god Caesar'.

There seemed to be a curious contradiction here. For, by family tradition and intellectual conviction, the emperor was committed to Republicanism. In addition to his family's long tradition, his own father Drusus the elder had been noted as one of the most strongly Republican influences in Augustus' entourage: and Claudius himself was predisposed by his profound historical studies to hold similar views. Indeed he may well have intended to express precisely this sort of opinion in the account of the civil wars which his mother and grandmother had cautioned him to abandon. And yet, in stark contrast, almost the entirety of his work as emperor could not fail to be directed towards the imperial absolutism which alone seemed to answer to the needs and wishes of his subjects.

It was therefore somewhat ironical that one of the novel designs of his first coinage was LIBERTAS AVGVSTA, Imperial Freedom, the Freedom permitted and granted by the government. Augustus had declared himself the Vindicator of the Liberty of the Roman People. But Claudius's choice of the additional epithet '*Augusta*' is more explicit in its claim that this Liberty is something inherent in the imperial regime.

After the late emperor's murder the senate had given the garrison *Libertas* as its watchword, for the first time for many decades. But what the senators, or some of them, had had in mind was the restoration of the old Republican right to conduct unrestricted struggles among themselves in the political arena, for public office and its dizzy profits, to the accompaniment of equally unrestricted freedom of speech. But the implication of Claudius' slogan, on the other hand, was that this would have meant the return of chaos, whereas the only true freedom to be had was not under a Republic at all, or for that matter under a tyrant such as Caligula, but by grace of his own beneficent government.

Although Claudius, for such reasons, was never popular among the senators, he had his personal friends and helpers among them. The most important of these helpers was Lucius Vitellius, whose son was to become the ninth of the twelve Caesars. Although Lucius' father was not a senator but a knight from Luceria (Lucera in Apulia), he himself became the most successful politician of the age. He owed his prestige largely to a successful governorship of Syria under Tiberius; but he had then received high favour from Caligula as well. Yet he attained even greater influence under Claudius, achieving the exceedingly rare distinction of a third consulship, in addition to serving as the emperor's fellow-censor. And when Claudius departed for his expedition to Britain, he left him in charge of the capital during his absence.

Yet Lucius Vitellius' reputation, even allowing for a good deal of jealous feeling among his fellow-senators, remained dubious. He was said to have flattered Caligula outrageously, and under Claudius, too, Tacitus described him as a byword for degraded sycophancy. He himself, however, or his admirers, made this quality into a virtue, since his memorial statue was inscribed with a reference to his 'immovable loyalty to the emperor'. Certainly he showed almost incredible adroitness in ingratiating himself with three such different emperors – and in becoming close friends with successive empresses as well.

In sharp contrast to his immediate forerunner, Claudius showed himself an appreciative friend. He was always testifying to his high regard for his associates, and to his respect for their experience and counsel. He was well aware how much he depended on their advice, and he emphasized this special relationship by entitling them to wear a ring stamped with his portrait in gold. Yet such trusted allies were inevitably few in number, because, until he came to the throne, he had been completely out of touch with the senatorial order, so that his social relations with its suspicious members remained limited.

In his earlier life he had been a knight, but now, although he extended the powers of some of the knights who represented him abroad, he could call upon less friends from among their ranks than Augustus or Tiberius. Moreover the knightly order suffered severely in Claudius's repressions of supposed plots. Perhaps their special concern with economic affairs had made them resentful of his tendency towards centralization, when this invaded the economic sphere and encroached on their profits: and that may have irritated the emperor.

At all events, he had to have more confidential helpers than either senate or knights could provide. Indeed his need was even greater than that of his predecessors, because he had concentrated such an unprecedented amount of work in his own hands. His solution was to increase the powers and duties of his personal staff, his assistants in the palace itself – Greeks or Hellenized orientals – who had formerly been slaves and were now of freedman rank. The utilization of such people for affairs of state was by no means completely novel. The titles allotted to their various functions went back to Augustus – though Augustus had never allowed them to become conspicuous. Nor did Tiberius, though his prolonged and permanent absence on Capreae must have meant that the freedmen of his entourage became somewhat more influential, owing to the shortage of other accessible advisers. Under Caligula, however, the palace freedmen did a great deal of his work and it was in his reign that some of them for the first time came to be among the most important figures in the empire.

Claudius, as so often, systematized an already existing tendency, and we find three or four freedmen not only assisting him in wide areas of his duties but enjoying greater power and fame than had ever fallen to the lot of freedmen before. Although they are sometimes described as his secretaries of state or ministers, they did not control anything comparable to the ministries or bureaux of a modern western state. The ancient authors who were so hostile to Claudius, and modern writers who have followed them, show him feebly submitting to the control of these men and allowing them to create his policy for him. But this version is mistaken. The inscriptions and papyri recording Claudius's speeches and letters show a unity of style which bears the unmistakable stamp of his own personality. The freedmen were *not* in charge of the government, but were organized and dominated by the emperor – as even the most unfriendly account cannot wholly conceal. At least until his last years, when he partly lost control, he himself remained the man from whom verdicts and decisions had to be obtained.

That does not mean, however, that his freedmen were lacking in power. For, although Claudius, until that final stage, was too conscientious and obstinate a man to be cajoled or hoodwinked about most matters, there was one exception to this. For, as we have seen, it must always have been fairly easy to work on his harrowing suspicions and fears. Furthermore, although the functions specifically assigned to the freedmen did not carry power, their proximity to the emperor inevitably did; and it is significant that the literary tradition never shows them performing their titular duties, but always acting as his agents in some wider field, being entrusted, for example, with important errands and missions. These tasks gave them great opportunities for patronage: how great, we can see from Seneca's obsequious treatise addressed to the imperial freedman Polybius, and from Suetonius's account of how a later emperor's household vigilantly watched for a suitable time to ply him with requests – in favour, perhaps, of some friend or relation who may, in view of the freedmen's oriental origin, have been a merchant or shipper in the east. By such means the freedmen of Claudius became extraordinarily, scandalously rich. Besides, even though it was he who made the decisions, it was open to a clever freedman to interpret or modify them before they passed into effect.

It is easy, then, to see why the historians, and the senators who inspired them, formed such a dislike of these secretaries. Whether they were hard, conscientious workers or not, whether there might not be a better side to them than all their rumoured nepotism and corruption, were questions which did not interest these representatives of the upper class. They loathed seeing such lowborn easterners giving themselves patronizing airs, and the prominence of such fellows was yet one more painfully conspicuous sign that the senate was no longer at the centre of power. When Seneca said to Polybius 'you owe the whole of yourself to Caesar', he was right. The freedmen devoted their entire loyalty to the emperor, and did not care about the interests of the senators at all.

At first the most important of Claudius's secretaries was Narcissus, the *ab epistulis* or minister of letters. For it was he who helped the ruler with the correspondence he exchanged with governors, commanders and imperial agents in the provinces. He was cognisant, therefore, of many important personal secrets. He made an enormous amount of money; and he was sent to northern Gaul in AD 43 with the responsible task of directing the embarkation of the British expeditionary force.

Narcissus declared his unlimited gratitude and devotion to Claudius, and there is no reason to doubt his word. In 48, as the emperor began to show signs of failing, it was he, virtually on his own, who conducted the suppression of the conspiracy in which the empress Messalina and her lover Gaius Silius were believed to be involved. But when Claudius, after the guilty pair were dead, decided to marry again, Narcissus failed to back the successful candidate, Agrippina the younger, who subsequently drove him into retirement and at about the time of the emperor's death compelled him to kill himself.

Agrippina's own principal freedman adviser was Pallas, the *a rationibus* or finance minister, whose retention in these duties since the beginning of the reign had given him obvious opportunities for influence. His private life was so grand that he did not deign to converse with his own slaves or freedmen, but jotted down his wishes and commands on tablets so as not to be obliged to address such inferior individuals. In 52 the senate was later felt to have humiliated itself gravely when, accepting the proposal of a great nobleman, it voted Pallas high honours and a huge sum of money in reward for his labours:

So that he, to whom all to the utmost of their ability acknowledge their obligation, should reap the just reward of his outstanding loyalty and devotion to duty: since the senate and the Roman people could have no more gratifying occasion for liberality than the opportunity to add to the means of this self-denying and faithful custodian of the imperial finances.[11]

Pallas declined the money – which he did not need, since he was enormously wealthy – but accepted the honours. Perhaps to some extent he had deserved them. Self-enrichment was a very general phenomenon among ancient functionaries, and if while enriching himself he had at the same time served Claudius well perhaps that was all that could be expected. But after Claudius died and Agrippina soon afterwards lost her power, Pallas fell from favour too, and when he died in 62 it was believed that Nero, to whom he had earlier been evasive about rendering his accounts, was responsible for his death.

Polybius, the *a studiis*, whose powerful position and imposing grandeur emerge so strongly from Seneca's adulatory words, has generally been regarded as Claudius' librarian and cultural adviser. But the term *studia* in his title may rather bear the meaning of favour and support, in which case it was he who arranged for the commendation and appointment of the men whom the emperor had earmarked for various promotions and offices. Seneca makes it clear that Polybius was obliged to listen to a great many entreaties from individuals. But in dealing with some of the many other petitions that he received, from cities and communities all over the empire, Claudius apparently had the assistance of another freedman, the *a libellis* or minister of notes. This was the post occupied by Callistus, who had already held an important secretarial post under Caligula. Perhaps Callistus also undertook the duties of an assistant *a cognitionibus*, who helped the emperor with his judicial work and sat in with him at legal proceedings.

Not content with overemphasizing the influence of his freedmen on Claudius's decisions, the ancient authorities likewise exaggerated the influence of his third wife Valeria Messalina, whom he had married in 39 or 40, when she was nineteen or twenty years of age (not fourteen or fifteen as is sometimes said). The match had seemed an excellent one, because she was the grand-niece of Augustus, both on her father's and her mother's side. Claudius lavished considerable honours upon Messalina – probably more than had been accorded to the wives of any of his predecessors, since the current tendency towards autocratic monarchy meant increased veneration of the empress as well as the emperor. She appeared frequently at official functions, and her status gave her considerable freedom of action, so that she was perhaps able, for example, to contribute to the downfalls of the freedman Polybius and the praetorian prefect Catonius Justus, and may also have prompted the execution of the senior Gallic senator Decimus Valerius Asiaticus for treason, though whether this was because she coveted his wealth, as people said, remains uncertain. For such reasons men spoke jeeringly of Messalina as queen. But in reality the decisive step towards a power-controlling or even truly power-sharing empress had not been taken. Claudius himself remained fully in charge.

Nevertheless Messalina was a portent, since she showed that not only emperors such as Caligula but empresses, too, had the opportunity to enjoy themselves unrestrainedly. Since the first six years of Claudius' reign fall within the missing portion of Tacitus' *Annals*, we lack a major part of his portrait of this woman. But he was right in concluding that for a long time she only 'toyed with national affairs in order to satisfy her appetites'. At the outset of the reign what she mainly desired – and this was her reason for attacks on others – was a visibly more brilliant position than all other young women, displayed in terms of luxury, magnificent parties and the sexual satisfaction her somewhat infirm husband, however lecherous, can scarcely have been able to provide. For if only one-tenth of the stories which have made Messalina a byword for lasciviousness are true, she was phenomenally oversexed.

> Hear what Claudius
> Had to put up with. The minute she heard him snoring,
> His wife – that whore-empress – who dared to prefer the mattress
> Of a stews to her couch in the Palace, called for her hooded
> Night-cloak and hastened forth, alone or with a single
> Maid to attend her. Then, her black hair hidden
> Under an ash-blonde wig, she would make straight for her brothel
> With its odour of stale, warm bedclothes, its empty reserved cell.
> Here she would strip off, showing her gilded nipples and the belly
> that once housed a prince of the blood.[12]

But there came a time in the year 48, when the last of Messalina's long line of lovers joined her in a desperately perilous political adventure. This was one of the consuls designate, Gaius Silius, rich, noble, reasonably young and extremely good-looking. One day, when the emperor had gone to Ostia to supervise the port of Rome he was creating there, Silius and Messalina planned a rebellion against him, and began it by going through a form of marriage. Tacitus makes a memorable set-piece of the occasion.

It was full autumn; and Messalina was performing a mimic grapeharvest in her grounds. Presses were working, vats overflowing, surrounded by women capering in skins like sacrificing or frenzied Maenads. She herself, hair streaming, brandished a Bacchic wand. Beside her stood Silius in ivy-wreath and buskins, rolling his head, while the disreputable chorus yelled around him. Vettius Valens, the story goes, gaily climbed a great tree. Asked what he saw, his answer was: 'A fearful storm over Ostia!'[13]

And a fearful storm there soon was over Rome as well, because Claudius came back. He found it hard to grasp the situation – it was perhaps the first time that he showed a serious loss of grip. His friend Lucius Vitellius, almost equally dismayed, took refuge in an unhelpful ambiguity. But the freedman Narcissus, on whom real power was momentarily thrust, assumed the initiative in stamping the sedition out. Taking over the temporary command of the praetorian troops in person, he had Silius arrested and executed, while Messalina, who lay moaning in the garden of her not very sympathetic mother, was assisted to die by an officer of the guard. Tacitus well realizes, he says, that this whole mysterious incident will seem fantastic and incredible. It appears less fantastic, however, if seen not just as a caprice, but as a serious plot. Its intention was probably to enthrone Britannicus, the seven-year-old son of Claudius and Messalina, with his mother and Silius as his regents.

The emperor never really recovered from the shock. Nevertheless it did not cure him of a taste for marriage, since he was incurably uxorious. Indeed in the very next year he was already taking yet another wife, his fourth. With the connivance of Pallas, who thus replaced Narcissus as the most influential freedman at court, his choice fell on Agrippina the younger. This woman, after growing up in an appalling atmosphere of malevolence, suspicion and criminal violence, had been sentenced by Caligula to banishment. By a former marriage she had a twelve-year-old boy by whom, now that she was married to Claudius, she proposed that Britannicus should be supplanted. She arranged for her son to be betrothed to Claudius's daughter Octavia, and a year later he was adopted by the emperor, with the name of Nero.

This was a time when something altogether new in Roman history appeared: the concentration of authority in the hands of a woman.

This was a rigorous, almost masculine despotism. In public, Agrippina was austere and often arrogant. Her private life was chaste – unless power was to be gained. Her passion to acquire money was unbounded. She wanted it as a stepping-stone to supremacy ... Complete obedience was accorded to a woman, and not to a woman like Messalina who toyed with national affairs to satisfy her appetites.[14]

That these words of Tacitus are scarcely exaggerated is confirmed by two points in which her position manifestly exceeded Messalina's. First, Agrippina was named Augusta: no living wife of a living emperor had ever been called this before. And equally unprecedented was the appearance of her portrait – together with those both of Claudius and of the youthful Nero – upon the official gold and silver coinage of the Roman mint itself. On state occasions Agrippina was seen in magnificent robes, or dressed in a cloak made of woven gold. And meanwhile she was striking venomously around her, with the intention of suppressing all possible opposition to herself and her son.

True, despite Tacitus' strong words, he himself has to admit that she did not have things entirely her own way. For example, the senate showed its resentment by venturing to condemn one of her agents, Tarquitius Priscus. Nevertheless for the most part she exercised a dominant influence over the course of events. The eminent writer and orator Seneca, one of Messalina's victims, was recalled from banishment to become Nero's tutor, and Agrippina also secured the appointment of another protégé as praetorian prefect, Sextus Afranius Burrus from Vasio (Vaison in southern France). Pallas, too, remained at her side.

When Claudius died in October 54, at the age of sixty-three, there were several divergent accounts of what had caused his death. But according to the version which subsequently prevailed most widely, Agrippina had killed him with poisoned mushrooms. This must be regarded as likely though not quite certain, since accidental loss of life frequently occurs in Italy owing to confusions between the harmless mushroom *boletus edulis* and the fatal *amanita phalloides*. Besides Agrippina had cleared the ground adequately for Nero's succession, and only had to wait. But perhaps that was just what she dared not do, because if Nero, who was nearly seventeen, did not come to the throne fairly soon, he might no longer be young enough to need her as his effective regent.

There is no reason to suppose that the good government of Claudius became worse under Agrippina's new regime. Yet his reign, like those of his predecessors, had been marked by a clear deterioration in his personal condition. The more thoughtful ancient writers, those who did not make the mistake of regarding him as a puppet all along, appreciated this; for example, Dio Cassius found it clearly recorded in his sources. And both he and Tacitus could pinpoint the date when this decline became most glaringly noticeable. According to Tacitus, it was from the time of his marriage with Agrippina that 'the country was transformed'.

Although it might, perhaps, be slightly more accurate to date the change from the plot and downfall of Messalina in the previous year, this verdict was evidently not far from the truth. For Claudius's temperament was peculiarly vulnerable to such emergencies. Like so many other emperors, he went in perpetual fear, and with good reason. Yet he was the most timorous of them all, and conspiracies upset him desperately. His profoundly flawed physical constitution, undermined still further by incessant overwork and too much drink and food, gradually made him more and more incapable of carrying on at the head of affairs: and the traumatic transference from Messalina to the masterful Agrippina proved the turning-point. When Augustus, in unhappy old age, was losing control, he had had at his side a reliable deputy and successor designate, Tiberius, who kept the state on an even keel. Claudius innovated alarmingly by relying, in his own worse plight, upon a woman and a terrifying one at that, and for the first time in its long history Rome momentarily found itself under female control.

6

Nero

Lucius Domitius Ahenobarbus, the future emperor Nero, was born at Antium (Anzio) on 15 December AD 37. His father was Cnaeus Domitius Ahenobarbus, of an ancient and extremely noble family; and his mother was Agrippina the younger, daughter of Germanicus and the elder Agrippina. When he was two, his mother was exiled by Caligula; and after Cnaeus Ahenobarbus' death in the following year, the same emperor seized the infant's inheritance. Under Claudius, however, Agrippina was recalled from banishment, and gave her son a good education. Then, after she had married Claudius in 49, the eminent Seneca became the tutor of the boy, who was betrothed to the emperor's daughter Octavia; she became his wife in 53. Meanwhile, in 50, he had been adopted as Claudius's son, and subsequently assumed the names of Nero Claudius Drusus Germanicus. On the death of the emperor in October 54 the claims of Claudius's own son by Messalina, Britannicus, were set aside, and Agrippina, with the help of the praetorian prefect Burrus, secured the throne for the seventeen-year-old Nero.

Agrippina arranged the deification of the husband she may well have murdered, and became the priestess of the new divinity. Moreover, she herself became, for a brief period, the effective ruler of the empire.

But already in 55 her position was rapidly declining. Although Nero did not yet abandon his imperial duties in favour of the artistic occupations and other amusements which he preferred, the empire was largely governed, and governed very well, by the harmonious cooperation of Seneca and Burrus. In 59 Nero, fearing a subversive movement, had his mother put to death. It is uncertain if Seneca and Burrus were involved in her death, but from now on they found it harder to keep Nero in order.

Meanwhile important military operations against the Parthians were taking place under Rome's leading general Corbulo in Armenia (58–60), and Gaius Suetonius Paulinus, in Britain, suppressed the ferocious revolt of Boudicca (Boadicea). In 62 Burrus died, and Seneca, finding it impossible to carry on in this new situation, went into retirement. The emperor's chief counsellor was now Tigellinus, who, jointly with Faenius Rufus, had succeeded to the praetorian command. Tigellinus presided over a revival of the treason law, and eminent nobles began to be executed on suspicion of conspiracy. Nero, long since estranged rom his young wife Octavia, divorced her and put h e r to death, marrying Poppaea, who presented him with a short-lived daughter (63). The next year witnessed the Great Fire of Rome; and work was started on Nero's new palace, the Golden House.

In 65, when the emperor made his first public performance on the Roman stage, the first of a series of plots against his life was detected and betrayed. As a result the eminent nobleman Gaius Calpurnius Piso was executed. Other casualties of this Pisonian conspiracy included Seneca and Faenius Rufus; his successor as joint prefect was Nymphidius Sabinus, who had helped to stamp out the plot.

In the following year a new security drive wiped out a group of senators of quasi-Republican and philosophical inclinations, led by Thrasea Paetus. Thereafter further conspirators were struck down, and leading commanders, including the great Corbulo and two brothers who governed Germany, were compelled to commit suicide (66). The order to kill themselves was conveyed to them after they had been summoned to Greece, where Nero was conducting an extended artistic and histrionic tour which culminated in his ostensible 'liberation' of the country. Meanwhile he had appointed Vespasian (the future emperor) to suppress the First Jewish Revolt, or, in Jewish parlance, the First Roman War. But no provincial governor or army commander felt safe any longer, and Nero's return to Rome in January 68 was followed, two months later, by the revolt of Vindex, governor of Gallia Lugdunensis. Vindex was defeated in May at Vesontio (Besançon) by his colleague in Upper Germany, Lucius Verginius Rufus. But then Galba, governor of Nearer Spain, was hailed emperor by his legionaries and the senate. Nero found himself abandoned by Nymphidius Sabinus and the praetorian guard, and on 9 June he was compelled to commit suicide.

•   •   •   •

Nero's genetic heritage from his disagreeable father and mother was atrocious. Moreover his childhood, like those of Tiberius and Caligula, had been full of disasters all too likely to leave a permanent mark on his character. But, in contrast to the second of those emperors, he had at least, in recent years, received some training to prepare him for what lay ahead.

His appearance was not outstandingly attractive. He was short-sighted, which made him blink or squint. And Suetonius gives further details, vividly translated by Philemon Holland:

He was for stature almost of complete height, his body full of specks and freckles and foul of skin besides, the hair of his head somewhat yellow, his countenance and visage rather fair than lovely and well-favoured, his eyes grey and somewhat with the dimmest, his neck full and fat, his belly and paunch bearing out, with a pair of passing slender spindle-shanks, but withal he was very healthful. For being as he was so intemperate and most riotously given, in fourteen years' space he never fell sick but thrice, yet so as he neither forbare drinking of wine nor any thing else that he used to do.

About the trimming of his body and wearing of his clothes he was so nice as was shameful . . .[1]

When Nero became emperor, he was not yet seventeen – far younger, that is to say, than any of his predecessors when they had first occupied the throne. This meant that for the first time in the history of the principate the reigning Caesar was temporarily disqualified by his age from effectively ruling.

For a few startling and unprecedented months, therefore, the empire was ruled by a woman. This was Nero's mother Agrippina the younger, unique, as Tacitus remarks, as the daughter of a great commander, and the sister, wife and mother of Roman emperors. On the first day of his reign Nero gave the tribune of the guard the watchword 'The Best of Mothers'. And on that very day, in the words of Dio Cassius, she began to 'manage for Nero all the business of the empire'.

That this was not an overstatement is confirmed by the official coinage. Coins of Claudius, in his last failing years, had portrayed the emperor on one side and Agrippina on the other. The first issues of the new reign display Nero and Agrippina together on the same side, facing one another. But Agrippina is pronounced by this coinage to be *more* important than her imperial son. For on these gold and silver pieces, which bear dates indicating that they were issued in December of the accession year, the obverse, the more important side of the two sides, bears Agrippina's name and titles, whereas Nero's are relegated to the less prestigious reverse. Moreover Agrippina's name and honours are framed in the nominative case normal to the rulers, whereas Nero's are in the dedicatory dative – the coinage, that is to say, is only dedicated to him, whereas the principal issuing authority is specifically stated to be Agrippina. This was the first and last time ever, in the entire history of the empire, that a woman was openly declared superior to the emperor himself.

There were also other sensational manifestations of her unparalleled position.

For a meeting in the palace a door was built in the back of the council chamber so that she could stand behind a curtain unseen, and listen. Again, when an Armenian delegation was pleading before Nero, she was just going to mount the emperor's dais and sit beside him. Everyone was stupefied. But Seneca instructed Nero to move forward and go to meet his mother. This show of filial dutifulness averted what would have been a scandal.[2]

Agrippina used her power by continuing to eliminate all possible rivals, notably Marcus Junius Silanus, who like Nero was a great-great-grandson of Augustus. However her dizzy eminence only lasted for an exceedingly short time. The second coinage of the reign, issued some time during the year 55, showed that her position was already weakening. Her head, it is true, still appeared in the company of Nero's. By now, however, the two portraits no longer faced one another, but faced in the same direction, so that the head in front partially eclipsed the head behind: and the head in front is the emperor's. Moreover his and Agrippina's designations have changed places, so that his names and titles are now transferred to the obverse side of the coins and take precedence. These changes were seen and noted, and they were meant to be, too. After 55 Agrippina's name and portrait never appeared on the Roman official coinage again. Although she had four more years to live, she was no longer at the centre of the political stage.

When, early in 55, the young Britannicus, the son of Claudius and Messalina, died at a dinner-party in the palace – allegedly murdered by Nero, though this cannot be proved – Agrippina was said to have been dismayed, since she was suspected of wanting to elevate him to the throne in place of her own ungrateful son. It is unlikely, however, that at this juncture she had become desperate enough to think of switching her allegiance to Britannicus, whom she herself had so recently displaced in favour of Nero. Nevertheless her acute consciousness that her influence was waning caused her to offer repeated displays of hysterical ill-temper. Even when Nero gave her a superb robe, she sourly commented that it was a mere fraction of what he owed her. The diminution of her power was sharply emphasized when the emperor transferred her residence to a separate mansion, thus putting an end to her imposing Palatine receptions. When he felt obliged to pay her a visit at her new residence, he used to arrive surrounded by guard officers. Then, after giving her a hurried kiss, he took his leave at the earliest possible moment. It was another sign that her reign had come to an end.

Its termination was a major achievement on the part of the two leading members of the court, Seneca, who had graduated from the tutorship of Nero to become his adviser, and Burrus, commander of the praetorian guard. It was remarkable for the two principal counsellors of an emperor to work in complete harmony. But Seneca and Burrus got on with one another extremely well, and, even if the literary tradition perhaps over-dramatizes their personal roles at the expense of the whole group of men they were working with, it was they, for the most part, during the years of Nero's youth, who governed the empire between them.

They had no part in the death of Britannicus; indeed it may have embarrassed them. But they were the men who successfully eased Agrippina out of her dominant role. This had to be done all the more quickly because Nero, without any prompting at all, had become utterly infuriated by her: and was already angrily recalling that Burrus had been her protégé. So before long the two men, in order to demonstrate their loyalty to the emperor, were interviewing the embittered Agrippina, in order to insist that she should keep out of imperial affairs. She was later heard sneering at Seneca's academic manner of speech and describing Burrus, who had a crippled arm, as a deformity.

Seneca, whose father, a knight, came from a conservative family of Italian expatriates settled at Corduba (Cordoba in Spain), was one of the most curious personages Rome ever produced. Interested in occult studies in his youth, he had been the victim of acute neuroses, and suffered from such persistent ill-health that he often contemplated suicide. Orator, philosopher, essayist, tragedian, he had already won a considerable reputation by the time of Caligula, with whose sister, Julia Livilla the younger, he allegedly committed adultery. For this he was exiled by the next ruler Claudius, until Agrippina recalled him and established him at court. And now, in collusion with Burrus, he had dropped her and was one of the rulers of the Roman world himself.

His control of the empire, however, depended on his control of the young Nero. It was Seneca who composed Nero's inaugural speech to the senate – a model of modest correctness. Seneca also wrote, a year or two later, a treatise *On Clemency* which eloquently recommends the young emperor to rule leniently, in terms much admired, in subsequent centuries, by Calvin and Corneille. But mercy is an autocratic quality, and Seneca was playing with fire when at the same time he stressed the unimaginably great power at Nero's disposal.

From out of all the host of mortal beings [he pictures the emperor as asking], have I been chosen and thought worthy to do the work of the gods upon the earth? I have been given the power of life and death over all the nations. To determine the condition and to control the destinies of every race and of every individual is my absolute prerogative.[3]

This assurance from his former tutor that he was omnipotent was heady stuff for a new young ruler, who was already receiving every incitement to be spoilt. Seneca's writings also contain interesting justifications of the role that he himself had assumed. He was a deeply sincere Stoic philosopher; but he had decided to serve and advise Nero, as Plato, too, had sought to guide monarchs. Yet to serve and advise a Roman emperor, amid all the crimes and extravagances of a flamboyant court, might have seemed incompatible with a philosopher's principles. But Seneca was able to explain how he could reconcile the two ways of life.

I must not add to his power for evil; I must not increase his destructive forces or confirm those he has. But if without injury to the commonweath I may return his kindness, I will do so. I would save his infant son from death, for that could not injure the victims of his cruelty; but I would not contribute a penny to the support of his mercenaries. If he hanker after marbles and fine clothes, that can do no mischief to any man, and I will help him to them; soldiers and arms I will not supply. If he entreat me as a great kindness to send him comedians and women, and other such delights which may temper his brutality, I will find them for him willingly.[4]

In recompense Nero made Seneca enormously rich. But that too could be accepted and endured by the philosophers.

To refuse a gift is to incense against ourselves an all-powerful monarch, who would have all that comes from his hands valued at a high rate. It matters not whether you are unwilling to give to a king or to receive from him, the offence is equal in either case, or rather even graver in the latter, since to the proud it is more bitter to be disdained than not to be feared.[5]

About Burrus, Seneca's loyal collaborator in the government of the empire, we know all too little, since Tacitus has decided to mislead us. As a foil to his cultured colleague, the historian presents Burrus as an experienced military man who displayed a soldier's blunt frankness. But this picture of him as a plain army officer is false: he had made his career, as an inscription reveals, in a civilian capacity, as the personal and financial agent of Livia, Tiberius and Claudius in turn. Only now had he assumed a military significance, having become the commander of the guard.

It was because he held this post that Seneca, who lacked military backing, needed his cooperation. And Burrus, reciprocally, needed Seneca, because, being only a knight, he could not on his own account have ensured the government's good relations with the senate, which Seneca, who became consul in 56, was better able to guarantee.

He did so effectively, since the new administration and the new emperor were as popular with the senate as with everyone else. Many favourable comparisons were made at the expense of Claudius, whose deification, now that his widow and priestess was no longer in power, became a good joke.

The keynote of Nero's accession speech had been his desire that the senate should fulfil its ancient functions once again, and the consuls theirs. And indeed, for the first part of the reign the senate, as well as the advisory council which Nero drew from its members, enjoyed more security and initiative than it had known for many years past. The public was reminded of this on the Roman coinage from the end of 55 to 60–1. For the inscription on these pieces, EX S(*enatus*) C(*onsulto*), indicates that they were issued by a decree of the senate, to which the formula represents a deliberately deferential, even if practically meaningless, gesture.

During these harmonious years a good many useful administrative reforms were pushed through. For example, provincial governors and their functionaries were prevented from extorting large sums from the local populations for gladiatorial shows. And at home there were measures to improve public order, careful provisions against forgery, and sensible reforms of treasury procedure.

Moreover during these years the emperor himself, as he grew out of his teens, did quite a lot of solid, useful work. At the beginning of his reign he had promised the senate judicial fairness and efficiency, and had undertaken not to persist in Claudius's practice of trying every sort of case himself. But he assiduously presided, in the correct imperial tradition, over such lawsuits as still fell within his sphere; and certain constructive and conscientious innovations date from this period.

Nero was reluctant to render a decision to those who presented cases, except on the following day and in writing. The procedure he favoured was, instead of continuous pleadings, to have each point presented separately by the parties in turn. Furthermore, whenever he withdrew for consultation, he did not discuss any matter with all his advisers in a body, but made each of them give his opinion in written form. These he read silently and in private, and then gave a verdict according to his own inclination, as if it were the view of the majority.[6]

Nevertheless certain events during these early years of Nero's reign instilled in his mind feelings of frustration, which exercised, in the end, a tragic effect upon his temperament. For the young emperor had some progressive and liberal ideas – which the ineluctable circumstances of Roman society made it impossible to put into practice.

For example, it was customary, whenever Games were held, for the circuses and theatres to be thronged by large contingents of praetorian guardsmen. But Nero did not think this practice appropriate. At the end of 55, therefore, instructions were given that these soldiers should be withdrawn. The aim was not only to remove guardsmen from temptations to bad discipline, but 'to give a greater impression of freedom ... and to test whether the public would behave respectably without their restraint'. But the measure, for all its good intentions, proved unsuccessful, since serious brawls broke out between the gangs favouring rival ballet-dancers; and in the following year troops had to be brought back again, while the dancers, despite the emperor's reluctance, were expelled from Italy.

Presumably Seneca, Burrus and the other imperial councillors had been obliged to intervene to persuade him of these regrettable necessities. And the same thing seems to have happened in connexion with another and more important matter. For in 58 Nero proposed that indirect taxation in all parts of the empire should be abolished. What induced him to intervene was a rising flow of complaints about the private tax-collectors to whom it had long been the Roman custom to farm out such taxes. Tacitus remarks that Nero's idea was a 'noble gift to the human race'. Yet the comment is sardonic, for if his suggestion had been implemented, *direct* taxes would have needed to be correspondingly increased; and any hope that the abolition of the indirect taxes might achieve this by stimulating trade was merely a gamble. Although, therefore, Nero's advisers loudly praised his aristocratic generosity, and although minor steps were subsequently taken to curb abuses, they dissuaded him from carrying out his main proposal.

More painful still to the young emperor was a conflict between his very genuine desire not to kill, and the grim facts of Roman society which operated against this humane wish. When, in 57, he built a wooden amphitheatre for gladiator and wild beast shows (the forerunner of the stone Colosseum) Nero's dislike of taking human life was so strong that he actually forbade the slaying of any gladiators in these contests – even convicted criminals were not to be put to death. This was in close conformity with the views of Seneca, who delivered the first unequivocal onslaught of all time upon such lethal gladiatorial duels, which were repugnant to his Stoic ideal of the brotherhood of man. But Nero's order soon became a dead letter: and he had to concur in the slaughter of gladiators, which was promptly reinstituted. This was done to preserve his reputation with the masses. Both for dynastic and personal reasons, he was regarded with affection by the Roman proletariat, to whom he did not forget to make free distributions of food and money. But to deprive them of the bloodthirsty massacres they so enjoyed would have been politically imprudent. When the matter was discussed in the imperial council, one wonders which side Seneca supported. It was the sort of dilemma which a philosopher seeking to advise a Roman emperor must have had to face on a good many occasions.

When Nero believed people were threatening his own safety, he was ready enough to put them to death. But otherwise his distaste for causing loss of life extended to official capital punishment, which he deplored.

157

When he was asked to sign an execution warrant, he exclaimed with a sigh, 'How I wish I had never learnt to write!' Seneca, too, was appalled by the horror of Roman executions – even if the sufferers were slaves, whom he, as a Stoic, acknowledged to be members of the human brotherhood.

It was, therefore, a peculiarly harrowing moment both for him and for his emperor when in AD 61 the city prefect or security chief Lucius Pedanius Secundus – a Spanish compatriot of Seneca – was found assassinated by one of his slaves; the man had resented his master's competition for the favours of another male member of the household. Ancient tradition, based on the Roman terror of slave risings, insisted that when such a crime was committed not only the murderer himself but every other slave living under the same roof should be put to death as well – and Pedanius owned four hundred of them, including many women and children.

Popular feeling in favour of the doomed slaves ran extremely high, and crowds eager to save all these innocent lives surged round the senate house where the issue was being debated. Yet when the debate ended, the old-fashioned view had prevailed: unless force was employed to hold the submerged slave population down, Roman society would collapse – and so the executions must go on. As huge throngs of people, armed with stones and torches, gathered to prevent the sentences from being carried out, Nero had to reprimand the population by an edict. And then all the slaves were put to death.

For Nero, as for Seneca, it must have been horrible. But Seneca was the tougher of the two, or at least the more able to console and calm himself by philosophy or casuistry. The effect of such nasty setbacks upon the temperament of Nero proved more serious. For they gradually induced him to feel an increasing distaste for governmental affairs. They made him lose interest in his job.

Indeed administrative work had never at any time enjoyed the highest of all priorities among his favourite occupations. For he was far more interested in the circus and theatre, and in singing, acting, dancing and writing poetry.

Caligula, too, had found the same activities very absorbing – with the exception of poetry, to which he preferred gladiatorial performances, a taste that Nero did not share. But there was also another difference between them. Caligula had been a man of eccentric, effervescent energy who heartily enjoyed these amusements, and even, from time to time, figured in one or the other of them as performer as well as spectator. But he had only participated in an amateurish way, whereas Nero loved the stage and circus so utterly and unrestrainedly that he longed to devote himself to them with systematic, professional thoroughness. But how could an emperor, who ought to be immersed in all the prolonged and incessant labours his office required of him, find time to be a professional artist as well? And how could he overcome the overwhelming distaste and shock which this incredible ambition must unfailingly arouse in the hearts of the senators?

Nevertheless, Nero got the star lyre-player Terpnus to give him intensive training, and submitted himself to every possible vocal discipline:

Even to wear before him upon his breast a thin plate or sheet of lead; to purge by clyster or vomit; to abstain from apples and fruit, with all such meats as were hurtful to the voice: so long until, his improvement still drawing him on (a small and rusty voice though he had), he desired to come forth and show himself upon the open stage, having among his familiar companions this Greek proverb evermore in his mouth, that hidden music was naught worth.[1]

The emperor also aspired to be a poet: and his poetry was not necessarily as poor as Tacitus reported. Indeed one of his allegations, that Nero's verses were totally derivative, is expressly denied by Suetonius. But he, too, may well have been unfair when he suggested that Nero's voice was 'small and rusty', or 'weak and husky' as a modern translator prefers to render it. Perhaps he did not sing so badly as the hostile pro-senatorial tradition liked to suppose: he would not have been quite so passionately intent on these activities if he had possessed no gift for them whatever.

When not engaged, however, in this rigorous training programme, he lived a self-indulgent life. When he was a very young man this took the form of rowdily rushing round the city at night. He himself, on occasion, returned from some of these excursions covered with bruises: and thenceforward, in order to prevent this from happening again, he was accompanied on his nightly wanderings by escorts of guardsmen and gladiators. Nero also wasted a great deal of time at excessively long and lavish dinner-parties. He was not, it is true, either a glutton or a drinker on the scale of his predecessor Claudius. All the same, allowing for an occasional break for diving into a warm pool, or, if it was summer, into a bath that had been cooled by snow, his dinners sometimes lasted for twelve hours, from midday until midnight. Although his health remained good, these prolonged parties must have largely cancelled out the good effects of his daily vocal exercises as well as leaving extremely little time for imperial duties.

Moreover, if even one-tenth of the tales are true, his varied sexual activities must have encroached on his time still further.

All emperors were the targets of an infinite amount of sexual gossip. But in Nero's case the rumours reached unprecedented heights or depths: and they credit him with a remarkable versatility. He was said to have gone to bed not only with perfectly normal, good-looking young women, but also with his mother Agrippina, with men older than himself, with eunuchs and with young boys including Britannicus; while graffiti on the walls of Pompeii include an inscription by a male prostitute alleging that he personally had served Nero's lust on four occasions. But perhaps the attention of the psychoanalyst might most profitably be directed towards Dio Cassius's assertion that 'the emperor would fasten naked boys and girls to stakes, and then, putting on the hide of a wild beast, attack them and satisfy his brutal lust under the appearance of devouring parts of their bodies'.[8] But whether this is how Nero really behaved, or whether Dio's unknown informant possessed a fertile imagination, is not easy to determine. Indeed, how far should we regard any of these various reports about Nero's lechery as true?

The tradition is so persistent that there was probably something in it. Permissiveness, after all, was the spirit of the age. Indeed the emperor himself was said to have assured his friends that it was all nonsense to suppose that anyone in the whole world was sexually chaste or pure, in any part of his body whatever; and the only reason, he added, why this had ever been believed of anyone was because they managed to hide what they were doing.

Moreover Nero had some support for this lax attitude among his senior advisers. In the words, for example, of the novelist and poet Petronius, who has been identified as a consul and arbiter of fashion enjoying a very close relationship with Nero,

> Then where's the shame in that,
> If loving men enjoy
> The pleasures of the night
> Whereby each girl and boy
> Experience delight?[9]

How the other principal policy-controllers reacted to Nero's sexual activities is less certain. But they are unlikely to have felt worried about them, except perhaps when he seemed inclined to take a favourite freedwoman, Acte, as his wife, which would have been a social impossibility for any emperor.

What was more worrying was his increasing abandonment of his imperial functions in favour of the equestrian and dramatic and musical arts. Seneca and Burrus, it is true, were accused of surreptitiously encouraging this tendency, so that they could keep the power in their own hands. More probably, however, realizing they could not suppress Nero's tastes altogether, they tried, as Tacitus said, 'to direct his deviations from virtue into licensed channels of indulgence' – in other words, to keep them from becoming a scandal.

But the person who must have found his flowering artistic tastes particularly deplorable was his own mother. Living a life of enforced retirement which readily prompted the most uncharitable thoughts about Nero, she could not fail to be disgusted by this painfully non-Imperial, anti-imperial behaviour. The whole business was so preposterously un-Roman: and so was the way he got himself up. It was one thing that he deliberately wore the hair-style of a vulgar charioteer, rising in steps or waves at the front. But that at least displayed a certain horsy virility. What she will have scoffed at much more acidly was the effeminate Greek clothing that he liked wearing so much. In particular he often appeared in a brilliantly coloured garment which resembled an amply flowing toga below the waist and a tunic above it, and was adorned by a garish scarf round the neck. Romans sometimes wore clothes of this kind in the relaxed privacy of holiday occasions, but only women were ever seen in them in public. And now Nero had joined their number. He also liked to sport a kind of flower-patterned mini-tunic, a short unbelted affair with a frilly muslin collar.

Agrippina's comments must have been unprintable. And we are already well on the way to seeing why he murdered her in 59, thus committing the matricide for which he has been pilloried throughout the ages.

The deaths of eminent men and women in Nero's reign follow a certain predictable time-table and pattern. First, after suspicion has been aroused against them for one reason or another, they are banished from the public scene – not killed at once, but sent into retirement or exile. Then, after a number of years, although they have not been in a position to fulfil any important political role since their withdrawal, they are executed or compelled to commit suicide. For in the interim period people appointed to keep a watch on these men, or other interested parties harbouring grudges against them, have reported to the emperor that they have been talking or conspiring against him. Whether they have really been indiscreet or even seditious we are rarely in a position to say. But no emperor – not even Claudius – was ever easier to frighten than Nero, and once he was frightened he forgot all his humane intentions immediately.

And so in 59, hearing how offensively Agrippina was speaking of him to such friends as she had managed to retain, he became convinced, not only that she was sneering at his beloved artistic life, but that she was actually plotting his downfall. And indeed, he may well have been right: though if she was plotting, her machinations can scarcely have been very dangerous, since she had not been of any political importance for four long years past. However this may be, Nero became so upset by her attitude that he finally arranged to have her killed.

The picturesque method he chose, involving the employment of a collapsible ship in the Bay of Naples, kindled the fancy of Tacitus, who describes the murder attempt in one of his most magnificent set-pieces. The story he tells is so macabre that Voltaire tried to believe it was not true. But although novelettish assessments of motivation are introduced and there are contradictions about the role, if any, played by Nero's elegant friend the future emperor Otho, the general lines of the historian's account can be accepted. However the initial plan failed in its purpose, since although the ship carrying Agrippina duly fell to pieces out at sea, she herself succeeded in jumping into the water and reaching a boat and subsequently the shore. Whereupon her son sent two naval officers who slew her in her bed.

Did Seneca and Burrus know in advance of the plan to kill her in the bay? We can only abide by Tacitus's verdict that nobody knows. But he added, no doubt correctly, that, whether or not they had been aware of the attempt beforehand, its failure convinced them she could no longer be allowed to stay alive.

After her death there may have seemed some danger that the frontier armies, which revered her father Germanicus, would react adversely to the news. But this peril did not materialize. In Rome, too, reactions were reassuring. About a week after the murder, on 28 March, the Arval Priesthood – an elite corporation including many of the most influential noblemen – held one of its periodical religious ceremonies in the city. These senatorial priests were accustomed to offer sacrifices to members of the imperial family. On this occasion, however, as an inscription informs us, they refrained from doing so, since it was too difficult, in the absence of full information, to get the emphasis exactly right. But then on 5 April they met again, and duly sacrificed. By now they had a senatorial decree to guide them. Nero had reported Agrippina's alleged plot to the senate, declaring: 'I can hardly believe that I am safe from her now. Nor do I derive any pleasure from the fact!' But he was enormously relieved, all the same; and so was the senate, which had hated her and was glad to pronounce her a perilous national enemy who had tried to murder the emperor, and had paid for the attempt with her life.

It was not a major political crisis, because Agrippina had long since been deprived of real authority. But Tacitus is probably right in suggesting that her death caused changes in her son's behaviour. For her highly critical attitude had irritatingly inhibited Nero's indulgence in chariot-racing and the theatre. Now that irritation and inhibition were removed; and nothing could curb his enthusiasm for the circus and the stage any longer.

Moreover he was perfectly prepared to justify these aspirations on sound, traditional grounds.

He had long desired to drive in four-horse chariot-races. Another equally deplorable ambition was to sing to the lyre, like a professional. 'Chariot-racing', he said, 'was an accomplishment of ancient kings and leaders – honoured by poets, associated with divine worship. Singing, too, is sacred to Apollo: that glorious and provident god is represented in a musician's dress in Greek cities, and also in Roman temples.'[10]

All the same the emperor's advisers still did their best to limit the inevitable damage. If he must perform, then he must. But at least they remained determined to ensure that his performances should be given to private audiences only.

In 62, however, the reign entered upon an entirely new phase, when both Burrus and Seneca vanished from the political scene. First Burrus died – not by the emperor's hand, as was inevitably suggested, but from an abscess of the throat, or perhaps cancer.

In his place two joint praetorian prefects were appointed. One of the pair was Faenius Rufus, who was popular but harmless. The other was Gaius Ofonius Tigellinus, a Sicilian of humble origin whose previous career had been picturesque but not entirely reassuring. Caligula, suspecting him of adultery with no less than two of his sisters, had sent him into exile. After earning his living for a time as a fisherman in Greece, he had subsequently reappeared in south Italy, where he bred racehorses successfully. Tacitus, who disliked upstarts, assigns him the nastiest of characters. However Nero probably relied on Tigellinus, not merely because they both liked horses and riotous parties, but because he was an intelligence expert, capable of dealing with seditious threats.

Seneca found Tigellinus too difficult to cooperate with, and offered the emperor his resignation. He was by this time the target of a good deal of criticism, because of the great wealth he had amassed; and without a reliable collaborator he felt he could not carry on. Besides it was becoming increasingly difficult to exercise any useful influence over Nero himself. Seneca had always claimed to be frank in his dealings with him; and his surviving writings describe his attitude with considerable realism. There was a limit, he wrote, to the extent to which collaboration with autocrats was possible. 'The wise man will shun a force that can hurt him; if the state is too corrupt to be improved, if it is entirely overwhelmed by evil, the philosopher should not continue to strive in vain.' The advent of Tigellinus, combined with Nero's growing neglect of his imperial duties in favour of amusements that alienated the senatorial class, suggested that this time to stop striving had come. And so Seneca took his leave of his master and retired into almost monastic seclusion. At the same time he offered to give up his wealth, though the emperor no doubt refused to accept it.

The new regime soon made itself felt. With the connivance of Tigellinus, Nero summoned up the courage to divorce Octavia and marry the glamorous Poppaea, who was the wife of his friend Otho. The removal of the entirely inoffensive Octavia, daughter of the emperor Claudius and descendant of Augustus's wife and sister, was certain to create a bad impression, especially in the army, and Burrus was said to have been opposed to her divorce. But now, after Tigellinus had shabbily framed her on an immorality charge, the measure went through, and she was exiled to an island and almost immediately put to death. Presumably it was felt unsafe, once she had been removed from the palace, to leave her at large, as a possible rallying point for rebellious elements. But the cruelty of her humiliating death showed that Nero was beginning to lose all control of his fears and suspicions.

Although Tigellinus was able to work so effectively on the emperor's terrors, his unfamiliarity with senatorial opinion may have caused him initially to underestimate the very real perils Nero ran by over-indulging his theatrical and musical interests. For now the restriction of his stage performances to private audiences became a thing of the past. In 64 the general public were being admitted to see him act.

His public début was at Neapolis (Naples), where the inhabitants were Greeks. For Nero was more passionately pro-Greek than any emperor before him, and it seemed to him only right to stage his inaugural appearance before Greeks, since they 'are the only people who have an ear for music, and they alone are worthy of my genius'. And so, taking the stage, and ignoring an earthquake which made it tremble, he sang his songs to the appreciative Neapolitan public. Day after day he came back and performed all over again. Even when he was resting his voice, he used to go to the theatre after his evening bath and dine there, while large crowds of people thronged all around him, and heard him calling out in Greek that as soon as he had put down a drink or two he would give them something to make their ears ring.

The time was clearly approaching when he would make public appearances in the capital as well. Before long the Roman populace were admitted to watch him chariot-racing – and they liked it. Then in 65, at the second performance of the Neronian Games which he had instituted on the Greek model, he began to appear on the Roman stage. The emperor's acting gave rise to innumerable mocking jokes. When he was playing the part of the mad Hercules, it was said that a young army recruit, seeing the emperor in rags and chains, rushed up on to the stage to rescue him. Moreover Nero was perfectly prepared to act female parts – wearing masks modelled on the features of whoever his mistress happened to be at the time. One of the mythological characters he represented was *Canace in child-labour*. 'What is the emperor doing?' went a story. 'He is having a baby.' Meanwhile, we are told, women in the audience were having babies, quite literally, on the spot; because the strict security measures made it impossible for them to get out of the theatre. 'We also read,' says Suetonius, 'of men being so bored with the music and the applause that they furtively dropped down from the wall at the back, or even shammed dead and got themselves carried away to be buried.'

In spite of his enthusiasm Nero suffered from intense, ludicrous stage fright when he was giving a performance.

He strictly observed the rules, never daring to clear his throat and even using his arm, rather than a handkerchief, to wipe the sweat from his brow.

Once, while acting in a tragedy, he dropped his sceptre and quickly recovered it, but was terrified of disqualification. The accompanist, however – who played a flute and made the necessary dumbshow to illustrate the words – swore that the slip had passed unnoticed, because the audience were listening with such rapt attention. So he took heart again.[11]

Such were the affairs of Rome and the palace after the termination of the first decade of Nero's reign. But these tragi-comedies were scarcely felt abroad, where the smooth government of the empire and its lavish prosperity, reflected in Petronius' *Dinner of Trimalchio*, continued undisturbed.

Only on remote frontiers had there been military operations. In Britain the expansion of Roman rule, signalized by Gaius Suetonius Paulinus' capture of the Druid stronghold Mona (Anglesey), was momentarily delayed by the revolt of Boudicca's Iceni in East Anglia, caused by Roman taxation and British reluctance to repay, with interest, a loan borrowed from Seneca. In 60 Boudicca captured Camulodunum (Colchester), Londinium (London) and Verulamium (St Albans), massacring seventy thousand Romans or Romanized Britons. But then she was defeated in a decisive battle near Atherstone in Warwickshire, and the war of British independence was over.

Meanwhile, in Asia Minor, Cnaeus Domitius Corbulo, invested with a large command, had been fighting a war with the Parthians for the control of Armenia. His occupation of that country, achieved in 58–60, was interrupted in 62 by the severe defeat of Caesennius Paetus at Randeia, near Elazig in eastern Turkey. But in the following year Corbulo reasserted Roman prestige and concluded a durable agreement with Parthia by which Tiridates, the Parthian nominee to the Armenian throne, formally accepted the position of a Roman client, visiting the capital in 66.

In Rome, however, by that time, the political situation was gravely undermined.

The end of the regime of Seneca and Burrus had meant a worsening of Nero's relations with the senate. One of Tigellinus' first actions was to revive the operations of the treason law; and he sent executioners to liquidate two Roman noblemen whose pedigrees compared too favourably with the lineage of the emperor. In 64 there were renewed security fears when the Great Fire of Rome, which made many families homeless, prompted widespread though unfounded suspicions that Nero himself had caused the conflagration, in order to make space for the Golden House he was planning to build for his own use. In consequence, his government turned on the small local Christian community as scapegoats.

As a counterblast to these ugly rumours, the same year witnessed the issue of the most magnificent brass coinages the empire ever produced. Nero's flamboyant features are portrayed with a superb blend of grandeur and realism; while a wide range of designs and inscriptions on the reverses enumerate the benefits he had conferred on the Roman people. Moreover these coins even allude tactfully to his love of horses and the theatre, which are shown within the framework of respectable tradition, by references to military manoeuvres and Apollo the lyre-player.

Yet no such propaganda could avail to bridge the growing gulf which these interests created between himself and the senatorial class. The following year witnessed the detection and suppression of the plot which is known as the Pisonian conspiracy, because according to Tacitus and Suetonius its figure-head was Gaius Calpurnius Piso, a handsome, eloquent, superficial nobleman. But in the version known to Dio Cassius, the two chief plotters did not include Piso at all: one of them was the joint praetorian prefect Faenius Rufus – and the other was Seneca. Faenius Rufus, who greatly resented his virtual eclipse by his colleague Tigellinus, presumably played a leading part in the plan. So did a number of his officers. Such men, however, were unlikely to support Piso, who shared Nero's unwelcome taste for singing and playing the lyre. Probably they intended to place not Piso, but Seneca, on the throne.

Whether Seneca himself became a party to the scheme has always been disputed. His treatises and tragedies are significantly redolent with political gloom. There is much talk of the hatefulness of tyrants, of suicide as a refuge from tyranny, and even of tyrannicide as 'an ultimate solution'. 'If,' Seneca wrote, 'I despair altogether of a ruler's improvement, this hand of mine shall at one blow discharge my debt to him and confer a benefit on all mankind.'[12] Such sentiments, however, were traditional philosophical utterances, and do not prove that he planned to kill Nero. All the same Seneca, by 65, had evidently fallen out of sympathy with the emperor, and the conspirators, even if they did not approach him as an accomplice, were obviously well aware of this alienation. Had they been successful they would have appealed to him to play a prominent part in their new regime – and perhaps some of them would even have asked him to become its leader and emperor.

Their design was to murder Nero in the Circus Maximus, while Games were being held. But the plan was never put into effect, because a leakage occurred. As a result fifty-one persons were charged with complicity, including nineteen senators, seven knights, eleven officers and four women. Nineteen executions or suicides followed, and thirteen sentences of banishment. Among those who lost their lives were Piso, Faenius Rufus and Seneca, as well as the latter's nephew Lucan, an epic poet who had formerly been a warm admirer of Nero but became transformed, perhaps from reasons of personal pique, into one of the severest of his critics. Another casualty was Claudius' daughter Claudia Antonia – a younger sister of Britannicus and Octavia – since if the coup had been successful her name might have used, by arranging a marriage connexion, to legitimize the projected new order.

The detection of the plot was celebrated by an issue of brass coinage inscribed SECVRITAS AVGVSTI (the safety of the Emperor), while gold and silver issues commemorated Jupiter the Protector. On the human plane, one of Nero's principal protectors had been Tigellinus, and statues were set up in his honour. Another who had helped to stamp out the conspiracy was a tall, grim praetorian officer named Nymphidius Sabinus, the son of a prostitute freedwoman and a gladiator, though Nymphidius himself put it around that his father was the emperor Caligula. It was he who was appointed to succeed Faenius Rufus as Tigellinus' colleague in the prefecture.

From now on there were constant suspicions and alarms of further plots. In the course of the single year 66 the government lashed out in no less than four different directions.

The first victims were a group of extreme conservative senators of philosophical, Stoic leanings – like those who had suffered under Caligula. Their current leader, Thrasea Paetus of Patavium (Padua), had displayed his uncompromising distaste for Nero's rule by a policy of passive resistance and absenteeism from the senate, for which he now paid with his life. Then – although at this point our text of Tacitus's *Annals* breaks off for the second time – a certain Annius Vinicianus, who had lost a brother and friends in the débâcles of Piso and Thrasea, was said to have been planning a revolt at Beneventum (Benevento in central Italy). This, apparently, is the 'nefarious plot' recorded by the Arval Priesthood on 19 June AD 66, when they gave thanks for its detection and the preservation, once again, of the emperor's life.

Vinicianus was the son-in-law of the great general Corbulo, who had been responsible for the eastern defences of the empire throughout the greater part of the reign; and Corbulo himself was the next to fall. Requested towards the end of the year to report to Nero, who was now in Greece, he received a written order to commit suicide. On reading this letter, Corbulo cried out the Greek word *Axios*, 'I deserved it!' – though whether this was an admission of guilt, or of remorse for his foolishness in accepting Nero's summons, it is hard to determine. At about the same time the emperor also requested the presence of two brothers, Scribonius Rufus and Scribonius Proculus, who as the army commanders of Upper and Lower Germany controlled a powerful proportion of the total military strength of the Roman world. And they too were ordered to kill themselves.

Under earlier emperors, too, there had been savage onslaughts on senators. But never before had so many distinguished nobles and commanders been struck down, and all within the space of a few months. Either the disaffection had indeed spread wide and deep, or, if this holocaust was unwarranted, Nero and his praetorian prefects, by committing such unnecessary crimes, must inevitably have intensified the very seditious feelings they were intended to stamp out. In either case the situation had become catastrophic.

Yet Nero himself, while not neglecting to send an experienced general Vespasian to deal with rebellion in Judaea, was unwisely staying on in Greece. For he was in the midst of an artistic, theatrical, cultural tour. He had Tigellinus with him. Nymphidius Sabinus presumably stayed behind in Rome, but Nero also left two personal deputies in the capital, his influential freedmen Helius and Polyclitus.

For Nero this visit to Greece, the home of the people who alone appreciated his efforts, was the joyful culmination of his career as actor, singer and charioteer. In a prolonged series of dramatic and athletic engagements at the principal centres, the prizes he was awarded by obsequious judges totalled no less than 1,808.

Occasionally there were untoward incidents, when improvisation proved necessary. At the Olympic Games, for example, during a race in which Nero was driving a team of ten horses, he had the misfortune to be hurled out of his chariot. Willing hands put him back in his place again, but he proved too severely dazed to complete the course. Nevertheless the judges prudently awarded him the first prize, and this elastic application of the rules earned them an enormous monetary recompense.

Nero's admiration of the Greeks, encouraged by such incidents, was finally expressed by an unprecedented gesture. For on 28 November AD 67, in an oration delivered in the stadium at the provincial capital Corinth, he declared Greece free.

It is an unexpected gift, Hellenes – though there is nothing that may not be hoped for from my magnanimity – which I grant you: one so great that you were incapable of requesting it. All Hellenes who inhabit Achaea and the land until now called the Peloponnese receive liberty and exemption from tribute, which not even in your most fortunate days did you all enjoy, for you were subjects either of foreigners or of one another.

Would that I were making this gift while Hellas was still at its height, so that more people might enjoy this boon! For this, indeed, I have a grudge against time, for squandering in advance the fullness of my boon. Yet even now it is not out of pity but out of good will that I bestow this benefaction upon you, requiting your gods, whose care for me both on land and on sea I have never found to fail, for affording me an opportunity to bestow so great a benefaction.

For to cities other rulers too have granted freedom: but Nero alone to an entire province![13]

He was not, of course, bestowing full political independence upon Greece, since it was irrevocably a part of the Roman empire. Yet he was proposing to grant its people immunity from Roman taxation, and for such a poor land this was an invaluable gift.

By the beginning of the year 68 Nero had already been absent from Rome longer than any other emperor since Tiberius; and as the surviving senators were still reeling from the blows that had felled so many of their colleagues in the previous year, the atmosphere in the city had become extremely uncomfortable. Indeed the freedmen who represented him in the capital were finding the secret reports that reached their ears so alarming that one of them, Helius, crossed hastily to Greece, mid-winter though it was, in order to beg him to come back. When Nero consented to do so, however, he displayed no feelings of anxiety, for his usual acute fears had been dulled by incessant, obsequious flattery. To the accompaniment of unprecedentedly lavish ceremonial commemorating his artistic victories in Greece, he made a grandiose, jubilant entry into Rome.

Very soon afterwards, however, he retired to the congenial Greek atmosphere of Neapolis. There he gave some consideration to the possibility of a massive military expedition to the Caucasus – which his courtiers declared would make him the new Alexander the Great.

However, his end could not now be greatly delayed. For after the destruction of so many senators, governors and commanders, no senior official in the provinces could feel safe any longer.

The first of the surviving governors to translate this disquiet into action was Gaius Julius Vindex in Gaul (Gallia Lugdunensis). When he raised the standard of revolt, he was obliged to rely on local auxiliaries, since he had no Roman legions at his disposal. He therefore appealed to his greatly senior colleague in Nearer Spain, Servius Sulpicius Galba, who commanded one legion. Whereupon Galba, who had particular reasons for anxiety because of strained relations with local imperial agents, came out openly against Nero, though without, in the first instance, claiming the empire for himself.

In these circumstances Nero, who could still have controlled the military situation without difficulty, failed to take the necessary action.

He was at Neapolis when he learned of the uprising of the Gallic provinces, on the anniversary of his mother's murder. He received the news with such calmness and indifference that he incurred the suspicion of actually rejoicing in it, because it gave him an excuse for pillaging those wealthy provinces according to the laws of war. And he at once proceeded to the gymnasium, where he watched the contests of the athletes with rapt interest. At dinner too, when interrupted by a more disturbing letter, he fired up only so far as to threaten vengeance on the rebels.

In short for eight whole days, making no attempt to write a reply to anyone, and no attempt to give any commission or command, he blotted out the affair with silence.[14]

When he was eventually persuaded, by an incessant stream of messages, to return to Rome, this tendency to escapism remained painfully apparent. For example, his principal advisers, summoned for consultation, were obliged to spend the greater part of the day watching him demonstrate novel types of water-organ. Nor was it by any means reassuring when Nero declared that he would go to Gaul, stand before the troops of Vindex unarmed, and just weep and go on weeping. And then, he said, after this pathetic demonstration had caused the soldiers to resume their loyalty, he would appear before them once again, and sing them paeans of victory – which he must go off at this very moment to compose.

On hearing of Galba's proclamation, he fell down in a faint. Yet the next news was good, for it was reported that at Vesontio (Besançon) Vindex had been defeated by Lucius Verginius Rufus the governor of Upper Germany, and was dead. But it was already too late for Nero to take advantage of this reprieve, even if he had at last summoned up the energy and initiative to do so. On 8 June he learnt that one of the two generals he had sent to north Italy had deserted his cause, thus immobilizing the other. At this juncture he decided that he himself should get away to Egypt, which he believed, probably wrongly, to be loyal. But he failed to make his escape, because the praetorians were no longer at his disposal. For their prefects had decided there was no longer any future in serving such an emperor, and had determined to abandon him.

Tigellinus, by this time, played only a passive part, perhaps because he was seriously ill. But Nymphidius had offered his guardsmen a large monetary gift, thus inducing them to abandon their loyalty and proclaim Galba emperor.

The senate, in collusion with Nymphidius, declared Nero a public enemy, and condemned him to be flogged to death with rods according to the ancient tradition. Fleeing to the house of one of his freedmen in the suburbs, he uttered the historic words *qualis artifex pereo* – 'what a loss I shall be to the arts' or 'how the National Theatre will miss me!'*

Then, as a troop of cavalry was heard down the road, he managed, with the help of a secretary, to stab himself in the throat, and so he died.

Nero's reign had come to grief because of the same trouble which had damaged or destroyed previous reigns: his relations with the senate and its leading members became disastrously bad. Tacitus rightly named the murder of Agrippina, the deaths of Seneca and Burrus, and the Pisonian conspiracy as landmarks in this fatal process.

The young emperor had started with the best intentions, but suffered from a series of setbacks which frustrated their fulfilment. These disappointments gradually diminished his interest in governmental affairs and increased his absorption in the theatrical and competitive activities which he found a good deal more interesting. But an emperor who was not prepared to devote a good deal of his attention to his imperial tasks could not survive. Besides Nero, when faced with suspected opposition, became panic-stricken, striking about him in a hysterical manner which, in self-defence, invited reprisals.

For all these reasons it is remarkable that he remained alive as long as he did. He remained alive because the legions, faithful to their paymaster who was the descendant of Augustus, did not cease to support him, despite his failure ever to take command of his troops. Even at the very end, most of the soldiers had not deserted his cause, and his downfall, like Caligula's, was primarily caused by his alienation of the praetorian command, which found willing allies among the senators.

Too self-centred to concentrate on checking the disaffection, too bemused by his artistic career to treat the empire as a serious full-time job, Nero had lost touch with hard realities, and he paid the penalty. With his bizarre figure the male line of Augustus came to an end.

* I owe the latter suggestion to Mr Anthony Powell.

Part III

The Civil Wars

7

Galba

Servius Sulpicius Galba, born in circa 3 BC, came of a family of conspicuous nobility and wealth. It had no direct connexion with the Julio–Claudian house which had hitherto provided all the emperors, but the young man was highly approved of by Augustus and all his three immediate successors, and became a special favourite of Livia, to whom his stepmother may have been related. Elected consul in AD 33, Galba held governorships of Upper Germany and Africa, and in 60 Nero appointed him governor of Nearer Spain (Hispania Tarraconensis), commanding a garrison consisting of one legion.

In March 68, when he was about seventy, he received an appeal for help from Vindex – who had revolted against Nero in Gallia Lugdunensis. This was followed by a conflicting appeal from the governor of Aquitania (south-western France), who wanted to suppress the rebellion. On 2 April, in a proclamation at Carthage Nova (Cartagena), Galba came out on the side of Vindex, proclaiming himself the general and representative of the senate and people of Rome.

Supported by Otho (who later became his successor) and by Caecina in the other Spanish provinces, he recruited a second legion, only to learn at the end of May that Vindex had been defeated and was dead. Retiring in despair to a remote Spanish town he emerged after learning that the senate, supported by the guard to which its prefect Nymphidius Sabinus was offering a large donative, had offered him the throne; and shortly afterwards came the news that Nero was no longer alive.

As Galba, now emperor, marched slowly towards Rome, the prefect of Egypt

Tiberius Julius Alexander transferred his allegiance to him with a promptitude that suggested earlier collusion; and in the capital itself an incipient rising by Nymphidius Sabinus, disappointed by his imperial protégé, was easily stamped out.

When the new ruler arrived outside the city in October, he killed a number of marines who had come to meet him. This and other inadvisable measures rapidly made him unpopular; and the conflicting influences of his three principal advisers, Titus Vinius, the new praetorian prefect Laco and the freedman Icelus, did nothing to provide reassurance.

On New Year's Day 69 the army in Upper Germany overthrew his statues and called upon the senate and people of Rome to chose a successor. On the following day the army of Lower Germany acclaimed its governor Vitellius emperor.

But meanwhile Galba, after hearing what had happened on 1 January, had decided that, in the absence of a son of his own, he must adopt an heir who could defend his throne and offer hope of continuity. His choice fell on a young man of as noble birth as himself, Piso Licinianus. But Piso's selection fatally offended Otho who, on 15 January, had both Galba and Piso murdered. Officers and men of the praetorian guard were in the plot, but not its prefect Laco, who likewise lost his life; and so did Vinius and Icelus as well.

The brief reign of Galba was chiefly important because of the circumstances in which it came about. These were summed up by Tacitus in the introduction of his *Histories:* 'A well-hidden secret of the principate had been revealed: it was possible, it now appeared, for an emperor to be chosen outside Rome.' The revelation of this secret showed the provincial garrisons their own power, incited them to display it in armed conflict one against the other, and led the way to endless military rebellions and revolutions in the centuries that lay ahead.

The proclamation of an emperor by a provincial army ought to have struck the members of the Roman governing class as deeply ominous, since it imperilled such shreds of independent action as they were still able to command. Instead, however, the senate and knights alike were so delighted by the removal of Nero that they happily confirmed Galba's acclamation by the troops.

A novel situation had been created by the accession of an emperor who, despite longstanding ties of friendship with the former imperial family, was not one of its members.

The change, it is true, was of as unabrupt a nature as could be imagined, owing to the extremely aristocratic nature of Galba's ancient house. But his lack of blood connexion with the Julio–Claudians raised unfamiliar and difficult points.

Should he, for example, adopt the designation of *Imperator* as a special prefix, and should he take the names of Augustus and Caesar? For all these appellations had belonged exclusively to the imperial dynasty that was now defunct. Galba evidently felt that to call himself *Imperator* was somewhat embarrassing.* He was hailed in this way at Carthago Nova, and initially used the prefix on his coins, but thereafter he tended to abandon its employment. However, following his election by the senate, he decided to adopt the name of Augustus; and after he had met a deputation from the senate at Narbo (Narbonne) in July or August 68, he added Caesar as well. This meant that the continuing tendency to regard Augustus and Caesar as titles of office rather than as proper names had now finally prevailed.

That the senate were able to gratify their desire for a blue-blooded emperor was due to an exceptional situation. For Galba was one of the very few distinguished noblemen to have been entrusted with an important command by the suspicious Nero, who thought he was too old and mild to rebel. And indeed Galba would never have lent his name to any revolt, had he not fallen out with the procurators who were Nero's local Spanish representatives – which made him fear that he might be the next to succumb.

Although bald and arthritic, and perhaps a sufferer from hernia as well, he was still an imposing looking man, with an aquiline nose and stern features. These, under the transforming attention of the exceptionally gifted artists who designed his coins, became magnificent embodiments of antique Republican, un-Neronian austerity and virtue – although Suetonius pronounced Galba to be too heavy an eater, and attributed to him a taste for sexual intercourse with grown men. On the reverse of the coinage was a fine and varied display of uplifting slogans, including references to the revival of public confidence, liberty, equity and concord, and a proclamation of the rebirth of Rome under the new regime.

Yet Tacitus analysed his personality in critical terms.

* Nero, in AD 66, had revived Augustus' use of the prefix.

In the course of seventy-three years he had lived a successful life spanning the reigns of five emperors – reigns which proved luckier for him than his own. His personality was something of a compromise: while free from serious faults, it scarcely achieved real virtues. Having won a reputation, he neither despised nor exploited it. He harboured no designs upon other people's property, was thrifty with his own, and where the state was involved showed himself a positive miser.

A tolerant attitude towards courtiers and officials attracted no censure when they happened to be honest. But his lack of perception if they were not was quite inexcusable. However, distinguished birth and the alarms of the time disguised his lack of enterprise and caused it to be described as wisdom. In the prime of life he attained military distinction in the Rhineland. As proconsul, he administered Africa with moderation, and his control of Nearer Spain in his latter years showed a similar sense of fair-play.[1]

The historian concludes this sketch with one of his most famous and penetrating epigrams: 'As long as he was a subject, Galba seemed too great a man to be one, and by common consent possessed the makings of a ruler – had he never ruled.' For the contrast between Galba the governor and Galba the emperor very soon became glaringly apparent.

By the time he came to the throne, he was too old to bear the exceptional strains of the imperial office. In consequence he had to lean heavily on his advisers: and their large powers soon showed that, despite governmental claims that Liberty had been restored, the senate was not going to regain its authority after all.

The imperial freedmen wielded excessive influence [declared Tacitus] and Galba's own servants had itching palms eager to catch at an unexpected windfall. For they knew their time was short in view of Galba's age. The new court exhibited the same evils as the old – equally serious, but not equally tolerable.

Besides, these over-powerful advisers of the new government by no means inspired public confidence. It is true that Tacitus, who hated the Civil Wars, took a jaundiced view of anyone they brought into power, but his condemnations seem justified by the outcome. It was true that one of these counsellors, Titus Vinius, was not without gifts. Admittedly he had started his military career by committing adultery with his commanding officer's wife, in the headquarters building of all places; and this had led to his arrest. Yet he subsequently became praetor and a successful legionary commander – though once again scandal pursued him when he was alleged to have stolen a gold cup at a banquet given by Claudius. Vinius had proved a strict and honest governor of the southern Gallic province, Narbonese Gaul. Yet he was accused of using his position, in the short reign of Galba, to amass great wealth. He was an ambiguous figure. 'Unscrupulous, cunning and quick-witted,' was the final summing-up of Tacitus, 'when and as he made up his mind he could be either vicious or hard-working, with equal effectiveness.'

Vinius, then, at least had possibilities, equivocal though they were. But Galba's replacement for Nymphidius in the praetorian prefecture, Cornelius Laco, was an unrelievedly unfortunate choice. A man with a minor legal background, wholly destitute of military experience, he remained 'quite out of touch with what his men thought; he regularly opposed any plan, whatever its excellence, which he had not himself suggested, and showed a stubborn disregard for expert opinion'.

The emperor's third principal counsellor, his freedman and supposed former bedfellow Icelus, had been imprisoned by Nero when reports of Galba's rebellion reached the capital, but was released when the senate changed its allegiance; and it was he who issued the instruction permitting Nero's body to be cremated, and conveyed to Galba the news that he had been declared his successor. Promoted to the status of knight, under the name of Servius Sulpicius Marcianus, he was said to have created an all-time record for the speed with which he enriched himself.

Such was the not very attractive trio who dominated the imperial council. But what was fatal was the hatred that each felt for the others. The great strength of Nero's counsellors Seneca and Burrus had been their harmonious relationship. Disharmony among imperial advisers only failed to be disastrous when their emperor was capable of controlling them; that was why the disputes between Agrippa and Maecenas had never dislocated the government of Augustus. But now Vinius, Laco and Icelus all pursued separate aims of their own, and Galba did not possess the force or understanding to impose a unified policy.

This was an open invitation to disaster, which almost immediately followed. And yet Galba had started well enough. Even before his arrival in Rome, his agents had suppressed a free-lance general in North Africa, Clodius Macer, and crushed the seditious designs of

Nymphidius Sabinus, who had prematurely supposed that the termination of the Julio–Claudian house meant that even men of his dubious origins now had a chance of the throne.

But the reasons why Nymphidius felt his revolt had a chance of succeeding should have provided Galba with a sharp admonition. For the emperor had launched a programme of financial retrenchment which, although greatly needed after Nero's extravagances, was badly received among civilians and soldiers alike. What displeased the praetorians was his refusal to pay them the large bonuses that Nymphidius had offered on his behalf. Indeed, the emperor had actually dismissed the prefect for having made the offer at all, and that was why Nymphidius, understandably, changed his allegiance.

Though his subsequent uprising came to nothing, the new regime's methods were scarcely likely to retain the support of the guardsmen for very long. 'I select my troops,' declared Galba, 'I don't buy them!' But, as Tacitus observed, such pronouncements, even if he had lived up to them consistently, were too high-minded and starry-eyed for the times. Moreover, when these words became known, they infuriated not only the praetorians but the legionaries in the provinces as well. And so the slide into chaos and anarchy gained momentum.

It was in Upper Germany, the southern part of the Rhine frontier, that the fatal crisis began.

In the previous year the commander in this region, Verginius Rufus, had taken his three legions into Gaul to suppress Vindex. Yet he had subsequently ordered them to swear allegiance to Galba; and although this meant that no rewards for their victory over Vindex would be forthcoming, they had reluctantly agreed. When, however, on 1 January AD 69, Verginius' old and sick successor Hordeonius Flaccus required the annual renewal of these oaths, the soldiers of the two legions stationed at Moguntiacum (Mainz) refused to comply, and toppled Galba's statues over on to the ground.

Then, finally, they agreed to swear an oath: yet it was no longer to Galba, but to the senate. For these legionaries of Upper Germany declared that they were not prepared to accept an emperor created by another army.

This revelation of the powerful *esprit de corps* felt by the soldiers on the German frontier was a first indication of the dangerous inter-garrison rivalry that was to bedevil the future history of the Roman empire. Nevertheless for the time being this rivalry expressed itself in a relatively cooperative form: since the Upper German troops, instead of nominating an emperor themselves, left the final arbitration in the hands of the praetorian guard, which they urged to appoint a ruler who would have the approval of all the armies.

These startling developments on the Rhine, when they became known at Rome about a week later, precipitated what was intended to be an appropriate counterblast from Galba.

For they accelerated a measure which he had for some time been debating in his own mind and with his friends – the adoption of an heir. In recent months, the matter had undoubtedly been the main topic of discussion throughout the country, for in the first place there was opportunity, as well as an unhealthy craving, for such talk, and in the second, Galba was old and failing.

Few Romans had any capacity to judge, or real desire for, the public good. But many day-dreamers talked glibly of the chances of this candidate or that in order to curry favour with a friend or patron, or else to vent their spite on Titus Vinius, whose daily growing influence only rendered him daily more detested.[2]

Other emperors had adopted sons before, and this had been generally understood to mean that they were adopting successors to the imperial power. But now this not unfamiliar situation must necessarily assume a somewhat novel character, because Galba was obliged by the lack of a son or suitable relative of his own to go outside his own house for his prospective heir – thus lining up yet another family for eventual succession to the principate.

According to Tacitus the emperor summoned a council to discuss the matter, and those present included Titus Vinius, the praetorian prefect Laco, an experienced consul-designate and the prefect of the city. Vinius was of the opinion that the appropriate nominee was Otho, who was his own personal friend: and as governor of Lusitania he had been Galba's principal supporter in his Spanish coup. Laco did not agree. Nor did Galba, who found Otho too reminiscent of Nero's lax court, and opted instead, probably with Laco's support, for a certain Lucius Calpurnius Piso Licinianus.

Piso, in his thirty-first year, came of a great ancient family which had suffered extensively at Nero's hands; and he himself was, and looked, impeccably well-behaved, and indeed strait-laced. Galba had long been an admirer of the young man's character. Yet Piso was a catastrophic choice, because he totally failed to appeal to the troops. He possessed no military experience, and what little they knew of him caused them no pleasure, since his relatives had been involved in palace conspiracies against Nero, whom many of the soldiers had liked.

In an effort, therefore, to try to obtain a better welcome for his decision from the guard, Galba decided to make his first announcement of Piso's adoption, not in the senate or Forum, but in the praetorian camp.

The occasion was a historic one. For even if Galba's choice of an heir was unfortunate, he was creating a precedent which was to be followed for the greater part of the century that lay ahead. That is to say, he was throwing the principate open to merit, in place of the system of dynastic inheritance which had produced such weird emperors in the recent past. Tacitus lived to see the first stages of this subsequent story, and was therefore careful to record the speech the emperor addressed to Piso in preparation for the significant ceremony. We may not be reading Galba's exact words, since the historian was clearly influenced by another imperial adoption of his own time, when Nerva, in almost equally critical circumstances, nominated Trajan as his successor. Nevertheless the oration ascribed to Galba sounds plausible enough, because it speaks the same sort of language as the slogans on his coins:

Could the vast frame of this empire have stood and preserved its balance without a directing spirit, I was not unworthy of inaugurating a Republic. As it is, we have been long reduced to a position in which my age can confer no greater boon on the Roman people than a good successor, your youth no greater than a good emperor. Under Tiberius, Caligula, and Claudius, we were, so to speak, the inheritance of a single family. The choice which begins with us will be a substitute for freedom. Now that the family of the Julii and the Claudii has come to an end, adoption will discover the worthiest successor. To be begotten and born of a princely race is a mere accident, and is only valued as such. In adoption there is nothing that need bias the judgement, and if you wish to make a choice, a unanimous opinion points out the man.

Let Nero be ever before your eyes, swollen with the pride of a long line of Caesars. It was not Vindex with his unarmed province, it was not myself with my single legion, that shook his yoke from our necks. It was his own profligacy, his own brutality – and that though there had been before no precedent of an emperor condemned by his own people.

We, who have been called to power by the issues of war, and by the deliberate judgement of others, shall incur unpopularity, however illustrious our character. Do not, however, be alarmed if, after a movement which has shaken the world, two legions are not yet quiet. I did not myself succeed to the throne without anxiety. And when men shall hear of your adoption I shall no longer be thought old, and this is the only objection which is now made against me.[3]

As Galba's heir, Piso Licinianus took over his name, adding the designation of Caesar, which henceforward became a special title of the heir to the throne. And so, on this day 10 January, the Arval Brethren record that they sacrificed in honour of the adoption of Servius Sulpicius Galba Caesar.

A day or two later, however, he and his adoptive father must have received a second instalment of disastrous news from Germany. The ceremonies of the adoption had been prompted by the information that, on 1 January, the legions of Upper Germany asserted their independence of action. But now it was also learnt that, on the following day, the garrison of Lower Germany had saluted its own governor, Aulus Vitellius, as emperor of Rome in Galba's place. This news greatly upset the praetorian officers in the capital, whether they were friendly to Galba or not. The Upper German legionaries had at least invited the guard to nominate a new emperor, and this showed a deference with which they could not be altogether displeased. But now the Lower German legions had brushed this suggestion aside, and named an emperor of their own. Just as the German legions had resented a nomination by the legion in Spain, so the praetorians, too, were most unwilling to accept the nominee of any legionary garrison.

This dissatisfaction, however, did nothing to shore up their loyalty to Galba. The ceremony at the praetorian camp at which the announcement of Piso's adoption was made – still unaccompanied by any bestowal of a donative – had fallen distinctly flat. 'The tribunes, centurions and front ranks raised a gratifying cheer by way of response, but throughout the rest reigned gloom and silence.'

Moreover, in another quarter the adoption had caused far more positive hostility. For it greatly upset Otho, who, after his leading part in elevating Galba to the throne, had confidently expected that he himself would be his chosen heir: and he was by no means prepared to accept defeat. Already for some time past he had been lavishing his attention on the praetorians, and the elevation of Piso instigated him to put the matter to the test. On 15 January, therefore, while their prefect Laco still remained wholly ignorant of what was going on, a small group of guardsmen publicly saluted Otho as emperor, and conducted him to their camp.

At this eleventh hour Galba and Piso at last conceded the praetorians the bonuses that had been so long denied. But when Galba came down to the Forum, he was attacked and pitched sprawling out of his sedan chair, and while the huge crowds gathered all around scrambled for safety the soldiers hacked him to pieces. Piso was dragged out of a temple and decapitated. Vinius, too, although he may have been privy to the plot, died transfixed by a legionary's sword. A veteran specially sent by Otho, now emperor, disposed of Laco. Icelus, as a former freedman, was reserved for public execution.

Galba's reign had lasted rather more than seven months. As he lay on the ground awaiting the fatal blow, he cried out: 'Why, what harm have I done?' But his short reign had been a dismal failure almost from the beginning.

To deny expected bonuses to the troops, while the men around him were seen enriching themselves, was simply asking for trouble. He had also allowed his advisers too much scope. Augustus, in his advancing years, had staved off catastrophe by appointing Tiberius as his deputy and virtual colleague. Claudius, when he too began to lose touch, had yielded much of his power to Agrippina the younger – a less acceptable solution, though at least it kept the administration going. Now, admittedly, Galba's adoption of an heir from outside the imperial house, though it was forced on him by the lack of a son of his own blood, was a very much better idea. But it did him no good, because things had already gone too badly awry before he acted, and in any case he chose an unsuitable man. Once again his age seems to have affectetd his judgement.

However, it is doubtful whether he would have been a successful emperor even if he had been younger. For there were hereditary reasons why he might be expected to fail. His family, in its prosperous Republican days, had gained a bad reputation for cruelty and rigour – and these characteristics were all too apparent in himself. His only real enthusiasm was for old-style disciplinarian severity, a bad recipe for retaining his army's loyalty in turbulent times.

He had shown that non-Julio–Claudians could attain the throne. But that they could keep it had still not been demonstrated – and was not to become apparent until two further reigns had come and gone. Meanwhile the claims of the old Republican families to control the Roman empire had received a poor advertisement from Galba. His brief, disastrous interlude extinguished the imperial prospects of Republican noblemen for ever.

8

Otho

Marcus Salvius Otho was born on 28 April AD 32. His grandfather had entered the senate under Augustus, and his father was given patrician rank by Claudius. Otho himself became an intimate friend of Nero, who was five years younger than himself. When, however, Nero became attached to Poppaea, who was Otho's wife, Otho, in spite of his youth and junior rank, was sent to govern Lusitania (Portugal and western Spain). That was in 58 or 59.

When Galba, his colleague in Nearer Spain, rose against Nero in 68, Otho was the first man of note to join his cause; and he accompanied the new emperor to Rome. When, therefore, Galba adopted another man, Piso Licinianus, as his son and heir, Otho found this wholly unacceptable. That was why, supported by praetorian officers and guardsmen, he had them both assassinated on 15 January 69.

And so Otho, in his thirty-seventh year, was declared emperor. Egypt, North Africa and the legions of the Danube and the Euphrates declared for him. His government, once the horrors of 15 January were over, displayed signs of moderation.

Nevertheless – as must have been known in Rome even before his accession – the Upper German rebellion against Galba had already been followed by the proclamation of Aulus Vitellius, governor of Lower Germany, as rival emperor. The German legionaries, under Vitellius' generals Valens and Caecina, moved rapidly southwards, and, after crossing the Alps in early March, were only held up by

Otho's advance-guard on the Po. Otho himself left Rome for the north on 24 March.

Without awaiting the expected Danube reinforcements, he decided to engage the enemy: and in the decisive First Battle of Bedriacum, Otho's army was completely defeated. His praetorian guard wanted to renew the struggle but he himself, who had not taken part in the battle, decided otherwise, and on 16 April, after a reign of three months, he committed suicide.

On the morning of the day when Otho's reign began, Piso Licinianus, who was to die before nightfall, had addressed the cohort on duty from the steps of the palace, and spoken of Otho's character in critical terms. 'Are we to believe,' Piso was said to have asked them, 'that he earned the principate by his mincing airs? Or by his characteristically effeminate love of finery? . . . Seduction, revelry and sex are the things that engage his imagination.' Later in the day, therefore, after his rival had been murdered, Otho indulged in distasteful gloating.

When Piso was dragged out and slaughtered in the entrance of the temple, there was, we are told, no death of which Otho heard with greater joy, no head which he surveyed with so insatiable a gaze. Perhaps it was that his mind was then for the first time relieved from all anxiety, and so had leisure to rejoice. Perhaps there was with Galba something to recall departed majesty, with Vinius some thought of old friendship, which troubled with mournful images even that ruthless heart; Piso's death, as that of an enemy and a rival, he felt to be a right and lawful subject of rejoicing.[1]

Otho himself had been privy to the assassination, both of Piso and of Galba himself. Originally it had been his aim to get himself adopted by Galba, with whom he would then have been willing to cooperate as his chosen heir. But after the adoption of Piso all such hopes were dispelled. Otho's subsequent claims that he had only accepted the purple under compulsion, and had been conducted to the praetorian camp against his will, cannot be accepted. For he had decided that Galba must die, and had connived at his death, or arranged it.

He was also the first emperor to win the imperial dignity for a new family (Augustus having escaped this category by his Julian adoption). True, Otho, who came from Ferentium (Ferento) in Etruria, was descended from Etruscan princes. Yet his family was 'new' from a Roman point of view, since his grandfather had been its first member to join the senate. The comparatively recent date of this promotion – in the time of Augustus – revealed a new secret of empire. That is to say, the Roman aristocracy, discredited by Galba's ill-success, need not necessarily be the only class to provide an emperor: for Otho came from a new social échelon that owed its elevation to no epoch earlier than the imperial age.

As for Otho himself, he had risen to a position of great influence under Nero, becoming his guide to the smart life of fashionable youth. His court life came to an end, however, after Nero came to believe that he was a competitor for the charms of Poppaea. Tacitus contradicts himself about the circumstances, which remain uncertain, but the most widely accepted version was that Otho was married to Poppaea, but that Nero took her away from him, and then resented Otho's continued affection for her.

> 'Otho in exile? Yes and no;
> *That is, we do not call it so.'*
> 'And may we ask the reason why?'
> *They charge him with adultery.'*
> 'But could they prove it?' No and yes:
> *It was his wife he dared caress.*[2]

The result was that Otho, by the tactful intervention of Seneca, was sent to Lusitania as governor. His governorship is variously assigned by Suetonius to AD 58 and 59, the latter date being required by the biographer's further assertion that Otho was privy to Nero's murder of his mother Agrippina the younger in that year. At all events, when Otho assumed the governorship he was only twenty-six or twenty-seven, so that by ordinary standards of promotion his appointment was a signal honour.

Nevertheless the former friendship between the two men was broken, because when Galba revolted in 68 in Nearer Spain, Otho was the first provincial governor to support his rising. When, however, he had overthrown Galba, his desire to ingratiate himself with those who looked back longingly to the munificent ways of the last Julio–Claudian emperor caused him to remember his pro-Neronian past once again. In consequence he added the name 'Nero' to his own designation in passports, though subsequently discontinuing this practice in the face of senatorial disapproval. He also reinstated Nero's statues and agents and freedmen; although he innovated by the appointment of a knight and not a freedman as his own principal secretary, so as to show that the old unpopular Claudian and Neronian regime of freedmen was not going to be revived.

Otho [says Suetonius] was of medium height, bow-legged, and with splay feet; but almost as fastidious about appearances as a woman. His entire body had been depilated, and a well-made toupée covered his practically bald head. He shaved every day, and since boyhood had always used a poultice of moist bread to retard the growth of his beard.[3]

This excessive personal vanity was mocked by the satirist Juvenal.

> Here's another clutching a mirror – just like that fag of an emperor
> Otho, who peeked at himself to see how his armour looked
> Before riding into battle. A fine heroic trophy
> *That* was indeed, fit matter for modern history-books,
> A civil war where mirrors formed part of the fighting kit.
> To polish off a rival *and* keep your complexion fresh
> Demands consummate generalship; to camp in palatial splendour
> On the field of battle, *and* give yourself a face-lack
> Argues true courage. No Eastern warrior-queen,
> Not Cleopatra herself aboard that unlucky flagship
> Behaved in such a fashion.[4]

Such practices, and most of all his close friendship with the young Nero, gave rise to rumours that his tastes included not only love for Poppaea but homosexuality as well. Yet even Tacitus, who regarded Otho as just the sort of thoroughly inferior person who is thrown up by times of civil war, had to admit that he governed his province of Lusitania 'affably', and lived a moderate and respectable life in his province – 'enjoying himself in his spare time, officially blameless'.

Otho's character and abilities, however, remain somewhat obscure, first because he ruled for so short time, and secondly because the ancient authorities, who loved moral contrasts, found an all too satisfactory rhetorical antithesis between his unvirtuous life and what they termed his virtuous end. On the whole he seems to have been a man of only moderate gifts, see-sawing between adequate statesmanship and short-sighted quick returns: the possessor of good connexions and useful experience, who happened to be in the right places at the right times.

When Otho committed the crime which made him emperor, he was acting under a misapprehension. For according to Suetonius's father, who was a military tribune in one of his legions, his elevation to the principate seemed to him unlikely to be contested by Vitellius, who, on hearing the news, would straightaway (he believed) withdraw his own claims. He himself, Otho was heard to say, would never have set himself up against Galba at all unless he had believed that his accession would be peaceful – since there was nothing he detested as much as civil war. It was in this spirit of misguided optimism that his mint forthwith produced coins bearing cheerful slogans, such as 'The Security of the Roman People' and 'The Peace of the Whole World'.

Nevertheless these phrases at once proved the emptiest of wishful thinking. For the German garrison, too, had already begun to issue its own coins, first without the mention of Vitellius, but then with his portrait and name, and even before Vitellius knew that Galba was dead, two large forces from his armies had set out from the Rhineland on the long march towards Italy and Rome. Vitellius himself was not with them, since he stayed behind in Germany to mobilize a reserve army and follow later at its head. But, contrary to Otho's hopes, the two Vitellian advance forces under Valens and Caecina were not stopped by the news of Galba's death. Otho tried to negotiate with Vitellius but tried in vain: so instead he tried, equally unsuccessfully, to have his rival assassinated, a procedure reciprocated by Vitellius.

Otho's chief hope, as far as the legions of the empire were concerned, lay with the troop concentrations on the Danube, whose sentiments of inter-garrison rivalry were excited to a high pitch of hostility by the pretensions of Vitellius's Rhine armies. And so the Danube legions started preparing to march to Italy in Otho's aid. But it would be a long time before they could get there, and meanwhile he was painfully dependent upon the sole support of the praetorian guard.

Indeed, so helpless was he in the guardsmen's hands that they even set about appointing their own prefects for themselves, in place of the murdered Laco. Moreover, they soon became almost uncontrollably undisciplined. A secret issue of arms to a unit of city troops (which was on its way to guard Ostia) was misunderstood by the praetorians, who suspected the senate of planning to kill Otho. Whereupon, helping themselves to the weapons, they rushed off, sword in hand, to the palace, where they broke into a large imperial dinner-party, wounding two senior officers who tried to stop their rush. Plutarch, whose Lives of

Galba and Otho are his only imperial biographies that survive, described what happened next.

Hearing that eighty of the senators were at supper with Otho, they declared it was a fair opportunity to take off the emperor's enemies at one stroke. A general alarm ensued of an immediate coming sack of the city. All were in confusion about the palace, and Otho himself in no small consternation, being not only concerned for the senators (some of whom had brought their wives to supper with them), but also feeling himself to be an object of alarm and suspicion to them, whose eyes he saw fixed on him in silence and terror.

Therefore he gave orders to the prefects to address the soldiers and do their best to pacify them, while he bade the guests rise and leave by another door. They had only just made their way out, when the soldiers rushed into the room, and called out, 'Where are the emperor's enemies?' Then, Otho, standing up on his couch, made use both of arguments and entreaties, and by actual tears at last, with great difficulty, persuaded them to desist.

The next day he went to the camp, and distributed a bounty of twelve hundred and fifty *denarii* a man amongst them. Then he commended them for the regard and zeal they had for his safety, but told them that there were some who were intriguing among them, who not only accused his own clemency, but had also misrepresented their loyalty; and therefore, he desired their assistance in doing justice upon them.

To which, when they all consented, he was satisfied with the execution of two only, whose deaths he knew would be regretted by no one man in the whole army.[5]

This incident seemed to ancient writers to represent one of the lowest points to which the authority, dignity and security of a Roman emperor had ever become degraded. Otho was a usurper who had gained his position by conspiracy and murder. It was he who had shown the soldiers that the imperial office was for sale, and that they possessed the power both to kill and to create a Caesar. And now he had been faced with the humiliating consequences of these acts. Such were the unedifying scenes of power-lust, mob violence and hysteria which civil strife, according to Tacitus, inevitably brought in its wake.

Faced with this difficult situation at home, Otho, despite a reputation for impetuosity, was too slow in his preparations to halt the Vitellian armies. His metropolitan units were not only disorderly but unaccustomed to active service, and time had to be taken to give them some training. Besides their numbers were inadequate, and to supplement them Otho had recourse to the unpopular measure of mobilizing two thousand gladiators. All this meant a delay of two months: and by then he was too late to close the Alpine passes. It was now imperative to hold the line of the Po, and it had to be held without waiting for the Danube armies, although their vanguard was already on the way.

Otho had first-class commanders at his disposal, but as Dio Cassius noted he made a fatal mistake by dispatching them northwards in command of separate forces, without the establishment of a unified command. He also sent an ineffective and abortive naval expedition to southern Gaul. Soon after it sailed he himself left Rome for the north Italian front, leaving the capital in the hands of his brother, Lucius Salvius Otho Titianus, an unenergetic man of questionable financial integrity. On the northward journey Otho created a good impression by marching on foot before the standards. Moreover, in contrast to his usual elaborate attention to his person, he was seen to display a soldierly disregard for washing and shaving.

On joining his troops, he received conflicting advice from his generals. Nor did he improve his situation by the belated appointment of a commander-in-chief, since the man he selected was his own inadequate brother, summoned for the purpose from Rome. His most experienced advisers urged that the enemy should not be engaged until after the arrival of the Danubian reinforcements. Otho and Titianus, however, perhaps unsure how long they could retain the loyalty of their men, declared for an immediate decisive action, even before they could oppose equal strength. But Otho himself was not to be present at the engagement. For his war council decided that he should retire, with a considerable contingent, to Brixellum (Brescello) to await the outcome. The intention, presumably, was to avoid risking his personal safety, and to keep him and his force in reserve. However the troops who stayed to fight were disheartened.

The decisive clash, usually known as the First Battle of Bedriacum (Calvatone), took place some twenty miles east of Cremona. Civil war engagements were invariably confusing, since the two armies wore similar uniforms and carried similar weapons. After a series of separate encounters, things were already not going too well for Otho's troops, when a large force of Vitellian auxiliaries, fresh from defeating the gladiatorial unit brought from Rome, turned and attacked the main body of the Othonians in the flank, and led the way to a resounding victory. The next day the defeated side, abandoned by several of their commanders, offered to surrender, and soon the two armies were fraternizing.

When news of the disaster reached Otho at Brixellum, assurances that the Danubian army would soon arrive to restore the position failed to convince him, and he decided to kill himself. He was dying, he declared, to stop the shedding of Roman blood. This was not in fact achieved, but his suicide in such a cause seemed to the ancients an impressive deed.

> She wavered yet, the fury of our fray,
> And wanton Otho still could win the day;
> But cursing war with all its price of blood,
> He pierced his heart and perished as he stood.
> Let Cato's life than Caesar's greater be:
> But in their death is Otho first or he?[6]

Tacitus devotes his most powerful rhetoric to the nobility of Otho's suicide, and echoes the general view that it went far to redeem the inadequacies of his life, and even the horror of Galba's murder. 'Two actions of his,' concludes the historian, 'one appalling, one heroic, have earned him in history an equal measure of fame and infamy.'[7]

Though his decision meant a sad let-down for his loyal officers and men, it was creditable that he felt an aversion to shedding further Roman blood. Nevertheless the motive for his suicide may not have been so glorious as it seemed. His secretary Secundus, who was in a position to know what he was talking about, indicated less high-minded reasons. It seemed to him (Plutarch records) that the emperor had become quite unable to weigh up the contrary risks of carrying on or giving in – and that in any case his nerve was not strong enough to endure the suspense any longer.

Otho's essential inadequacy had found him out. Yet his reign of ninety-five days was significant. The fact that it occurred at all, however briefly, was a demonstration that a Roman emperor need not come from an antique noble clan. 'In armed competition for the purple,' remarked Sir Ronald Syme, 'the premium on ancestors fell sharply.' But Otho also provided a much more sinister demonstration: that a man could gain the throne by assassinating his predecessor. During the centuries ahead, this was all too often destined to happen again, and became a characteristic feature of the succession crises which continually racked Rome and the empire.

And Otho also provided a further unwelcome precedent – that of a ruler who was the slave of the praetorian guard which had created him. The fact that he nevertheless so rapidly fell was encouraging, since his downfall revealed that praetorian power had its limits: though this outcome scarcely justified great optimism, if the only result was that other military units elevated subsequent emperors instead.

9

Vitellius

Aulus Vitellius, born in AD *15, was the grandson of a knight from Luceria (Lucera in Apulia), who was an agent of Augustus; and the future emperor's father was Lucius Vitellius, Claudius' most intimate friend and adviser. Aulus himself was consul in 48 and governor of Africa. Galba appointed him governor of Lower Germany, where he assumed office in November 68.*

On 2 January 69, at the instigation of Caecina and Valens, his soldiers hailed him emperor, and the Upper German army, which had already withdrawn its allegiance from Galba, joined his cause on the following day. Gaul, Raetia, Britain and Spain also rallied to his standards. Even before receiving the news of Galba's death, Caecina and Valens had already started for Italy. They pressed on, crossing the Great St Bernard and Mont Genèvre passes, and won the First Battle of Bedriacum against the generals of Otho, whose suicide was followed by the senate's recognition of Vitellius on 19 April.

He followed his generals slowly to Rome, which he reached in July. But there he learnt that the eastern legions, which at first seemed prepared to accept him, had transferred their allegiance to Vespasian, the governor of Judaea, and the Danube armies did the same.

While preparing for the new war that lay ahead, Vitellius disbanded Otho's praetorian guard and replaced it by a much larger force of his own supporters among the soldiery. As Vespasian and his main armies proceeded with more cautious plans, his partisan the Danubian legionary commander Primus made a dash for Italy with some of his legionaries. Vitellius planned to hold the line of the Po, but neither Valens nor Caecina was available any longer to command his troops, since the former was ill and the latter deserted. In late October, while Civilis launched a nationalist revolt in Germany, the almost leaderless Vitellian army was utterly defeated by Primus at the Second Battle of Bedriacum, and, as the victors advanced on the capital, Vitellius' surviving forces melted away.

On 18 December Vespasian's brother Sabinus, who was the prefect of Rome, almost succeeded in persuading Vitellius to abdicate. But the Vitellian troops and city populace prevented this, and Sabinus, joined by Vespasian's younger son Domitian, had to barricade himself on the Capitoline Hill. There on the following day, when his fortifications were overrun and the Temple of Jupiter went up in flames, Sabinus lost his life, while Primus forced his way into the city. Domitian managed to escape. A day later the hiding-place in which Vitellius had taken refuge was discovered, and he was brutally murdered.

A product of the same class as Otho, the stratum of society which became important after the principate began, Vitellius had received an excellent start in life owing to the uniquely powerful position of his father Lucius at Claudius' court: and he himself, too, was the friend of every emperor from Tiberius onwards. His associations with those rulers, however, if gossip is to be believed, were not always edifying. He was said, for example, to have served Tiberius as a male prostitute; Caligula liked him because they shared a taste for chariot-racing; Claudius and he shared a common passion for gambling; and Nero employed him as master of ceremonies at his début on the Roman stage. On that occasion, when the public wanted to see the emperor performing, it was Vitellius who overcame his coyness. And at senatorial meetings, too, he made himself conspicuous by exceptionally sycophantic behaviour towards Nero. Tacitus' comment on these manifestations is that 'like other cowards, Vitellius would insult anyone decent, but kept quiet when people answered him back'.

In his leisure time he enjoyed coarse company, and frequented disreputable bars. But what made him notorious was his appetite. He used to drink a good deal, at mid-day as well as in the evening, but above all he ate, enormously: and a good deal of his most outrageous over-eating was undertaken at the cost of others, as a ruinously expensive diner-out, especially after he became emperor.

The most notorious feast of the series was given him by his brother on his entry into Rome: 2,000 magnificent fish and 7,000 game birds are said to have been served.

Yet even this hardly compares in luxuriousness with a single tremendously large dish which Vitellius dedicated to the goddess Minerva and named 'Shield of Minerva the Protectress'. The recipe called for pike-livers, pheasant-brains, peacock-brains, flamingo-tongues, and lamprey-milt; and the ingredients, collected in every corner of the empire from the Parthian frontier to the Spanish Strait (Straits of Gibraltar), were brought to Rome by warships.[1]

He himself survived well enough by taking regular emetics. Some of his fellow-diners, however, had a tougher time. One of them, Quintus Vibius Crispus, who often had to be host or guest at these gigantic meals, was once compelled by illness to absent himself for some days from the convivial board. But this, he commented privately to an associate, had saved his life. 'If I had not fallen ill,' he declared, 'I should have died.'

To speculate on the reasons for Vitellius's gastronomic over-indulgence is not particularly profitable, since we do not know enough about these ancient personages to explain such aberrations. Perhaps it was caused by some sort of compensatory compulsion. Or it may have been just that old-fashioned sin of gluttony, given free rein by his imperial position. But whatever it was, and however much it cost, among the misdeeds of the epoch it did not rank very high. As Tacitus points out, it was not comparable to the criminality of Otho, who had murdered the emperor before him. Whereas Vitellius, he comments, 'as the slave of his belly and his palate, was felt to have brought discredit chiefly upon himself'.

He was an extremely tall man, with a thigh crippled by a blow received from a four-horse chariot when he had been in attendance on Caligula. His heavy eating and drinking habits gave him a high complexion and a large stomach.

However even the hostile Tacitus, although attributing his career merely to his father's distinction, and his elevation to the throne to the hatred he felt for Galba, is obliged reluctantly to admit that his character possessed certain positive features.

He was a man of some frankness and generosity, qualities indeed which turn to a man's ruin, unless tempered with discretion. Believing that friendship may be retained by munificent gifts rather than by consistency of character, he deserved more of it than he secured.[2]

Dio Cassius presents a slightly more positive picture.

Though he lived the kind of life he did, he was not entirely without good deeds. For example, he retained the coinage minted under Nero, Galba and Otho, evincing no displeasure at their likenesses; and any gifts that they had bestowed upon any persons he held to be valid and deprived no one of any such possessions. He did not collect any sums still owing from earlier taxation, and he confiscated no one's property.

He put to death only very few of those who had sided with Otho, and did not withhold the property of these from their relatives. Upon the kinsmen of those previously executed he bestowed all their funds that were still to be found in the public treasury. He did not even find fault with the wills of such as had fought against him and had fallen in the battles.[3]

Tacitus complains that he was cruel – it is a charge he brings against Otho as well. Yet in view of Vitellius's restraint towards his political enemies there was some justification for his revival of the coin-type CLEMENTIA, which had not been seen on the coinage of the previous five reigns.

Unfortunately, however, he knew nothing whatever about military affairs. No doubt that was why Galba had felt it safe to trust him with a large army command. Yet such ignorance was a notable disadvantage for a leader in civil war. During his last fatal months 'the most portentous spectacle of all was Vitellius himself, without knowledge of military matters and without forethought in his plans, even asking others about the order of march, about the business of reconnoitring, and the discretion to be used in pushing on or protracting the campaign'.[4]

All the same he was by no means unpopular with the army. This was partly because of his slack discipline, which led to many disorderly scenes during his southward journey. 'Few commanders,' remarks Tacitus, 'have made themselves so popular with the army by their good actions as he made himself by doing nothing at all.' Yet Vitellius also possessed a winning though somewhat crude affability.

On his arrival the army, already disaffected towards the emperor and disposed to mutiny, received him gladly, with hands upraised to heaven, as though he were a gift sent by the gods, being the son of a man who had thrice been consul, in the prime of life, and of an easy, extravagant disposition.

This earlier good opinion of him Vitellius had strengthened by fresh and recent proofs, for all along the road he warmly kissed even the common soldiers whom he met, and at every post-house and inn he was so extraordinary affable to muleteers and travellers that in the morning he used to ask them one by one if they had breakfasted yet, and let them see that he had done so by belching.[5]

Nevertheless a comradely talent for eructation was not enough to win battles, and Vitellius' military incompetence meant that he depended entirely on the commanders of his two advance forces, Caecina and Valens.

Aulus Caecina Alienus, born at Vicetia (Vicenza), was young, tall, handsome, soldierly and an excellent public speaker. A man of considerable superficial charm, he liked to wear a brightly coloured cloak and German trousers, while his wife rode beside him in a purple robe. Caecina was believed to be inordinately ambitious. While a member of the governor's staff in Baetica (southern Spain), he had joined the rebellion of Galba, who rewarded him with the command of an Upper German legion. When, however, Galba ordered his prosecution for the embezzlement of funds he decided to play a leading part in the uprising of Vitellius.

Fabius Valens came of a family of knights from Anagnia (Anagni in central Italy). Tacitus describes him as an able man of loose character and excessive financial greed, who 'had tried to pass himself off as a man of fashion by behaving extravagantly ... In the theatricals performed by young men during the reign of Nero, at first apparently from compulsion but afterwards of his own choice he repeatedly acted in farces, with more cleverness than propriety.' As commander of a legion in Lower Germany he became one of Galba's supporters, and even murdered his own governor, Fonteius Capito, on the suspicion that he did not hold the same views. But when Galba showed Valens less gratitude than he expected, he, like Caecina, incited Vitellius to declare himself emperor – though thereafter their two armies moved southwards so quickly that the revolt must have been planned before Vitellius appeared on the scene at all.

Such were the two personages who led the Vitellian armies on their southward march, Caecina moving through Switzerland and Valens through France. Although a series of unpleasant incidents incurred, and Valens' legions at one point broke into violent mutiny, both forces succeeded in crossing the Alps before the winter snows had dispersed. Before long they effected a junction at Cremona, and fought the First Battle of Bedriacum against the Othonians.

After their victory Vitellius gave consulships both to Caecina and to Valens. Like Galba's advisers, however, they proved unsatisfactory lieutenants, because of their intense mutual jealousy and dislike. Caecina was heard describing Valens as a sordid and seedy individual, while Valens declared Caecina a pompous ass. According to Tacitus there was nothing to choose between them; both were equally degraded and unscrupulous. But the historian was eager to show what poor types were thrown up by the Civil War, and they may not have been quite as bad as all that.

Vitellius himself had just left Lower Germany with his reserve army of about sixty thousand men when he learnt that his two generals had been victorious, and that Otho had killed himself. The senate immediately declared him emperor in the dead man's place.

Leaving his army to proceed by road, Vitellius himself took a ship and sailed down the River Saône, disembarking at Lugdunum (Lyon). There he held a victory parade, with Caecina and Valens at his side. The ceremonies included a significant feature, for Vitellius 'ordered the whole army to march out to meet his young son, who was solemnly conducted to the spot and enveloped in a general's cloak. Holding the child in his arms, Vitellius gave him the name "Germanicus" and surrounded him with all the emblems of imperial rank.' This child of his second wife, Galeria Fundana, was apparently only six years of age, and was so tongue-tied by nature that he approached total dumbness. Nevertheless his father was now the emperor, and Vitellius was announcing the foundation of a new dynasty.

This, whatever his other disadvantages, he was almost unprecedentedly well placed to achieve – just because he happened to possess a son of his own blood. Of all the eight Caesars and seven emperors before him not more than two had been similarly blessed, and one of those, Tiberius, had been bereaved of his son long before his own death, whereas the other, Claudius, had been forced by Agrippina to set his offspring aside. After the downfall of the Julio–Claudian dynasty, Galba had been well aware of the need for dynastic continuity, to which the soldiers were so deeply attached; and in consequence, lacking a son of his own, he had adopted one from outside his family. But if Galba had had a son, he would have declared him his heir. Vitellius had one, and did.

Moreover, he openly proclaimed his dynastic intentions by issuing coins which displayed the heads of his young son and his daughter, inscribed 'the children of the Imperator Germanicus'. His adoption of the designation Germanicus, as well as its bestowal upon his son, represent a novel usage. When it had first been conferred on Drusus the elder, the stepson of Augustus, it had meant 'the conqueror of Germany'. The senate, at the time of its original conferment, had ordained that Drusus's descendants, too, should bear the same name in honour of his conquests: and it was proudly retained by Germanicus, Claudius and Nero. But now, as part of Vitellius's nomenclature, it meant something entirely different – *the nominee of the German legions.* This was a fateful and imprudent admission that he was a protégé of one of the great frontier garrisons, and not the unanimous candidate of the army as a whole.

Otho's defeated legions had at first tried to give the throne to Lucius Verginius Rufus, the governor of Upper Germany, but he had evaded this honour, not for the first time, by escaping through the back door in order to avoid the menacing delegation. Not long afterwards Vitellius, belying his generally merciful behaviour, ordered leading Othonian centurions to be executed, an act which greatly damaged his reputation with the Danubian legions. He had also ordered the demobilization of Otho's praetorian guardsmen, who thus became eager to serve with Vitellius' enemies. Vitellius' new praetorian guard, a larger force, was taken from his German legionaries and auxiliaries.

On arrival at the gates of Rome, he was induced by his advisers not to ride into the city in full uniform, but to proceed on foot, wearing a civilian toga. However Rome was soon full of his victorious soldiers, who behaved with the same ungovernable licence that they had displayed on the march. To distract attention from this conduct, the imperial mint produced coinage filled with propagandist uplift. One coin records the concept TVTELA AVGVSTI, the Emperor's Guardianship of his People, which had always been implicit in the imperial office but had never received numismatic commemoration before. Vitellius was also the first ruler to proclaim LIBERTAS AVGVSTI, the Freedom Conferred by the Emperor, which is more pointed and personal than Claudius' LIBERTAS AVGVSTA, the Freedom inherent in the Imperial Regime.

Those Romans who were suffering from the indiscipline of the victorious army cannot have been very impressed with this concept of liberty. But the message was primarily directed towards the senate, with which Vitellius, like most emperors, was wisely eager to make a good start. In order to do so, he tactfully reckoned the beginning of his reign not from 2 January, when he had first been hailed emperor in Germany, but from 19 April, when the senate recognized his accession. Moreover he attended senate meetings scrupulously, allowed the free expression of opposing views, and did not disdain to support his consular candidates in person. He also continued with Otho's policy of excluding freedmen from important secretarial posts. The desirability of such conciliatory gestures towards the senate became abundantly clear when he felt obliged, in the final emergency, to flout senatorial susceptibilities by having consuls elected for ten years ahead, in order to reward his partisans.

Vitellius also revealed, during these critical months, that he held certain reservations about using the appellations of 'Caesar' and 'Augustus', so closely associated with the rulers of the past whom he could not yet aspire to emulate. Although, like Otho, he was happy enough to honour the personal memory of his former patron Nero, he would have preferred to get away from the characteristic titles of the defunct dynasty, since he planned to found a new, Germanican, house. Nevertheless, his reluctance to assume these designations was overborne. Even after his final victory he still declined to be called Caesar, but withdrew his refusal when matters later became desperate, out of a superstitious hope that this portentous title might still turn the tide: though it never once appears upon his Roman coinage. His unwillingness to call himself 'Augustus' had already been overcome at the time when he entered the city – although Tacitus scornfully observed that 'his acceptance was as pointless as his previous rejection'. He also eventually accepted a perpetual consulship. Augustus, three-quarters of a century earlier, had decided to terminate his own continuous series of consulships, so as not to deprive nobles of these coveted posts, and Nero, in 58, had likewise turned down a similar offer. But Vitellius probably calculated that he needed the prestige. For the consuls who took office at the beginning of each year still headed the official calendar, and Vitellius, who did not belong to the Julio–Claudian house or the ancient nobility, could not afford to despise such outward signs of privilege. Had he survived, the perpetual consulship might have become one of the central features of the imperial structure.

However, if Vitellius showed certain signs of possessing constitutional ideas of his own, they all came to nothing, because before the summer was over an army from the disaffected Danubian garrison, commanded by Antonius Primus who had declared for Vespasian, was already across the Julian Alps on Italian soil. For Vitellius had reacted too slowly. On hearing of the initial acclamation of Vespasian, he had been absurdly complacent; and now once again, Tacitus pictured him lounging in the shady arbours of his villa at Aricia 'in the manner of miserable animals that are content to lie and doze so long as food is put in front of them'. Like Otho in face of the Vitellian generals, he wasted too much time.

Like Otho again, however, he at least realized it was imperative to hold the line of the Po. Since the invader was coming from the east, the point of the greatest strategic importance seemed to be Hostilia (Ostiglia), where Primus would attempt to cross the river. So, Valens being unfortunately ill, Caecina was set to occupy a strong position near that town. But at this point Caecina decided to desert, on the simple calculation that the other side appeared the more likely to win. His troops refused to follow him, and placed him under arrest. Nevertheless, left virtually leaderless, they decided to withdraw to Cremona, and it was near that city once again that the Second Battle of Bedriacum was fought.

It was bitterly contested, until after nightfall, when the moon began to shine full into the faces of the Vitellians, making them into an easy mark. They broke and ran, and Primus subjected Cremona to a blood-thirsty sack. Then he pressed on towards the south, fortified by the news that Valens, who was now sufficiently recovered to have been sent to organize a second army in Gaul, had failed in his mission and was under arrest. Soon afterwards he was put to death.

After learning the news of his army's defeat, Vitellius sent most of his remaining troops to Mevania (Bevagna), eighty miles north of Rome, where the road enters the Apennines; and he followed them there in person. But when he heard that the fleet at Misenum had deserted him, he withdrew his force from Mevania to Narnia (Narni), only thirty miles north of the city, and himself retreated headlong to Rome. There his discussions with Vespasian's brother the city prefect Sabinus, aimed at the surrender of his imperial power – a novel sort of negotiation for a Roman emperor – were frustrated by his own soldiers and the crowd, who stormed the Capitol and killed Sabinus, though his nephew Domitian managed to get away. Just after Primus had entered the city, Vitellius himself was murdered with an extreme savagery which seemed to Tacitus a fitting culmination of the harrowing Year of the Four Emperors.

He had not been a monster. However, elevation to the purple increased the already excessive amount he ate and drank, and his inability to keep the throne he had so recently gained was due not to chance or ill-luck, but to his own mediocrity. The combined faults of torpid hangover, military inexperience, and reliance on two mutually hostile advisers were a clear prescription for failure.

Admittedly such verdicts, offered nearly two thousand years later, must be doled out with care. All these shortlived emperors, Galba, Otho and Vitellius, have been stigmatized in the present pages as inadequate. Certainly they all failed, within the space of a few months. Yet Hegel's utterance that the will of God reveals itself only in historical outcomes, if interpreted to mean that the good and competent succeed and the bad and incompetent fail, is sometimes fallacious. For example, those late imperial Caesars who failed to assert their claims to the throne are habitually described as 'usurpers', and those who clung on to the purple are called 'emperors': whereas none, in reality, were usurpers any more than the others.

For the same reason we are justified in wondering whether Galba, Otho and Vitellius were any more incapable or mediocre than, say, Caligula and Nero, who lasted longer. But even if Caligula or Nero had come to the throne in the catastrophic year 69, they could scarcely have made worse mistakes than those which the emperors of that time contrived to commit. They sowed crops that were truly disastrous, and reaped their harvests forthwith.

At the time their triumphant successor, Vespasian, did not look like proving any better than they had been. But as it turned out, to the general surprise, he outclassed Vitellius and his other transient predecessors altogether; and an attempt will now be made to show why this was.

Part IV

The Flavian Emperors

10

Vespasian

Titus Flavius Vespasianus, the founder of the Flavian dynasty, was born at Reate (Rieti in central Italy in AD *9. He was the son of a Sabine tax-collector knight, but his mother's brother became a senator. Vespasian, who owed his early career to Claudius' freedman Narcissus and adviser Lucius Vitellius (the father of the emperor), distinguished himself as a legionary commander in the invasion of Britain (43–4), and became consul in 51 and governor of Africa (the modern Tunisia). But then he underwent a period of considerable poverty. Subsequently, accompanying Nero to Greece in 66, he narrowly escaped trouble by falling asleep while the emperor was singing. Yet in February of the following year he was appointed governor of Judaea with the task of suppressing the First Jewish Revolt, known to the Jews as the First Roman War. The Jewish historian Josephus describes the high hopes entertained by the Jewish rebels:*

> *I spoke of this upheaval as one of the greatest magnitude. The Romans had their own internal disorders. The Jewish revolutionary party, whose numbers and fortunes were at their zenith, seized the occasion of the turbulence of the times for insurrection.*
>
> *As a result of these vast disturbances the whole of the eastern empire was in the balance. The insurgents were fired with hopes of its acquisition, their opponents feared its loss. For the Jews hoped that all their fellow-countrymen beyond the Euphrates would join with them in revolt; while the Romans, on their side, were occupied with their neighbours the Gauls, and the Celts were in motion. Nero's death, moreover, brought universal confusion. Many were induced by this opportunity to aspire to the sovereignty, and the soldiery were eager for changes which might make their fortune.*[1]

Nevertheless, by June 68 Vespasian had reduced almost the entire land of Judaea with the exception of Jerusalem and a few outlying fortresses. But when he heard the news of Nero's death, he stopped his campaign, and although ostensibly extending recognition to each successive new emperor in turn, soon began to plot with Mucianus and Alexander, the governors of Syria and Egypt, who both agreed to support his bid for the throne.

In July the Egyptian, Judaean and Syrian legions acclaimed him, followed by the Danubian garrisons and plans for the attack on Italy were drawn up. While Vespasian himself remained in Egypt to cut off Rome's grain supply, it was decided that Mucianus should lead the main army westwards.

But meanwhile the commander of one of the Danubian legions, Primus, forced his way into Italy, won the Second Battle of Bedriacum, and entered Rome during the night of 19–20 December. He found that Vespasian's brother Sabinus, who had been Vitellius's city prefect, had lost his life in the burning citadel, though Vespasian's younger son Domitian had managed to escape. Vitellius was lynched by Primus' troops, and the senate declared Vespasian his successor.

A week or two afterwards Mucianus arrived in the city, repressed the ambitions of Primus, reduced the praetorian guard to its smaller pre-Vitellian dimensions, and directed the government on behalf of Vespasian, until the new emperor himself reached Rome in about October 70. His general Cerialis put down the German revolt of Civilis very soon afterwards, and the new emperor and his elder son Titus, who had by this time captured Jerusalem, celebrated a magnificent Triumph in the following year.

With the help of Mucianus (until his death in 75–7), Vespasian now addressed himself with unflagging industry to the reconstruction of the empire after the Civil Wars. In 73–4 he revived the censorship, and employed this office not only to purge the senate but to augment it by many new members, provincials as well as Italians.

His fellow censor was Titus, whom he also employed as his praetorian prefect, openly declaring his intention of founding a new dynasty. The first emperor to have a son of his own whose maturity and distinction already fitted him for this role, Vespasian, although in his later sixties his health and energy deteriorated, was able with Titus' help to palliate the process of decline which overwork and constant fear had imposed on most of his predecessors. For example, after a period in which political opposition had not been lacking, Titus effectively put down a conspiracy in the very last year of his father's life.

This was 79; on 23 June Vespasian died what appears to have been a natural death, from a stomach chill due to excessive bathing in the cold waters at Aquae Cutiliae (Bagni di Paterno) near his birthplace. Titus succeeded him without incident.

The circumstances surrounding the origins of Vespasian's rebellion are enveloped in a fog of his own side's publicity, because the winning party presented the course of events retrospectively according to its own interpretations. Thus the Flavians pretended that the determination to seek power was forced on the reluctant Vespasian by the insistence of the armies, and that this decision was reached only after Vitellius had come to the throne and begun to behave badly. But Tacitus rightly refused to accept this view, and understood that Vespasian and his fellow-governors in the east had started planning their rebellion much earlier.

Vespasian, the governor of Judaea, and Gaius Licinius Mucianus, the governor of Syria, had not been on good terms during the last years of Nero's reign; for, whereas Judaea had hitherto been under a minor governor of knightly rank who owed deference to the governor of Syria, the Jewish revolt had resulted in the elevation of the Judaean governorship to a major, independent military command under Vespasian, and Mucianus resented this. After the suicide of Nero, however, the two men composed their differences. While dutifully inducing their troops to swear allegiance to the successive short-lived emperors who followed, they continued to watch the situation with minute care. Galba's reign did not disturb them unduly, since he appointed Vespasian's brother Sabinus as his city prefect. But it was probably Otho's violent accession that prompted them to consider moving into active revolt.

Vespasian and Mucianus secretly secured the support of Tiberius Julius Alexander, the influential renegade Jew who was prefect of Egypt. Neither Alexander nor Mucianus, however, entertained claims to the throne on his own account. Alexander's knightly and Jewish origins made him ineligible, and Mucianus, too, renounced any such ambitions – partly because he had no sons who could help him found a dynasty. It was therefore Vespasian, the father of two sons, who by common agreement must be elevated to the throne.

The victory of Vitellius only served to crystallize this decision, although his father had been Vespasian's patron and the latter for the time being recognized the new emperor. So did Mucianus and Alexander, and Alexander's relative by marriage Agrippa II, the Jewish king who was collaborating with the Romans against his compatriots. But Agrippa, who was in Rome at the time, learnt secretly that Vespasian was planning rebellion, and hastily returned to the east to be at his side.

On 1 July AD 69 Alexander ordered the Egyptian garrison to swear an oath of allegiance to Vespasian. Some days later Vespasian's own legions in Judaea likewise acclaimed him as emperor, and before the middle of the month Mucianus and his Syrian army had done the same. The plan that the leaders adopted was that Mucianus, with twenty thousand soldiers, should set out on the long westward march, while Vespasian himself was to remain for the time being in the east, based on Alexandria. For Vespasian believed that by thus controlling the grain supply of Egypt, which was vital to Rome, he might be able, with the help of his brother Sabinus the city prefect, to compel Vitellius to capitulate without fighting.

Vespasian also received impressive declarations of support from the Danubian armies, so that these for the first time began to assume the historic emperor-creating role that was to become such a prominent feature of the later history of Rome. The initiative in the Danube armies was seized by Marcus Antonius Primus, the commander of one of the legions in Pannonia, and it was he who dashed forward into Italy ahead of Mucianus, and defeated the Vitellians at the Second Battle of Bedriacum. Then, in succession, Primus, Mucianus, Vespasian (nine or ten months later), and Titus (who had been left to capture Jerusalem), returned to Rome, and the new Flavian dynasty could embark on its mission of healing the wounds of the Civil War.

Vespasian was a new kind of ruler, from a lower social class than Otho or Vitellius: and he became the first emperor to place on his coins the figure and name of the goddess Fortuna with the specific addition AVGVSTI, 'the Fortune of the Emperor', the remarkable destiny of the man who had become emperor from comparatively humble origins. Indeed this imperial destiny, it was said, had been widely predicted for him by astrologers, as well as by his Jewish captive and collaborator Josephus. The accession of a man with such a comparatively humble background alerted a whole new range of candidates, in the centuries to come, to the chance that they, too, might gain the throne, and in the later years of the empire there were many indeed who sought, with varying degrees of success, to grasp the prize for which he had made them feel eligible.

Vespasian deliberately stressed his modest rank, and correspondingly plain tastes.

From the very beginning of his reign until the end, he was unpretentious and undespotic, never making any effort to conceal his former mean estate, but often glorying in it. Indeed, when some tried to trace back the origin of the Flavian family to the founders of Reate and the comrade of Hercules whose memorial still stands on the Via Salaria, he just laughed at them.

So far was he from any desire for adventitious decorations that, on the day of his Triumph, exhausted by the slowness and tediousness of the procession, he could not keep from observing: 'It serves me right for being so silly in my old age as to hanker after a Triumph, as if it were either due to my ancestors or had ever been among my own ambitions.'[2]

He spoke Latin with a peasant's accent, and tradition cherished a picture of the plebian ruler seen carting away rubbish on his shoulder from the site of the temple of Capitoline Jupiter which he was rebuilding after its destruction by fire. Reluctant, in his youth, to enter an official career, he had subsequently been compelled, by poverty, to become a mule-dealer, and mortgage everything he possessed: and, even now that his fortune had so greatly changed, there was no one, according to Tacitus, who promoted a general vogue for simplicity more than Vespasian, with his old-fashioned, unpretentious way of life.

For example, his drinking habits were noted for their unusual abstemiousness; though caution in this respect was in any case imposed by a tendency to gout. And the somewhat prosaic character of his sex-life likewise reflected this novel, unsmart image. His wife Flavia Domitilla, who was of such undistinguished origins that even her claim to Roman citizenship was disputed, had died before he came to the throne. After that Vespasian lived with a mistress from his younger days named Caenis, a woman who more than thirty years earlier had been a freed-woman and secretary of Claudius's mother Antonia. Vespasian's younger son Domitian saw no reason to treat Caenis with respect, but she became powerful and rich, and her secretarial experience had given her an extremely retentive memory. She and Vespasian lived together in cosy domesticity until she died in 75. Subsequently he formed the habit of taking a concubine to join him in his afternoon nap. Despite fine Flavian hair-styles, all this was a far cry from the glamorous imperial noblewomen of the previous dynasty.

Vespasian was also thoroughly good-natured and affable, and greatly addicted to lightening the gravity of serious matters by buffoonish jokes, which were frequently of a crude sexual or lavatory character. Moreover, unlike most of his compatriots, he enjoyed humour at his own expense. Squarely and powerfully built, he displayed the facial expression of one who was straining to evacuate his bowels, and this is sometimes apparent in his many admirable portrait busts. Artists were strongly attracted to his knobbly features, and often – no doubt with his approval – represented them with a realism that was wholly unflattering.

He and they were well aware that the humdrum, prosaic, cautious commonsense apparent in his countenance and his life – the traditional soundness that had made the Roman nation what it was – would prove precisely the quality which was needed in order to restore confidence after the horrors of the Civil Wars.

Vespasian and his principal supporter Mucianus were men of strongly contrasted personalities.

Vespasian was an energetic soldier. He could march at the head of his army, choose the place for his camp, and bring by night and day his skill or, if the occasion required, his personal courage to oppose the foe. His food was such as chance offered. His dress and appearance hardly distinguished him from the common soldier.

Mucianus, on the contrary, was eminent for his magnificence, for his wealth, and for a greatness that transcended in all respects the condition of a subject. Readier of speech than the other, he thoroughly understood the arrangement and direction of civil business.

It would have been a rare combination of princely qualities if, with their respective faults removed, their virtues only could have been united in one man.[3]

Mucianus was clearly the more picturesque figure of the two:

He was a man much talked of, in fair days and foul alike. In his youth, he had courted the great with an eye to his own advancement. Then he ran through a fortune and his standing became precarious, for even Claudius was thought to disapprove of him. Removed to an isolated corner of Asia, he came as near to being an exile as later to being emperor.

Mucianus' character was a compound of self-indulgence and energy, courtesy and arrogance, good and evil. A libertine in idle moments, he yet showed remarkable qualities once he had set his hand to a thing. To the world, his activities might seem laudable; but there were ugly rumours about his private life. Yet by a supple gift for intrigue he exercised great influence on his subordinates, associates and colleagues, and found it more congenial to make an emperor than to be one.[4]

Mucianus 'had the art of displaying to advantage whatever he said and did'. He found men who failed to praise him quite insufferable, lavished honours on those who had given him even the slightest help and fiercely hated anyone who had withheld such assistance. 'He had eyes,' adds Tacitus, 'only for the depths of a man's purse, not for equity or truth.' For the historian rejects the patriotic motives of the traitors who helped Vespasian to power, and sees the new imperial entourage as 'a change of individuals rather than outlook'. Nevertheless Mucianus, even in Tacitus' cold portrayal, emerges as a diplomat of extraordinary cunning and skill.

However both he and Vespasian were initially outsmarted by Marcus Antonius Primus, a Gaul aged about fifty from Tolosa (Toulouse), who, acting on behalf of the Flavian high command but without awaiting its instructions, dashed ahead and won the decisive battle on his own. This adventurer, nicknamed 'Beaky', was seen by Tacitus as a particularly unsavoury product of these years of disturbance and indiscipline.

The man had a criminal record, and in Nero's reign had been sentenced for forgery. It was one of the unfortunate results of civil war that he had managed to get back his rank as senator. By Galba he was given command of the Seventh Legion. It was believed that he had written more than once to Otho volunteering his assistance as a party leader. But the offer was disregarded, and he rendered no service in the Othonians' campaign.

Switching his allegiance to Vespasian as Vitellius' star waned, he gave a powerful impetus to the Flavian movement. A man of drive and eloquence, a skilful propagandist who came into his own in a period of dissension and revolt, light-fingered and open-handed, he was at once a vicious influence in peacetime and a general to be reckoned with in war.[5]

Primus' victorious entry into Rome was immediately preceded by what seemed to be a tragedy for his cause, when Vespasian's elder brother Sabinus, the city prefect, was slain by enraged Vitellians on the Capitol. The sixty-one-year-old Sabinus, who had enjoyed a long and distinguished public career, was a man who talked too much and had lost some of his former energy, but was widely regarded as honest. His death was not an unrelieved disaster, since it removed one possible personal complication from an already sufficiently complicated political scene. For although Sabinus had served under Vespasian in Britain, he was not only the older and richer of the two, but it was he who, as a condition of saving his younger brother from bankruptcy, had demanded a mortgage upon his house and land. It would have been a miracle if Vespasian could have wholly forgotten this. Moreover Sabinus and Mucianus, people said, would inevitably have become unfriendly rivals.

Mucianus arrived in the city only a short time after Sabinus' death, and from that time onwards Primus found himself gradually but firmly thrust aside. He had failed to prevent his troops from committing horrible atrocities at Cremona, followed by a four-day orgy of pillage in Rome itself. He was also to blame, it was now maintained, for egging on the German leader Civilis against the Vitellians, and thus precipitating Civilis' revolt against Roman rule in general.

But Primus's worst indiscretion was to be heard asserting that it was he himself, not Mucianus, who had won the war. What he said was the truth, for the opposite claim that a bloodless victory would have been won but for Primus's impetuosity was untenable. Nevertheless these boastful words led to a serious rift between the two men, in which 'Primus showed what he felt with greater frankness, whereas Mucianus hugged his grievances with wily, and hence more implacable, cunning'. After his entry into the capital he behaved obstructively towards Primus, who left for the east to complain to Vespasian. The new emperor received him with amiability and gave him the insignia of a consul. But thereafter Primus lapsed into private life, and in due course went back to his native Tolosa, where he spent a quiet old age.

Meanwhile Mucianus was for the time being in charge of Rome, though he had to pay some suspicious, though outwardly deferential, attention to the emperor's eighteen-year-old younger son Domitian, who was basking in the heroic aura of his escape from the burning Capitol. Moreover, in his capacity as temporary head of state, Mucianus was obliged to deal with a momentary outburst of liberty in the senate, whose members felt free to air their quarrels and feuds amid sharp exchanges of vindictive sentiments. Mucianus also felt it necessary to proceed to harsh precautionary measures. One of his victims was the

handsome young Calpurnius Galerianus, son of the late Piso, conspirator against Nero. He was executed because his aristocratic origins, so
sharply contrasting with those of the new emperor, were causing people
to speak of him as a possible candidate for the throne. Vitellius's seven-
year-old son and heir was also put to death, in case he should provide a
focus for similar movements.

After Vespasian's return to Rome in autumn 70, Mucianus retained
an extremely important advisory role until his death, which took place
between five and seven years later. Yet during these years he did not
possess enormous influence over the emperor. Although he had quite
deliberately, from the very outset, renounced the supreme power for
himself, his temperament was ill-suited to the part of a loyal subordinate.
Shortly before entering Rome he had sent the senate a dispatch tact-
lessly claiming the credit for Vespasian's accession for himself, and even
after the emperor's arrival his ostentatious behaviour still caused
eyebrows to be raised.

Moreover, although Mucianus, as author of a book on geographical
wonders, was a serious literary figure, the emperor found his luxurious
and effeminate private life hard to take. Augustus had bravely endured
Maecenas' extravagance, but Vespasian, discussing the sexual tastes
of Mucianus privately with a friend, was said to have burst out with the
remark, 'I personally find it quite satisfactory to be a male.'

Mucianus had probably hoped for a much greater share of the
imperial power than he eventually got. Nevertheless, in 72 he received
the exceptional honour of a third consulship; and he continued to be
greatly honoured right up to his death. For Vespasian, despite his
private criticisms, preferred (as Tacitus put it) 'to hide the weaknesses
of his friends rather than their merits'.

Vespasian gave the empire the gift of peace, and after the experiences
of the Civil Wars an overwhelmingly splendid gift it was. His resplen-
dent Temple of Peace, justly calling the world's attention to this
achievement, was ranked by Pliny the elder as one of the Wonders of
the World, and it was in this reign that Pliny coined his famous phrase,
'the immense majesty of the Roman Peace'. Vespasian's successful
termination of the long-drawn-out internal strife that had racked and
imperilled the empire created a powerful, widespread predisposition in
his favour.

He persistently appealed to this sentiment through the abundant publicity of his coinage. For, despite this generally favourable attitude towards him, he still needed all the help and sympathy he could raise. He had grave difficulties to contend with. The many wounds of the Civil Wars were still wide open: and seeing that three successive Caesars had fallen within the space of a few months, there was no particular reason why another should not suffer the same fate. Moreover, since each of them in turn had failed to inaugurate a new dynasty, why should he, whose family was less distinguished than all of theirs, prove any more successful?

The ingredients of power remained the same as ever, and the principal ingredient was still the army, which Vespasian handled with a tactful blend of fairness and firmness. In consequence, his reign witnessed no repetition whatever of the recent military rebellions. Regrouping the legions in order to forestall trouble from dissatisfied Vitellians, Vespasian not only succeeded in reconciling the frontier armies to the idea of his own rule, but managed to ensure that they kept right out of politics altogether. It is he therefore who deserves the credit for the prolonged internal stability which lasted almost throughout the whole of the following century. Yet he kept his soldiers occupied, notably in the conquest of a considerable frontier territory in the Upper Rhine – Upper Danube reentrant. Nor did he let the troops forget his own military distinction, since he allowed them to salute him as *imperator* no less than twenty times.

Vespasian chose to date his accession not, like Vitellius, from the day on which he had been recognized by the senate, but from 1 July 69, when he had first been acclaimed by the troops. This was an honest admission that he owed them the job. It was also a realistic warning to the senators that the old days when Republican pretensions might still mean something were gone for ever.

Vespasian's coinage, it is true, shows how careful he was to appear as a traditionalist. He assiduously attended the senate, and consulted it with great thoroughness about any measures he proposed to take. Indeed his relations with the senate as a whole compared favourably with those of any emperor before him.

All the same, it was not part of his plan that it should regain even a single shred of autonomous power. The Civil Wars had shown the necessity of a strong monarchy, and a strong monarchy there was going to be. At first Vespasian's coinage spoke of the Restoration of Liberty (LIBERTAS RESTITVTA), that concept to which the senate was so devoted, but after AD 71 the inscription disappeared, and was not seen again. Although he paid a great deal of lip-service to Augustus, the ostensible restorer of the Republic, he himself was more like the central-izing Claudius.

Indeed, he went further even than Claudius in that direction. When, for example, in 73-4, Vespasian revived in his own favour, in association with Titus, the office of censor which Claudius alone among former emperors had held, he used that office to control the senate more openly than Claudius ever had; and his intention that this should be so was deliberately advertised by the appearance of the title CENSOR on his coins, whereas Claudius in the previous generation had not felt it desirable to proclaim his control of the senate so openly.

The body that emerged from this operation possessed a much less aristocratic and metropolitan, and more Italian and municipal, mem-bership than it ever had before. The carnage of previous reigns, includ-ing the many months of civil strife, had facilitated this process, because the great patrician houses of the Republic were almost extinct; only thirty senatorial families could claim to go back to the Republic at all. Vespasian, while not averse to strengthening his position by marriage ties with such of the old nobility as could still be found, filled the many gaps in the senatorial ranks from knights who had served loyally as his own supporters – men who came, very often, from Italian towns such as his own – and they provided him with a team of excellent collaborators.

The senate that emerged from these changes was to a considerable extent his own personal creation. For out of 148 of his Roman and Italian senators whose origins we can identify, no less than fifty-five were introduced by himself. There was also an increase in senators from the provinces: exactly half of the twenty-eight who are known (all westerners except four) were his own appointees.

For after the Civil Wars there could be no rational justification for strictly Republican sentiments any longer. Nevertheless such feelings still existed; and Vespasian was carped at a good deal.

His critics included a number of itinerant moralists, describing them-selves as Cynics, who preached unconventionality and anarchy, and earned the particular distaste of Mucianus. But there were also small groups of senators and others, of different ideological viewpoints, who likewise refused to accept the Flavian dispensation.

Particularly noteworthy among them was Helvidius Priscus, praetor in 70. The son-in-law of Nero's victim Thrasea, Helvidius had insulted Vitellius publicly, and although a former friend of Vespasian, criticized his regime, too, from the start, and subsequently his attacks rose to a violent crescendo. Helvidius had been greatly disillusioned when the new regime declared an amnesty for Nero's informers. But he was also a keen student of philosophy, and his objection to Vespasian's government was partly based on philosophical grounds. Dio Cassius credits him with a widespread programme of social revolution, including the total overthrow of the imperial system. If, however, as we are told, he was a Stoic, he ought to have objected, not to monarchy as an institution (as the Cynics did), but only to individual monarchs who ruled badly. To us, Vespasian's rule seems the best monarchy Rome was ever likely to get. But that is not how it seemed to Helvidius.

Presumably he was an adherent not so much of Stoic theory as of the practice of former Stoics who had personally opposed the autocrats of their own day – Stoics of the calibre of Cato, and even the Tyrannicides Brutus and Cassius, whose birthdays he was known to celebrate each year. Perhaps what Helvidius objected to most of all was Vespasian's obvious intention to leave the throne to Titus and start a dynasty; though if he hoped that the senate might name some alternative heir instead he could not be described as by any means realistic. In any case, he opposed the government so ferociously that Vespasian was obliged to banish him, and finally, in about 75, to order his execution. Yet he did so with great regret, and at the last moment tried to countermand the order; though he left it too late, for Helvidius had already been put to death.

To another opponent, Demetrius, whose violence had caused philosophers to be exiled in 71, the emperor exclaimed: 'You are doing your utmost to get me to kill you, but I don't kill dogs for barking.' However, the barking of these Republicans and quasi-Republicans went on. But they had to bark louder and louder, since their audience was becoming more and more indifferent.

Far more dangerous, if true, was the report in 79 that two senior senators supposedly committed to Vespasian, Aulus Caecina Alienus and Titus Clodius Eprius Marcellus, were conspiring against his life.

They were condemned by the senate, and committed suicide. The incident indicated that even an emperor so untyrannical as Vespasian could not assume that senatorial plots would ever cease.

The danger was all the greater because the emperor, out of his eagerness to lead an unassuming life, had considerably relaxed security precautions. He put an end to the indiscriminate searching of his visitors. And he spent most of his time at the Gardens of Sallust, where anyone and everyone who wanted an interview was able to see him.

This genial accessibility was highly praised by his friend Pliny the elder, who, like his other intimate advisers, used to go and see him before dawn. He talked to them while he was dressing and putting on his shoes. But even that was not the beginning of his day's work, because before their arrival he had already looked at his letters and read whatever official reports had come in. During the rest of the day he was assiduous in the administration of justice. Indeed he was assiduous in everything: and that was the unspectacular reason for his success. Although he allowed himself a daily drive and a siesta, he worked extremely hard for every other available minute, driving himself on with unremitting conscientiousness.

When he was on the point of death, he tried to struggle to his feet, and said to his friends: 'An emperor ought to die standing.' This was typical of his concept of the principate: the man who occupied it must always be on the job. Tiberius had called the imperial office a miserable servitude. Vespasian was more uncomplaining, but he too held the same conviction that it was his task to give unremitting service to the community. Vitellius had expressed this idea by his coin-type TVTELA AVGVSTI – the Emperor's role as watchful guardian. Vespasian repeated the design, and gave it substance by the way he behaved.

Moreover his concept of the people he had to serve embraced the populations of every territory in the empire. Although Italy was still dominant in the senate, the provinces, aided by judicious grants of citizenship, were rising fast. Vespasian, who knew the provinces well, possessed an empire-wide viewpoint. From his time onwards Roman history becomes increasingly the story not of a palace but of a vast common civilization. And that was to a considerable extent the achievement of the seemingly unimaginative founder of the Flavian dynasty. By his incessant, unexciting devotion to these empire-wide labours, he created a durable norm to which the best of his successors adhered. The rulers destined to govern a peaceful Roman world throughout the greater part of the second century AD were not melodramatic eccentrics of the Julio–Claudian type. They were industrious public servants like Vespasian.

However his reluctance to cut any sort of a dash could easily be misunderstood. In particular, he was widely accused of excessive parsimoniousness. Innumerable jokes, good and bad, centred round his supposed avarice, and quite a number of them were cracked by himself. And when people told him his agents were making money for themselves, he said he regarded them as his sponges – he put them in to soak, only to squeeze them dry himself later on.

Once, on a journey, his muleteer dismounted and began shoeing the mules. Vespasian suspected a ruse to hold him up, because a friend of the muleteer's appeared and started busily discussing a lawsuit with the emperor. Vespasian made the muleteer tell him just what his shoeing fee would be, and insisted on being paid half . . .

When Titus found fault with him for contriving a tax upon public lavatories, he held a piece of money from the first payment to his son's nose, asking whether its odour was offensive to him. When Titus said 'No' he replied, 'Yet it comes from urine.'[6]

Yet the man who sponsored a gigantic building programme at Rome including not only the Temple of Peace but the first stages of the Flavian Amphitheatre or Colosseum, cannot justly be described as mean; and Vespasian was also the first emperor to endow Chairs of Greek and Latin Rhetoric at Rome.

All the same he had inherited an empire ruined by the ravages of civil war, and he was ready enough to remind people of the financial deficit which these disasters had left behind them – and to raise rates of taxation quite sharply in order to remedy it. Oppression, it is true, was the last thing he wanted. He was keen, for example, not to burden the provinces with excessive costs in connexion with the imperial post. But he also showed considerable vigilance in putting a stop to tax evasions.

All the jests about his careful financial methods were very far removed from the traditional idea that munificence was a quality of monarchs; and people found these economies distasteful. But their distaste was not nearly strong enough to endanger his position. Vespasian was far too sensible to allow parsimony to bring him down, as Galba had been brought down. Like Augustus, he was an expert at delicate, precise calculations of what was possible and what was not.

When he died in 79, he was only five months short of seventy years of age. For some time past the punishing nature of his daily routine had been making itself felt. Yet Tacitus remarks that Vespasian was the only ruler who, instead of getting worse as time went on, actually became better.

This proved possible because of a uniquely advantageous circumstance. Unlike all the nine Caesars before him, he had a mature son of his own to assist him as his powers began to fail. Titus represented him in the senate, and in other state occasions. But he was also a highly experienced soldier and administrator, who acted in every way as his father's deputy and partner. Seventy years earlier, when Tiberius was deputizing for his stepfather Augustus, the two men had been temperamentally at odds. Vespasian was more fortunate in Titus, whose aid enabled his father's reign to continue under firm control until the end.

II

Titus

The future emperor Titus, born in AD *39, was named Titus Flavius Vespasianus like his father Vespasian. His mother Domitilla had died before her husband came to the throne. Educated with Nero's step-brother Britannicus, Titus subsequently held successive military posts and in 67 accompanied his father to Judaea to help put down the Jewish revolt, in the capacity of a legionary commander.*

After Nero's death in the following year, he was sent to convey Vespasian's congratulations to Galba. But on learning at Corinth of Galba's death, he turned back and returned to the east. There he helped to promote the reconciliation between Vespasian and Mucianus, governor of Syria, which led to their alliance and Vespasian's successful rebellion against Vitellius. When Vespasian began his revolt, he entrusted the control of the Jewish War to Titus, who captured Jerusalem in September.

His father shared his Triumph with him, gave him many state offices as his own colleague, and appointed him to the praetorian prefecture. Indeed he openly proclaimed him his deputy and successor, and this was probably the cause of the conspiracy of Eprius Marcellus and Caecina which Titus forcibly suppressed in the year of his father's death.

Earlier he had incurred criticism by his liaison with the Jewish queen Julia Berenice, sister of Agrippa II. *In about 75 she came to Rome with her brother and lived openly with Titus, but after a time he dismissed her. When he had come to the throne in 79, Berenice returned to Rome, but almost immediately he sent her away for the second and last time.*

226

Although Titus' succession was unchallenged, certain aspects of his record and character created widespread misgivings; but Titus successfully dispelled them. This was partly achieved by lavish expenditure, notably upon the completion of the Colosseum. In the provinces, attention was mainly concentrated on Britain, where Agricola advanced as far as the River Tay and consolidated the Forth–Clyde line.

In September 81, in his forty-second year, Titus died, in the farmhouse in which his father, too, had breathed his last little more than two years earlier.

His youthful military service in Germany and Britain had earned Titus a reputation, and many statues subsequently celebrated the successes he had achieved in these posts. When, later, he was given leave of absence from Judaea to convey Vespasian's message of allegiance to the new emperor Galba, it was said that, as he proceeded westwards in the company of the Jewish collaborator King Agrippa II, he entertained hopes of ingratiating himself with Galba and by-passing Vespasian, so as to become the heir-presumptive. This is unlikely, but if any such idea arose it probably had Vespasian's approval. Mucianus, whom Titus helped to reconcile with Vespasian, was impressed by the young man, ascribing his own renunciation of the throne to Vespasian's possession of two grown sons, and especially the older of them with his military experience: 'It would be illogical not to concede the imperial supremacy to one whose son I should set about adopting if I were emperor myself.'

When Vespasian had been acclaimed by the eastern legions in summer 69, he left Titus in charge of the suppression of the Jewish revolt, which was now, apart from outlying strongholds, reduced to the defiant city of Jerusalem. In May 70 Titus began the siege of the city, and, amid harrowing scenes, it fell to his troops after resisting for four months. In the words of Racine's *Bérénice*:

> At last, after a cruel, long-drawn siege,
> He quelled the haggard, bloodstained rebels spared
> By hunger, flames and internecine broils,
> And left a plain where ramparts once had stood.[1]

Before the end the Temple had been burned to the ground, a catastrophe which is annually commemorated on the Jewish fast-day of 9 Ab. The Jewish historian Josephus, who became the prisoner and then collaborator of the Romans, declared that Titus had done his utmost to prevent this disaster.

A runner brought the news to Titus as he was resting in his tent after the battle. He leapt up as he was and ran to the Sanctuary to extinguish the blaze. His whole staff panted after him, followed by the excited legions with all the yelling and confusion inseparable from the disorganized rush of an immense army.

Titus shouted and waved to the combatants to put out the fire. But his shouts were unheard as their ears were deafened with a greater din, and his hand signals went unheeded amidst the distractions of battle and bloodshed . . . As the soldiers neared the Sanctuary they pretended not even to hear Titus' commands and urged the men in front to throw in more firebrands.

Round the Altar the heap of corpses grew higher and higher, while down the Sanctuary steps poured a river of blood and the bodies of those killed at the top slithered to the bottom. The soldiers were like men possessed and there was no holding them, nor was there any arguing with the fire . . .

Yet the flames were not yet effecting an entry from any direction but were feeding on the chambers built round the Sanctuary. So, realizing that there was still time to save the glorious edifice, Titus dashed out and by personal efforts strove to persuade his men to put out the fire, instructing Liberalius, a centurion of his bodyguard of spearmen, to lay his staff across the shoulders of any who disobeyed. But their respect for Titus and their fears of the centurion's staff were powerless against their fury, their detestation of the Jews, and an uncontrollable lust for battle.

Most of them again were spurred on by the expectation of loot, being convinced that the interior was bursting with money and seeing that everything outside was of gold. But they were forestalled by one of those who had gone in. He, when Titus dashed out to restrain his men, pushed a firebrand into the hinges of the gate. Thus the Sanctuary in defiance of Titus' wishes was set on fire.[2]

Another writer, however, Sulpicius Severus, indicated that this account of Titus' role was entirely untrue, since, on the contrary, he deliberately played a leading part in the destruction of the Temple. Although Sulpicius did not write until the fifth century AD, the suspicion that his may be the truer version is confirmed by two further considerations. First, Josephus had been a determined propagandist for Titus, and would naturally have wished to defend him against this terrible accusation from the Jews. Secondly, Sulpicius may have

derived his information from an almost contemporary source, Tacitus'
Histories, of which the relevant portions are lost.

At all events Titus' destruction of Jerusalem, honoured by his Arch
and honorific inscriptions at Rome, reverberated right down the centuries. Although he himself did not by any means intend his obliteration
of Jerusalem as a favour to the Christians, whom, according to Sulpicius, he regarded as the pestilential offshoot of a pernicious stock,
Christian tradition lauded his destruction of the city as vengeance upon
the Jews for their slaying of Christ. Conversely, the writers of the
Hebrew Talmud believed that Titus' death at an early age was retribu-
tion from heaven. For not only had he captured Jerusalem, but he
behaved with extreme brutality to his hordes of Jewish prisoners.

While at Caesarea Maritima, he celebrated his brother Domitian's birthday in the grand style, reserving much of his vengeance on the Jews for this
notable occasion. The number of those who perished in combats with wild
beasts or in fighting each other or by being burnt alive exceeded 2,500. Yet
all this seemed to the Romans, though their victims were dying a thousand
different deaths, to be too light a penalty.

Titus next went on to Berytus (Beirut), a town in Phoenicia and a Roman
colony. Here he made a longer stay, celebrating his father's birthday with a
still more lavish display, both in the magnificence of the shows and in the
originality of the other costly entertainments. Vast numbers of prisoners
perished in the same way as before.[3]

Titus' capture of Jerusalem caused honours to be showered upon
him in the east. At Memphis, in Egypt, as part of a traditional ritual, he
allowed himself to be crowned with a diadem. For a short time, too,
eastern coinages issued in his name gave him the prefix of *imperator*, to
which only the emperor was entitled; and his legionaries, who greatly
admired him, were said to have hesitated initially whether to offer the
throne to his father or to himself.

Moreover, after Titus's success in Judaea, the senate voted him an
independent Triumph. But this was soon afterwards converted into a
joint Triumph with his father. For the situation had begun to get somewhat out of hand. Titus was conceited about the position he had won,
regarding himself as the decisive factor in the rise of the dynasty to
power, and showing little backwardness in parading this conviction.

But he still did not harbour the slightest intention of behaving
disloyally, and, when, early in 71, he began to see how dangerous

the gossip about his ambitions might become, he hastened back to Italy.

Titus sailed at once in a naval transport, touching at Rhegium [Reggio Calabria] and Puteoli [Pozzuoli]. Hurrying on to Rome, he exploded all the false rumours by greeting Vespasian, who had not been expecting him, with the simple words: 'Here I am, father, here I am.'[4]

From the very outset Vespasian piled honours upon Titus, displaying him as his deputy and indeed, apart from outward details of regalia, virtually as his colleague. Joint Triumph with the emperor, joint priesthood, joint consulship (from 70), joint tribunician power (from 71), joint censorship (73–4), all were his.

For his father, remembering the anarchic discontinuity of the Civil Wars, was determined that Titus should succeed him. Coins of 71 made this unprecedentedly clear when they described Titus by the appellation *designatus imperator*. In this context, '*imperator*' does not mean general but emperor: it declares unequivocally that Titus is destined for the throne. 'Either my son,' Vespasian was heard saying, 'shall be my successor, or no one at all.'

He was provoked into this assertion by the insolence of Helvidius Priscus, who subsequently died for his hostility to Vespasian's policy: and, as we have seen, the policy which angered Helvidius most of all may have been this wholly unambiguous dynastic intention. It was anathema to conservatives since it destroyed the last vestiges of hope that the senate could decide who the next emperor should be. There must also be doubts whether this open enhancement of Titus' position was welcome to Mucianus, upon whose position as Vespasian's chief collaborator it encroached. Indeed one of the reasons why Titus hastened home so rapidly in 71 may have been his desire to provide a counterblast to Mucianus' influence.

If so he succeeded in his aim, because Mucianus, although still prominent, found he could not compete with him. For one thing Vespasian now proceeded to appoint Titus as his praetorian prefect. The guard which he thus commanded was a new formation, since Vespasian had decided to get rid of the guardsmen of Vitellius, though he allowed some of them to join his own new praetorian force. It was diminished in size from his predecessor's swollen unit, reverting to the dimensions originally fixed by Augustus. However the prefecture was evidently regarded as even more important than before. From the very outset of his reign Vespasian had entrusted it not to knights as was habitual, but to senators; and indeed the man from whom Titus took over was himself a member of the imperial family by marriage – his own brother-in-law. Now the post had gone to the emperor's eldest son himself.

Moreover, Titus interpreted the security aspects of the job with severity or even harshness. 'For wherever any men had aroused his private suspicions very strongly, he first sent secret emissaries into the theatres and camps to demand their punishment as if by general consent, and then without scruple put them to death.'⁵ This made him unpopular with the civilian population. But the guardsmen and their officers were flattered by his appointment as prefect, since he was so manifestly the emperor's deputy and heir. And the legionaries, too, must have been pleased by Vespasian's clearly stated plans for the succession, not only for the usual reason that these guaranteed them the continuation of their salaries and rewards, but because Titus himself had gained their favour.

The only potential threat to his position was caused by his love-life. For he was deeply attached to the Jewish queen Julia Berenice, the daughter of King Agrippa I of Judaea, and sister and royal colleague of Agrippa II, who was ruler over regions of southern Syria and northern Palestine as a client-monarch dependent on Rome. In 66 Berenice had attempted, at first single-handed and then with the aid of Agrippa II, to prevent her co-religionists' revolt, weeping at its catastrophic consequences which she correctly foresaw. When, in the following year, Titus came to Judaea, they soon became lovers. He was in his twenty-eighth year, and she in her thirty-eighth, a wealthy, beautiful, politically capable woman with three marriages and at least three affairs behind her, as well as an incestuous relationship, if rumour could be believed, with her brother the king. Later Juvenal wrote of a present she received from him:

A ring, the diamond of Berenice,
Well-known in legend (which adds to the cost), the stone King Agrippa
Gave his incestuous sister in that barbarian country
Where, on the Sabbath day, the kings will go around barefoot,
Where the pigs are free to live to a ripe old age.⁶

Berenice also attracted the attention not only of Vespasian's son but of Vespasian himself. Her support, and her brother's, for his claim to the throne was very valuable and timely. For one thing her great wealth could be called upon by Vespasian; and besides, she was related by a former marriage to his leading adherent Tiberius Julius Alexander, the prefect of Egypt.

As for Titus, he had already been married twice in earlier years. But his first wife, the daughter of a praetorian prefect of Caligula, had died, and he divorced the second in about 64–5 soon after the birth of his only child Julia. He was also believed to have a sexual taste for male prostitutes and eunuchs. Now, however, he seemed in love with Berenice, and indeed according to gossip the abrupt conclusion of his western trip early in 69 was mainly caused, not by political considerations at all, but by his eagerness to be with her again.

When Vespasian's regime became established at Rome, Berenice did not lose her influence at court. In addition to her connexion with Alexander, who may have become joint praetorian prefect with Titus for a time, she probably enjoyed the encouragement of Vespasian's mistress Caenis, whose patroness Antonia had been a close friend of Berenice's father.

The Jewish queen no doubt expected that Titus, on returning to Rome in 71, would invite her to join him there immediately. But he did not, and she had to wait. This was conceivably because Mucianus did not favour her visit; and when she was finally invited to the city in 75, Mucianus may have been dead. Her brother Agrippa II was asked to the capital at the same time, and during the visit many compliments were lavished upon the royal pair for their loyal collaboration during the Jewish revolt. Agrippa was granted the insignia of a praetor, and Berenice was lodged in the imperial palace itself, where she lived openly with Titus. The historian Tacitus reassures us that 'practical efficiency never suffered from the attraction he felt for her'. Nevertheless the unusual arrangement caused a good deal of criticism, which resulted in severe retaliatory measures, described by Dio Cassius:

Berenice expected to marry Titus, and was already behaving in every respect as if she were his wife.

But when he perceived that the Romans were displeased with the situation, he sent her away.

For, in addition to all the other talk that there was, certain sophists of the

Cynic school managed somehow to slip into the city at this time, too. First Diogenes, entering the theatre when it was full, denounced the pair in a long, abusive speech, for which he was flogged. And after him Heras, expecting no harsher punishment, gave vent to many senseless yelpings in true Cynic fashion, and for this was beheaded.[7]

But how soon Titus 'sent her away' on this first occasion, we cannot tell: perhaps she remained as his mistress in Rome for several years before this happened. Meanwhile the hostility aroused by their association was undoubtedly more formidable than Dio suggests. The historian chooses to refer to attacks by off-beat anti-establishment 'philosophers', but these men were probably prompted to make their abusive remarks by some of the Roman senators who held similar views. For the ruling class was totally unwilling to tolerate an emperor, or an emperor's heir, who associated with an oriental queen. When Antony lived with Cleopatra, their liaison had given their enemy Octavian, the future Augustus, the strongest weapon in his propaganda armoury, and he found it easy to stir up a storm of hate against them. It was very much the same situation now, and Theodor Mommsen was justified as describing Berenice as a 'Cleopatra in little'.

However, in one respect she was even less acceptable than Cleopatra. For if the Romans disliked the Greeks, the Jewish faith was far more alien from their own classical background; and they had just had to suppress a terrible revolt among the Jews. It was true that Berenice had collaborated with them, against her own co-religionists. Nevertheless the rebellion had filled the Romans with bitter feelings against the whole Jewish race. Very many of their leading men must have dreaded a union between Titus and Berenice; and its prospect spread considerable doubts about his suitability as successor to the throne.

The leader of the movement against Berenice may have been one of the emperor's principal counsellors, Titus Clodius Eprius Marcellus. Born of humble parentage at Capua in Campania, and elevated to the consulship, Marcellus was a blustering, fanatical prosecutor who had had become one of the accusers of the Republican-minded Thrasea, a service for which Nero had presented him with an enormous reward. Nevertheless Marcellus, who remarked he was perfectly ready to work for any emperor at all, whoever he might be, subsequently became an adherent of Vespasian's government, and entered into fierce controversies with its critic Helvidius Priscus, whose ruin he no doubt helped to bring about. Honoured with a second consulship in 73, Marcellus was promoted by Mucianus' death to a dominant position among the emperor's friends.

But he clashed seriously with Titus, who in the very last year of his father's reign used his powers as praetorian prefect to strike him down. With Marcellus fell Caecina, the general who had deserted from Vitellius ten years earlier. At that time he had been graciously received by Vespasian; and he became sufficiently intimate with Titus to be seen, in the Flavians' Sabine homeland, fighting a friendly gladiatorial duel against the prince. But now Titus put an end to him. According to Suetonius:

He invited Caecina to dinner and then ordered him to be stabbed almost before he left the dining room. He was induced to do this by a pressing danger, having got possession of an autograph copy of a harangue which Caecina had prepared to deliver to the soldiers.[8]

And Dio Cassius, too, believed that Titus had him killed 'in order to forestall an act of revolution that very night: for Caecina had already got many of the soldiers in readiness'. Moreover Eprius Marcellus, too, was denounced for involvement in the conspiracy. He was brought to trial in the senate and condemned, whereupon he cut his throat with a razor.

The plot seems to have been a genuine one, but its circumstances remain obscure. A later writer maintained that Titus had Caecina killed because he suspected him of being Berenice's lover. Certainly the controversy about Berenice may well, in some way or other, have had something to do with the supposed plot. Perhaps, however, Caecina was not a lover of Berenice at all, but her enemy – and Marcellus is likely to have been her enemy as well. It is possible that she had still not left Rome when the two men met their fates, and that it was this serious indication of her unpopularity which impelled Titus to send her back to the east.

But whether or not the position of Berenice was one of the issues at stake, the principal motive behind the plot was probably something different – namely the reluctance of the two men to accept that Titus had to be the ageing Vespasian's successor. For if a family as humble as the Flavians had gained the throne, why should the families of Marcellus or Caecina not try their hand at repeating the same success on their own account?

Nevertheless the death of Vespasian on 23 June 79 left Titus as his unchallenged successor. This eleventh of the twelve Caesars, strangely enough, became the first of them who had ever succeeded his own father: moreover it was not to happen again for more than another hundred years.

The emperor Hadrian later believed Vespasian was killed by Titus, who had long been disloyal to him. Such rumours about the deaths of rulers never failed to appear. Yet it is surprising that a successor on the same imperial throne should have adopted such an improbable view, which even Hadrian's own secretary Suetonius, in spite of all his addiction to gossip, did not consider worth mentioning.

The new emperor displayed an impressive charm.

Though not tall, he was both graceful and dignified, both muscular and handsome, except for a certain paunchiness.

He had a phenomenal memory, and displayed a natural aptitude alike for the arts of war and peace; handled arms and rode a horse as well as any man living; could compose speeches and verses in Greek or Latin with equal ease, and actually extemporized them on occasion. He was something of a musician too: sang pleasantly, and had mastered the harp.

It often amused him to compete with his secretaries at shorthand dictation, or so I have heard; and he claimed that he could imitate any handwriting in existence and might, in different circumstances, have been the most celebrated forger of all time.[9]

In spite of his talents, however, Titus came to the throne with an unfortunate reputation. People did not like the severity with which he had carried out the duties of praetorian prefect, and his recent suppression of Eprius Marcellus and Caecina had left an unpleasant taste. Besides, Titus was considered extravagant and greedy, as might be expected from one who spent his youth at Nero's court; and his association with Berenice had provoked widespread alarm.

However he seemed peculiarly well aware that his elevation to the throne made it imperative for him to present an entirely different image. To dispel the picture of himself as a harsh organizer of repression, he took unprecedentedly strong measures against informers, refusing to recognize the charge of high treason; and when two patricians came under suspicion of plotting against his life, he refrained from taking retaliatory action.

He also rapidly disillusioned Berenice, in whom his accession had aroused renewed hopes. Immediately after he ascended the throne, she came to Rome once again, believing that he would make her his empress.

> And, if I can believe his friends' reports
> If I believe his oft-repeated vows,
> He'll over all these states crown Berenice,
> And to these titles add an empress' name.
> He will come here himself to tell me so.[10]

But Racine, whose verses those are, was right to point out that he had produced his *Bérénice* out of almost nothing at all. For this marvellous play, like the contemporary *Titus et Bérénice* of Corneille, was constructed out of a brief seven-word sentence of Suetonius, and nothing more: '*Berenicen statim ab urbe dimisit invitus invitam.*' Philemon Holland felt he needed twenty-five words to reproduce the succinct Latin: 'As for Queen Berenice, he sent her quickly away from the city of Rome, but full loath they were both of them to part asunder.'

It was the end of all Berenice's ambitions.

> Mine ears are stopt. For evermore Farewell!
> For evermore. My Lord, cans't thou not feel?
> To one who loves, the fearful word's like steel.
> A month gone by, a year; how anguished we,
> When we're disparted by the sundering sea.
> Come, dayspring, come: thou, night, thy shades restore:
> Titus shall ne'er see Berenice more.[11]

Moreover, as Suetonius declared, it was a deeply painful parting for Titus as well as Berenice. But if he had married an eastern queen, his chances of harmonious relations with the Roman governing class would never have stood the shock, and his throne and his life could barely have been preserved. How long Berenice lived on, we do not know. But her epitaph is well pronounced by Stewart Perowne: 'Only Berenice can claim the quadruple tiara of the Bible, the Palatine, the Salle Richelieu and Covent Garden.'

Her dismissal prompted Tacitus to observe that 'Titus led a life of pleasure in his youth, and proved more self-disciplined in his own reign than in his father's'. However in one respect he showed less restraint, and this was quite deliberate. For he was particularly eager that the criticisms of meanness directed against Vespasian's regime should now cease. In consequence he cultivated the traditional monarchic virtue of generosity and munificence.

When the stewards of his household reminded him that he was promising more than he could perform, he replied, 'None should ever go away sad at heart from an interview with his emperor.'
Further, when on one occasion he recalled at dinner that he had bestowed nothing on anyone during the entire day, he gave utterance to that memorable and justly praised saying: 'Friends, I have lost a day!'[12]

> 'I've lost a day!' The prince who nobly cried,
> Had been an emperor without his crown.[13]

Combining, therefore, personal largess with lavish public expenditure, he did everything he could to aid the surviving victims of the two great disasters which disfigured his short reign, the destruction of Pompeii and Herculaneum by Mount Vesuvius in 79, and a plague and fire in the capital in 80. During June of the same year the completion of the Colosseum begun by Vespasian, and of the Baths which were named after himself, was celebrated by magnificent gladiatorial games. Titus was not, it is true, unlimitedly extravagant, since he followed some of his father's economical practices, notably the reclamation of land illegally occupied by squatters. But the simultaneous profusion of popularity-seeking measures makes it hard to agree with Dio Cassius' conclusion that his government could be described as frugal.

Dio also records that on the last day of the spectacles for the Colosseum and the Baths Titus broke down and wept in public. Were his tears, perhaps, prompted by the knowledge that he had an incurable disease? Such a conclusion would also account for the historian's further statement that, although he lived on for another fifteen months, he 'did nothing more of importance'.
Then, in autumn 81, his health took a fatal turn, at the same Sabine watering-place that had witnessed his father's death.

At the very first station on the road he got a fever, and as he was being taken away in a litter, it is said that he drew back the curtains and looked to heaven, complaining bitterly that his life was being snatched away from him quite undeservedly; for there was no action of his which he had reason to be sorry for, except one, and one only.[14]

A later poet, Ausonius, declared 'we believe no one speaking thus of you – not even yourself.'[15] Yet Titus evidently had something on his mind. Almost every event of his career has been ransacked to try to find what it was. Most probably his expression of sorrow relates in some way or other to the greatest of his embarrassments: his bad relations with his younger brother Domitian, to whom he had allotted proper honours as his evident heir, but no real share in his power. Some thought, for example – and they included Domitian himself – that Titus' conscience was pricking him because he had suppressed his father's intention that his two sons should succeed him jointly after his death. Dio Cassius, however, favoured those who believed Titus felt sorry because he had failed to kill Domitian, whose imminent succession he regarded as a disaster; and this may be the right answer.

And so, on 13 September, Titus died.

As usual there were rumours that he had been murdered: Domitian was said to have given him a poisoned fish. Certainly his brother was glad of his death, but the story that he brought it about can be discounted, like many other stories hostile to Domitian. According to Plutarch, the immediate cause of Titus' death was the excessive coldness of the waters at Aquae Cutiliae. Although it seems strange that both father and son should have shared this fatal over-confidence in their native spa, this may well – whether he had a fatal disease or not – be the true explanation. It was also the diagnosis, according to Plutarch, of the people who were looking after him at the time.

Titus was in his forty-second year when he died, and he had ruled for only two years and two months. Suetonius deplored his death, declaring him the 'delight and darling of the human race'. But the problem of his reign was more convincingly summed up by Dio.

It is maintained that Augustus would never have been loved had he lived a shorter time, nor Titus had he lived longer. For Augustus, though at the outset he showed himself rather harsh because of the wars and the factional strife, was later able, in the course of time, to achieve a brilliant reputation for his kindly deeds. Titus, on the other hand, ruled with mildness and died at the height of his glory, whereas if he had lived a long time, it might have been shown that he owes his present fame more to good fortune than to merit.[16]

There is good reason for his hesitancy, since even Nero would have left a name as a first-class ruler if he had died only two years after his accession. Moreover, the high praise of Titus in the ancient tradition is all too often attributable to an over-schematic, diametrical, contrast with the abhorred Domitian. And is there not something corny about that saying which Suetonius found so laudable: 'Friends, I have lost a day'?

Perhaps the verdict of Ausonius is the appropriate one. For the poet, despite his disbelief that Titus had anything on his conscience, nevertheless felt it right to conclude that he was 'happy in the brevity of his reign'.

I2

Domitian

Titus Flavius Domitianus, son of Vespasian and younger brother of Titus, was born at Rome in October AD 51. On 18 December 69, during the Civil War between Vitellians and Flavians, he took refuge on the Capitol with his uncle Sabinus, escaping into hiding when their defences were stormed by Vitellian troops and Sabinus was killed.

On Vitellius' death two days later, Domitian was saluted as Caesar, but his temporary position as the titular head of affairs, while Mucianus directed the government on Vespasian's behalf, came to an abrupt end in October of the following year, when Vespasian himself arrived in the capital. Thereafter, although his father and then Titus gave Domitian a number of honours, he was allowed no useful employment.

When he came to the throne in 81, Domitian followed a meticulously thought-out policy of systematic absolutism – in contrast to the ostensible Republicanism of the old Augustan monarchy. As time went on, and particularly after his adoption of the title 'perpetual censor', this tendency seriously dismayed the senate.

As a counterblast, and in order to satisfy his ambitions, he realized that he must be popular with the army and achieve martial glory. However, after a successful extension of the German territories of the empire (83), the imperial generals suffered two grave defeats in Dacia (Rumania) before the situation on that front could be rectified.

In 89 Antonius Saturninus, governor of Upper Germany, rose in revolt, and his

240

rebellion, which was fiercely suppressed, greatly increased the emperor's suspicions of the senators. Leading figures of philosophical, Stoic inclinations were among the considerable number of personages who suffered under revived treason procedures, and as Domitian, with good reason, became increasingly fearful of plots, his last three years (93–6) spread terror among the senatorial class.

The legionaries continued to support Domitian strongly. However he alienated his praetorian prefects, who eventually joined his wife Domitia and palace officials in the conspiracy which struck the forty-five-year-old emperor down on 18 September 96.

Nerva, who was declared his successor on the very same day, must have been privy to the plot. But it caused such great anger in the army, and particularly among the praetorian guard, that he was compelled in the following year to allow Domitian's assassins to be executed. Immediately afterwards, to save his throne, he adopted a son and heir from outside his own family, the eminent and popular military man Trajan, who duly succeeded him when he died in 98.

Domitian's early years had not been happy. When he was a boy, there was no money to spend on his education or comforts, whereas his elder brother Titus, growing up when the family was more prosperous, had enjoyed a luxurious youth. At some point during this period, too, their mother Domitilla died.

It was a memorable change when, at the age of eighteen, after a narrow escape from death in the burning Capitol Domitian found himself presented to the praetorians as Caesar at the instigation of Mucianus, who installed him in the palace as visible representative of his father, the newly recognized emperor. Moreover, it was the name, not of Mucianus, but of the young Domitian which stood at the head of official edicts and letters. After he became emperor, Domitian ensured that his adventures of that time should be celebrated by relief sculptures and court poetry. 'Although,' declared Martial, 'alone he already held the reins of Julian power, he gave them up, and in a world that had been his own remained but the third – after both Vespasian and Titus.'

Yet in those early months of Vespasian's reign, until the emperor himself arrived from the east, the real power had largely rested with Mucianus. And even if he exercised his famous diplomacy as best he could, causes of friction with Domitian soon arose. For example, the young prince wanted to give a staff appointment to Primus, the victor of the Second Battle of Bedriacum, but the jealous Mucianus refused to allow this. He also removed the first praetorian prefect of Vespasian's reign, Arrius Varus, because Varus seemed too close to Domitian – though he replaced him by another of the youth's friends. Domitian was also determined to go and head the German legions against the rebel Civilis. He moved northwards with Mucianus: but when they reached Lugdunum (Lyon), Domitian apparently made contact with the Rhine headquarters, and urged its commander Cerialis to transfer his army to himself. Cerialis returned an evasive answer; and Domitian got no farther north than Lugdunum. Yet people's tongues were now wagging about his possible aims. 'He may', concludes Tacitus, 'have been toying with the idea of fighting his father, or it may have been a manoeuvre to gain support and advantage against his brother.' Rebellion against his father is unlikely to have entered Domitian's mind. Yet he was jealous of Titus, and would have welcomed some victories of his own to set against his brother's Jewish triumph. Ugly stories about his ambitions had reached Vespasian in the east, and Titus himself intervened to assure his father that there was nothing in these tales.

During the rest of Vespasian's reign Domitian shared in the outward privileges of the regime, receiving, for example, conspicuous attention on the imperial coinage: for since Titus had no son it was understood, even if not officially stated, that brother would eventually succeed to brother. Nevertheless Domitian was Vespasian's fellow-consul only once, whereas Titus received that honour on no less than six occasions. Worst of all, Domitian was given no position of influence or authority, and never allowed by his father to go campaigning.

In consequence he took to literary activities instead, writing poems about the siege of the Capitol and the Jewish revolt, and reciting his compositions at public gatherings. Pliny the elder implies that, although Titus was a poet as well, Domitian was the more accomplished versifier of the two.

Tacitus' comment, like everything else he had to say about Domitian, is disagreeable:

He realized that his elders despised his youthfulness, and ceased to discharge even the slight official duties he had previously undertaken. Assuming an ingenuous air of abstraction and looking as if butter would not melt in his mouth, he posed as a connoisseur of literature and poetry. What he was after was to hide his real character and avoid competing with his brother, whose gentler nature, quite unlike his own, he totally misconstrued.[1]

242

Certainly Domitian was compelled to make the best of a bad job, and had to avoid appearing to compete with his brother. But his relegation to unemployment for so many years, after the sudden emancipation in 69–70 from his dismal upbringing, meant that he was seething with disappointed ambition. Under Titus matters did not improve, and in spite of continued honorific awards Domitian still was not officially designated as successor. His suspicions that Vespasian had meant to leave him co-emperor, but that Titus, a handwriting expert, had cut this provision out of his father's will, were probably unfounded. However Titus, who knew his brother would one day follow him on the throne and was distressed by their unfriendly relations, should have given him more experience of government.

Although Domitian was said, not very plausibly, to have helped Titus out of this life – perhaps partly because he forbade memorial games on his late brother's birthdays – he duly arranged his deification and celebrated it on coinage. It was essential to enhance the dignity of the Flavian house. For not only did Domitian himself lack the prestige of his father and brother, since he had been given so little chance to win distinction, but the prestige of Vespasian and Titus, too, could not be compared with the veneration which had overflowed from Augustus to his Julio–Claudian successors. This was evidently a source of worry to the court's epic poet Valerius Flaccus, who bravely asserted that the Flavian dynasty was superior to the Julians.

Even Pliny the younger, who detested Domitian's memory, had to concede that he had been a fine looking man. As always Suetonius adds curious details.

> He was tall of stature, with a modest expression and a high colour. His eyes were large, but his sight was somewhat dim. He was handsome and graceful, too, especially when a young man, and indeed in his whole body with the exception of his feet, the toes of which were somewhat cramped. In later life he had the further disfigurements of baldness, a protruding belly, and spindle legs, though the latter had become thin from a long illness.[2]

Domitian wrote a book *On Care of the Hair*, but his knowledge of the subject evidently did not do much to remedy his own lack of it. Moreover he was so sensitive about this condition that if he heard anyone else being mocked for being bald he took it as a personal affront. Or so we are told, but since Martial, who flattered him abysmally, nevertheless makes a good deal of fun of men who are bald, Domitian can scarcely have been so touchy on the subject as all that. The exact nature of the trouble with his feet cannot be identified; perhaps he suffered from a claw-like curvature of the big toes. The strong colour noted by the biographer is described by Tacitus as a marked tendency to blush, which the ancients regarded as a sign of good breeding, especially in the young.

Domitian's politically influential wife, Domitia, daughter of the great Neronian general Corbulo, was made Augusta, but subsequently dismissed, and then brought back again; whereupon she had to share the emperor's affections with his niece Julia, the daughter of Titus, of whom he was very fond – although he was said to have caused her death by an abortion.

Domitian was extremely over-sexed, describing his continual copulations as 'bed-wrestling'. He was said to enjoy bathing with prostitutes, and his many adulteries were contrasted with the strict legislation he initiated against loose morals in others. The same contradiction between his private practice and public professions occurred in his affection for eunuchs, since this perversion, shared by Titus, did not prevent him from declaring castration illegal. Domitian was credited with other eccentric tastes, too, such as the depilation of his mistresses with his own hands. He was also very much addicted to watching gladiatorial fights between women and dwarfs – and he enjoyed pulling the wings off flies and seeing them suffer.

Although not, people said, outstandingly hardworking, he was the possessor of a clear, chill intellect. He displayed a strong tendency towards theoretical rigidity, and a liking for austere legal correctness. In 83 he sentenced three Vestal Virgins to the traditional penalty of execution for immorality, and in 90, according to another antique custom, the Chief Vestal, Cornelia, condemned to death for a similar offence, was buried alive in an underground chamber while her lovers were beaten to death with rods. Grim official savageries of such a kind seemed curiously discordant with Domitian's alleged aversion to bloodshed, which was so emphatic at the beginning of his reign that he even planned to forbid the sacrifice of oxen.

But the punishment of the Vestals harmonized with his reverence for the ancient Roman religion, which caused him to celebrate age-old rituals with great pomp. He showed a deep and almost obsessive veneration for the early Italian goddess Minerva – a divinity particularly esteemed in his own Sabine country. It was she, presented in four different guises, who formed the main theme of Domitian's coinage, and whose temple was to be the centre-piece of the new Forum he started to build.* Yet Domitian also used this very Italian goddess, who was identified with Pallas Athene, as the patron of his own profound admiration for Greek culture, inviting large audiences to his villa on the site of Alba Longa (Castel Gandolfo) to witness not only Roman wild beast shows, but plays and oratorical and poetic contests in the Greek style. These and other Hellenizing entertainments, repeated in the provinces, were condemned by conservatives as corrupting influences, like the similar Games formerly given by Nero. The coexistence in Domitian's character of phil-Hellenism and devotion to Roman tradition may point also to yet another and more deep-seated contradiction in his personality. For this cultural passion existed in the heart of a man whose early education, arranged by a father who was as impoverished as he was uncultured, had been scrappy. When Domitian became emperor, this was yet another of the frustrations he had to work out of his system.

Unlike Nero he never allowed his literary and artistic ambitions to go to his head. As Mommsen observed, Domitian was one of the best administrators who had ever governed the empire – firm, far-sighted and meticulous. 'He took such care', declared Suetonius, 'to exercise restraint over the city officials and the governors of the provinces that at no time were they more honest or just.' He relied extensively on his council, upon which senators and knights were equally represented. At first there were few changes among his principal advisers, who remained the same men who had served Titus and Vespasian. Prominent among them was Quintus Vibius Crispus, who had rivalled Eprius Marcellus in the last years of Vespasian's rule but, unlike him, possessed the bland tact necessary for survival.

Next came the aged, genial Crispus,
Whose manners – like his morals – were mild and pliable.

* The Forum Transitorium, later known as the Forum of Nerva.

No one could better have served to advise a monarch with absolute sway
Over seas and lands and nations – if only he had been free,
Under that scourge, that plague, to tender honest counsel,
Speak out against cruelty. But what could be more capricious
Than a tyrant's ear, when the fate of his so-called friends and advisers
Hung on his word? Best play safe, stick to the weather –
How rainy or hot it's been, how spring showers are here again.
So Crispus never struck out against the current, never
Uttered his private opinions, or staked his life on the truth;
And so he survived many winters, to reach his eightieth year,
Safeguarded, even in *that* Court, by such defensive techniques.[3]

Subsequently Domitian did not rely very much on advisers at all – as befitted a man who was said to feel genuine affection for no one, with the exception of a few women.

He developed an extensive programme of buildings and other public works, including not only the commencement of his new Forum but the completion of the restored Temple of Capitoline Jupiter. He also constructed, beside earlier imperial residences, a grandiose palace on the Palatine hill, which suited his exalted concept of an emperor's importance. He gave exceptionally lavish public shows, and distributed considerable gifts to the city populace.

These munificent projects meant that government expenditure was very large. In consequence Domitian had to be vigilant in the collection of official revenue, and there were many stories of his extortions.

Any charge, however slight – to have spoken or acted in prejudice of the emperor's welfare was enough – might result in the confiscation of a man's property, even if he were already dead. An unsupported claim that someone had been heard, before his death, to name the emperor as his heir, even though he were unknown at court, was sufficient pretext for taking over the estate.

Domitian's agents collected the tax on Jews with a peculiar lack of mercy; and took proceedings not only against those who kept their Jewish origins a secret in order to avoid the tax, but against those who lived as Jews without professing Judaism. As a boy, I remember once attending a crowded Court where a magistrate had a ninety-year-old man stripped to establish whether or not he had been circumcised.[4]

Some of these reports need to be discounted; for example, he may not have been any more stringent in his enforcement of the tax on Jews, the *fiscus Judaicus*, than Vespasian who had introduced it after the Jewish revolt. But since Vespasian's posthumous reputation was much the more favourable of the two it is round his son that such hostile tales tended to gather.

Quick to anger but treacherous and secretive, Domitian displayed a scowling vigilance that inspired terror, especially among highly educated persons whom his own lack of formal education caused him to resent. His social manners did little to allay these fears. Pliny the younger shows him eating heavily and alone before mid-day, and then sitting, satiated, among his dinner-guests as a spectator, while the dishes were thrown down casually in front of them.

They also had to suffer from his unpleasant sense of humour.

On one occasion, he entertained the foremost men among the senators and knights in the following fashion. He prepared a room that was pitch black on every side, ceiling, walls and floor, and made ready bare couches of the same colour resting on the uncovered floor. Then he invited his guests alone at night without their attendants.

And first he set beside each of them a slab shaped like a gravestone, bearing the guest's name and also a small lamp, such as hangs in tombs. Next comely naked boys, likewise painted black, entered like phantoms, and after encircling the guests in an awe-inspiring dance took up their stations at their feet. After this, all the things that are commonly offered at the sacrifices to departed spirits were likewise set before the guests, all of them black and in dishes of a similar colour.[5]

Meanwhile, Domitian discoursed to his silent guests on topics relating to death and slaughter. But when they returned, petrified with terror, to their homes, an imperial messenger soon arrived bringing, not the expected order to die, but costly gifts, including the boy who had served them, 'now washed and adorned'.

Nevertheless Domitian did not spend all his time on macabre practical jokes. Above all he intended to be a triumphant military emperor. His wife was the daughter of the greatest general of his age, and nothing would enhance his own prestige better than the martial success which his father and brother had conspired to deny him. Moreover, appreciating as well as anyone an emperor's dependence on the army, he drew the logical conclusion, by spending more time with the troops than any emperor ever had before. He also raised the soldiers' pay. It was their first rise since Augustus; and it made yet another heavy demand on the national exchequer.

The operations he personally conducted in Germany in AD 83 completed his father's conquest of the Agri Decumates, the territory between the upper Danube and the upper Rhine inhabited by the powerful tribe of the Chatti. The transports of delight displayed by grovelling poets were not as wholly without justification as later historians declared.

> Crete gave the mighty name Metellus bore,
> Scipio a mightier gained on Afric shore,
> But yet more grand the name from conquered Rhine
> That, when a child, Germania made thine.
> Thy sire and brother won the Jewish crown.
> The wreath the Chatti send is all thine own.[6]

Meanwhile Gnaeus Julius Agricola, who had been governor of Britain since the last year of Vespasian, continued his campaigns into Caledonia (Scotland) for several seasons until 84. Agricola's daughter was married to Tacitus, who loyally declared, in his eulogistic biography of his father-in-law, that Domitian had recalled him prematurely, withholding proper appreciation of his achievements from motives of personal jealousy.

The news of these events, although reported by Agricola in his dispatches in the most exact and modest terms, was received by Domitian with the smile on his face that so often masked a secret disquiet. He was bitterly aware of the ridicule that had greeted his sham triumph over Germany, when he had bought up slaves to have their dress and hair made up to look like prisoners of war. But now came a genuine victory on the grand scale. The enemy dead were reckoned by thousands. The popular enthusiasm was immense.

There was nothing Domitian need fear so much as to have the name of a subject exalted above that of his prince. He had only wasted time in silencing forensic eloquence and all that was distinguished in the civil career, if another man were to snatch his military glory. Talents in other directions could at a pinch be ignored; but the quality of a good general should be the monopoly of the emperor. Such were the anxieties that vexed him and over which he brooded till he was tired – a sure sign in him of deadly purpose. Finally, he decided to store up his hatred for the present and wait for the first burst of popular applause and the enthusiasm of the army to die down. Agricola, you see, was still in possession of Britain.[7]

Yet Agricola does not seem to have been treated unfairly by Domitian,

THE ROMAN EMPIRE
IN A.D. 96

who retained him in his British command for longer than the average duration. In spite of a victory at the unidentifiable 'mons Graupius' (perhaps not far from Inverness), his endeavours had not resulted, and did not seem likely to result, in any permanent annexations beyond Titus' Forth-Clyde line.

Domitian's next target, Dacia – extending eastwards from the Transylvanian plateau – was a tougher proposition. Unified under their monarch Decebalus, the warriors of this important state inflicted resounding defeats upon two Roman armies (85–7) before one of Domitian's generals steadied the situation by a victory at Tapae, not far from the Iron Gates (88). Nevertheless the planned knock-out blow by the Romans never materialized, since at this stage a grave threat from the Germans beyond the middle Danube, farther to the west, engaged their attention instead.

Meanwhile the emperor, after handing out bonuses to his troops, returned to Rome. Very soon, however, he received the same sort of news that had so greatly dismayed Caligula and Claudius in turn, and had subsequently brought Nero and Otho down – a report of sedition in a legionary garrison. As had been feared in AD 39, and in 69 had disastrously occurred, it was one of the commanders of the great German armies who had raised the standard of revolt.

He was Lucius Antonius Saturninus, the governor of Upper Germany. His motives for his rebellion were partly personal, for he was a homosexual who went in fear of the emperor's puritanical disapproval. Yet he was also, surely, in touch with other disaffected governors and senators.

By seizing the savings banks of the two legions at Moguntiacum (Mainz), Saturninus virtually compelled his legionaries to hail him as emperor. However Domitian moved into action with lightning speed. After ordering the single Spanish legion, under the command of the future emperor Trajan, to make for the Rhineland, he himself immediately left Rome and hastened to the scene of the rising. Saturninus had proclaimed himself on 1 January 89. By 12 January Domitian was on his way to suppress him. And already on the twenty-fifth of the same month the Arval Brethren at Rome were celebrating the collapse of the revolt.

For Saturninus' plans had gone wrong. Germans who intended to cross the frozen Rhine and reinforce him were obliged to abandon their plan, because the river suddenly thawed; and the governor of Lower Germany, Lappius Maximus Norbanus, instead of supporting the rebels, had led his legions against them. Saturninus was overwhelmed, and lost his life.

When Domitian arrived he punished the disloyal officers mercilessly. He also tried to secure the archives of the rebel headquarters, in order to see what other leading men had been involved. But Lappius Maximus had deliberately destroyed all these documents. That was taking a great risk with a man of Domitian's temper, but presumably Lappius calculated, rightly, that he himself, after his striking victory, was immune from punitive measures. Yet his destruction of the files further upset the emperor's peace of mind, since it left a lingering suspicion that there had been important accomplices in the revolt.

For it was already painfully clear to the Roman governing class that Domitian felt less concern than any of his predecessors with the establishment of any sort of meaningful dialogue with the senators, other than those who served him faithfully as officers of the army. His father Vespasian had shown absolutist tendencies, but Domitian strongly accentuated them, regarding it as inessential to maintain even an ostensible partnership with the senate. It was true that he worked hard to protect the dignity of the senatorial class, as part of a set policy of upholding the status of the different traditional Orders of the hierarchical Roman state. But his willingness to discuss administrative matters with his council was counterbalanced by a refusal to consult the senate itself, which he only addressed in the most perfunctory fashion and habitually compelled to vote in accordance with his wishes, without even attempting to conceal his intention to exercise total domination.

This purpose was further displayed by his adoption, in 85, of the unprecedented title Perpetual Censor, which henceforward appeared prominently on his coinage. Earlier emperors, too, had exercised occasional censorial powers in order to introduce new senators and expel old ones; and Claudius and Vespasian had held the censorship itself for limited periods. But Domitian's assumption of the office in perpetuity was an unequivocal pronouncement that he intended to control the senate, and its composition, for as long as he lived: and he very soon showed that he meant exactly what he said.

His policies were coldly and logically thought out. Every previous emperor, too, had, in the last resort, ruled entirely by force. But Domitian felt that the time had come to drop all their more or less threadbare assurances to the contrary: and so he deliberately presented himself as the autocrat he was determined to be. Up to a point Caligula had acted in the same way, but Caligula, although attracted towards oriental monarchy, was an eccentric who had not displayed great perseverance in going after his aims. Domitian intended to be far more systematic. Moreover, despite his strong personal interest in Greek culture, and a new willingness to have his divinity on earth quite openly indicated – like the divinity of Hellenistic kings – he intended, nevertheless, to exercise these monarchic powers through purely Roman forms.

This tendency towards absolutism was accentuated by the revolt of Saturninus, which violently stimulated his natural bent towards harshness. The first result of the rebellion was the reintroduction of treason trials. It was evidently not fortuitous that the memoirs of Tiberius were Domitian's favourite reading. For both emperors alike had been driven to treason trials by senatorial hostility. But the circumstances were different, since Domitian, unlike Tiberius, had openly provoked this hostility by his calculated progress towards autocratic rule.

The revival of treason trials meant the revival of informers. The emperor did not propose, however, to make their lives any easier than those of other members of the upper class.

So disloyal was he even to those who showed him some favour or helped him in his most revolting crimes that, whenever persons provided him with large sums of money or lodged false information against large numbers of people, he was sure to destroy them, being especially careful to do so in the case of slaves who had given information against their masters.

Accordingly, such persons, though they received money and honours and offices in which they were his colleagues, lived in no greater honour and security than other men. On the contrary, the very offences to which they had been urged by Domitian were commonly made the pretext for their destruction, his object being that they alone should appear to have been the authors of the wrongdoing.

It was with this same purpose that he once issued a proclamation to the effect that, when an emperor fails to punish informers, he himself becomes responsible for their being informers.[8]

Yet this severity provided little or no consolation to their enemies in the governing class, who experienced increasingly drastic treatment. When a senator fell the properties of the victim were promptly confiscated; yet the motive for the persecutions was not so much the emperor's greed, to which people ascribed them, as his suspicion.

A drive against possibly subversive free-thinking philosophers was undertaken as early as 89. But it was during the last three years of the reign, to the accompaniment of every sort of security measure, that the senate was reduced to abject terror by tougher treatment than it had ever received from any previous emperor. While Domitian barricaded himself in his strongly defended Alban palace, executions of prominent men in the capital multiplied as never before. Among the victims was Helvidius Priscus the younger, the son of Vespasian's victim of the same name. His alleged crime was to have composed a satire on the emperor's matrimonial affairs. Yet he may also have been involved in a genuine plot, because Domitian did not strike entirely at random.

His childlessness increased his fear that someone would attempt to supplant him. In AD 95 the purges were still further intensified. One of the casualties was his own cousin Clemens, whose young sons had until now been Domitian's destined heirs: from now on nothing more was heard of them. But the emperor's most fatal move, which had already brought down both Caligula and Nero, was to lose the sympathy of his own joint praetorian prefects – whom he prosecuted and eliminated. Their successors, Petronius Secundus and Norbanus, found it easy to deduce that their position, too, was very far from safe. In consequence, with the connivance of the empress and an imperial chamberlain and secretary, they enlisted a freedman, Stephanus, who, while handing Domitian a document, succeeded in stabbing him in the groin. 'He grappled with his assailant and bore him to the ground, where they struggled for a long time, the emperor trying now to wrest the dagger from Stephanus' hands, and now to gouge out his eyes with his lacerated fingers.' Another conspirator rushed in, and Domitian was finally overpowered and killed; though Stephanus, too, did not survive, since men who had come belatedly to his victim's help made a concerted rush at him and stabbed him to death.

Senators such as Tacitus and Pliny who lived through Domitian's last years worked off their pent up feelings afterwards by attacking his memory. Indeed they attacked it with all the more vigour since they themselves had held high office during his reign; for complicity in his ferocious repressions had given them a guilty conscience. And Tacitus very fully appreciated his dilemma. For, although he loathed imperial tyranny, and knew that martyrs like Helvidius Priscus were courageous, he did not feel all the same, that this sort of prickly obstruction was the answer. Instead he praised men like his father-in-law Agricola, who had obediently gone on doing their jobs, even under the tyrannical Domitian. For that was just what he himself had done – and so had Trajan, the emperor under whom he was writing.

Domitian, as such authors fail to inform us, never ceased to be very popular with the army. Moreover the government of his empire as a whole still continued to be excellent – tales of imperial freedmen and favourites running amok are little more than fabrications.

Nevertheless he was a perfect text for one of Tacitus' main theories: that emperors generally deteriorated. For, in spite of all the merits of his administration, his relations with the senate and governing class unmistakably took a series of turns for the worse as time went on. The decisive dates were AD 89, when the revolt of Antonius Saturninus brought it home to the emperor how much the senators hated him, and 93, when their repression at his hands reached unprecedented heights of severity. Yet his basic attitude which had caused them to hate him, namely his intention to preside over an undisguisedly absolute monarchy, had apparently been in his mind since the very beginning of his reign; ever since then he had been continuously engaged in putting progressive stages into practice.

It was a curious flaw in Domitian's powerful intellectual equipment that he felt he could do this, and prevail. He failed to understand that his policy towards the senate was an open provocation and invitation to conspirators, setting up a vicious circle of plots, executions and more plots, which he could not expect to survive for an indefinite period.

For his theory of the principate was premature. The immediate future lay with the more discreet and less oppressive, though still autocratic, formulas of his father Vespasian. But a hundred years after they were both dead, Domitian's was the idea of imperial power which instead began to prevail. From the military monarchy of Septimius Severus onwards, the emperors were as unabashedly absolute rulers as Domitian: the fictions Domitian so despised had been well and truly cast away. Yet, even then, the concept can scarcely be described as effective.

For, although Severus himself reigned for three years longer than Domitian, very few of Severus' autocratic successors ruled for even half as long, and many survived for practically no time at all. Their downfalls were as violent as the death of Domitian, and due to the same basic reason: because undisguised one-man rule invites reprisals and competitors.

Conclusion: The Success and Failure
of the Caesars

Almost every one of the Twelve Caesars left his substantial, individual mark on the civilization from which our own is largely derived. Julius Caesar terminated a whole epoch in the affairs of the world, and set the stage for a new one, though the elusive formula for its establishment escaped him. It was discovered by Augustus, who, profiting by the warnings of Caesar's fate, devised an autocracy that was more cunningly veiled, and introduced it to the accompaniment of one of the most far-reaching reorganizations which any great state has ever known.

But Tiberius, for all his ability, showed how impossible the Augustan precedent was to follow, and then Caligula paid the penalty for a premature attempt to cast the Augustan veil aside. Claudius devoted his powerful but eccentric brain to the evolution of a bureaucratically efficient monarchy, and Nero revealed that a ruler who preferred the arts to administration could not hope to remain alive.

As the empire plunged into civil war, Galba's accession displayed that an emperor might be made by a provincial army. Otho was the first of many rulers to bring about his own predecessor's death, and the first also to owe his position to the praetorian guard. The elevation of Vitellius revealed the emperor-making capacities of the great frontier garrisons.

Vespasian, after this chaotic year, succeeded in founding a second dynasty, and restored stability to the Roman world. He was the prototype of the enlightened, hard-working autocrats of the second century AD, just as, after the enigmatic interlude of his older son Titus, Titus' brother Domitian foreshadowed the third century's military autocrats.

The Twelve Caesars had stamped their indelible imprint upon history, by performing vast achievements or leaving solemn warnings behind them.

Yet every one of them, too, in some way or another, had found his immense office too much for him. Each of their reigns – or at least those that were not cut off almost at the outset – ended in personal deterioration. Some rulers deteriorated simply because they were growing old. But others began to decline long before they reached an age when decline might be expected.

Lord Acton, in the Appendix to his *Historical Essays and Studies*, wrote: 'Power tends to corrupt, and absolute power corrupts absolutely. Great men are always bad men.'

In the second part of that statement there is a great deal of truth. To gain or keep an important political position without performing unpleasant or at least self-seeking action is almost impossible. As Peregrine Worsthorne writes even about our comparatively staid modern scene: 'There are always skeletons in the cupboard, always incidents where even the most illustrious and heroic figure behaved with less than total honesty or truthfulness.' In speaking of the less inhibited days of the Roman empire, that would be a mild expression of the steps that were found necessary in order to prevail and survive.

However Acton's further assertion about absolute power corrupting absolutely does not convey the whole truth about the Twelve Caesars.

True, this sensational, almost unlimited, power was highly relevant – for another reason. It was not so much that it corrupted them after they had obtained it, but already, before that, it was what had tempted most of them to try to obtain the imperial office. In view of the alarming perils involved, it may seem difficult to understand why anyone could be eager to become ruler of the Roman empire. Yet signs of reluctance were not greatly in evidence. Even in the third century AD, when a would-be usurper scarcely needed to be a statistical expert to note that the average reign ended rapidly and violently, candidates for the throne still proliferated on every side – and by no means all of them sought it merely because their soldiers compelled them to do so.

As for the Twelve Caesars, most of them emphatically wanted the job. Unwillingness was only shown by Tiberius who took on the imperial functions out of the well-warranted conviction that no one else but himself was capable of performing them. In a number of other cases, too, this same sense of duty played a part in driving emperors on. But a far more frequent inducement was the plain love of immense power and its breathtaking possibilities.

Having once obtained all this power, however, the Caesars were not always corrupted by it. True, Julius, Vitellius and Domitian, in their different ways, display signs of such corruption. But when we consider the others, this verdict may, at most, be applicable only to two of them – Caligula and Nero. For each of these young men, in turn, after a particularly insecure and hazardous childhood, discovered that absolute power gave them unlimited opportunities for self-indulgence. Their seizure of these opportunities distracted them from the work which they ought to have been doing, and which had to be done to ensure their political and personal survival.

For the labours that a successful emperor found himself compelled to undertake were not only terrifyingly responsible, but enormously extensive, and never ending. In fact the burden was intolerable, especially if a ruler had a bad record of health, like Julius Caesar, Augustus and Claudius, or lived to a considerable age, like Augustus, Tiberius, Claudius, Galba and Vespasian.

And this load of work had to be borne amid an atmosphere of almost unremitting fear and suspicion. One ruler after another, except for the very few who arranged things better, went through the familiar motions of first seeking an accommodation with the former governing class, then realizing that these attempts had failed, and subsequently entering a period, likely to be terminal, of hostile and terror-ridden relations with the groups they had failed to win over. If Shakespeare's Henry IV had been speaking of the Roman emperors, his declaration 'Uneasy lies the head that wears a crown' would have been a classic under-statement.

Excessive work and nagging fear, then, rather than absolute power, were the principal troubles which caused the Twelve Caesars, each in his turn, to deteriorate. This formula does not, it is true, completely suit Julius Caesar, who suffered from grave over-exertion, but not apparently from fear – though in his case an additional undermining factor was his weak physical health. Augustus, too, was a chronically sick man, and he overworked for many years longer than Julius Caesar did. He was also severely afflicted with the continual suspicions which had failed to disturb Julius. Augustus' inevitable demoralization, in such circumstances, was only masked by his introduction of a confidential helper and prospective heir to supplement his failing powers and ensure the avoidance of catastrophe. When however this deputy, Tiberius, himself came to the throne, he provided a more emphatic example still of the same damaging blend of overwork and suspicious fright; and his reign ended grimly owing to his failure, in his ageing years, to remedy these hazards by finding a lieutenant whom he could trust.

Caligula rapidly declined into a disastrous relationship with the senate and praetorian guard, and this caused his destruction. Claudius, like Tiberius, was perpetually nervous and worked far too strenuously, with the additional handicap of his subnormal physical condition. He, too, as these pressures began to affect his abilities, needed someone to help him rule the empire or even, as time went on, take on the bulk of the task instead of him. For this he turned to his wife Agrippina the younger, who thus gave Rome its first unwelcome taste of female government.

Nero divested himself of this encumbrance, and his comparative lack of interest in the serious tasks of government did the empire no harm for a time, under the efficient rule of Seneca and Burrus. When they were gone, however, his failure to apply himself to his duties eventually caused him to lose control of the situation. The consequent worsening of his relationship with the senate greatly increased his natural tendency to panic-stricken fright, and eventually struck him down.

Galba, Otho and Vitellius all left in quick succession because of serious personal faults, and not by chance. And once again it was not by chance that Vespasian survived, since he avoided their mistakes and proved a much more effective ruler. But although he was not subject to the suspicious fears of so many of his predecessors he worked more strenuously than any of them; and he could not have won through, as he did, until his seventieth year, if he had not enjoyed the services of a wholly reliable deputy. Like Augustus, he employed his chosen heir in this capacity, but he went one better than Augustus owing to the fortunate possession of a son of his own blood to sustain his final years.

This son, Titus, when his turn came to ascend the throne, died too soon for his quality as an emperor to become clear. His brother and successor Domitian displayed, in full measure, the traditional imperial quality of suspicious fear and the consequent fear which envenomed his relations with the senatorial class duly brought about his ruin.

The Twelve Caesars exhibited a remarkable variety of individual characteristics. But they were alike, those of them who ruled long enough to present a reasonably clear picture, in that they found the burdens of their position scarcely endurable. And although absolute power, no doubt, sometimes proved a corrupting influence, Lord Acton might usefully, though less elegantly, have rewritten his assertion in the following terms: 'Overwork combined with fear tends to corrupt, and continual overwork and fear corrupt absolutely – with all the greater rapidity when combined with old age or ill-health.'

Human beings though the Caesars were – despite the efforts of their subjects to declare them otherwise – and human beings subject to shattering pressures, they performed the almost superhuman task of governing many millions of men and women over a gigantic area: and on the whole, with the aid of an efficient system, they governed well. Despite the political convulsions that troubled and decimated the small metropolitan uppei class of the capital, the vast territories of the Roman empire, from the time of Augustus onwards, were an excellently administered going concern. Moreover, for all the inadequacies and inequalities of the ancient social structure, among free men at least a large measure of justice prevailed wherever the imperial writ ran.

And this was the doing of the Caesars. True, we must not credit them with everything that had happened, for that would be to perpetuate the personality cult in which the ancient writers excessively revelled: and to a considerable degree the government of the empire continued whatever the character of the emperor at Rome. Yet the success of this imperial machine was also, and to quite a large extent, the achievement of the Caesars who guided it. The most able of them, whatever their personal peculiarities, changed the course of history for the better, and demand our awed respect and admiration.

Notes

Introduction: The Significance and Strangeness of the Caesars
1 Pliny the younger, *Letters*, 24, 1-4 (trans. B. Radice).
2 Suetonius, *Augustus*, 6 (trans. P. Holland).
3 Virgil, *Georgics* I, 466ff. (trans. Robert Fitzgerald).
4 *The Times*, 30 May 1974.
5 Andrew Marvell, *Horatian Ode upon Cromwell's Return from Ireland.*
6 Dio, LIII, 19, 1-6 (trans. E. Cary).
7 Petronius, *Satyricon*, fragment 28 (trans. J. Sullivan).

Part I FROM REPUBLIC TO EMPIRE

Chapter I Julius Caesar
1 Suetonius, *Caesar*, 45 (trans. R. Graves).
2 Suetonius, *Caesar*, 57 (trans. R. Graves).
3 Pliny the elder, *Natural History*, VII, 91.
4 Caesar, *Civil War*, III, 73, 5.
5 Cicero, *Philippics*, II, 116.
6 Lucan, *Pharsalia*, II, 657; I, 144ff. (trans. J. W. Duff).
7 Caesar, *Civil War*, I, 9, 2. The word for 'position' is *dignitas*.
8 Lucan, *Pharsalia*, VII, 500ff. (trans. E. Ridley). 'Magnus' (not in the Latin here) was the surname adopted by Pompey.
9 Suetonius, *Caesar*, 80 (trans. R. Graves).

Notes

Chapter 2   Augustus

1 Pliny the elder, *Natural History*, II, 94 (trans. A. H. M. Jones).

2 Cicero, *Letters to Atticus*, XIV, 8, 1 (trans. A. H. M. Jones). Casilinum (the modern Capua) and Calatia (Maddaloni) were towns in Campania. The *denarius* was the standard silver coin (worth four *sestertii*).

3 Virgil, *Aeneid*, VIII, 678ff. (trans. R. Humphries). But Antony was not married to Cleopatra according to Roman law, and probably not according to Egyptian law either.

4 Virgil, *Aeneid*, VI, 847ff. (trans. P. Dickinson).

5 *Sibylline Oracles*, VIII, 91ff., 121ff. (trans. M. S. Terry).

6 Virgil, *Georgics*, II, 167ff. (trans. G. Highet).

7 Horace, *Odes*, III, 14, 14ff.; IV, 15, 17ff.; IV, 5, 17ff. (trans. J. Michie).

8 Dittenberger, *Orientis Graecae Inscriptiones Selectae*, 458 (trans. A. H. M. Jones).

9 Strabo, *Geography*, VI, 4, 2, 288 (trans. H. L. Jones). Strabo ascribes the same happy conditions to the reign of Augustus' successor Tiberius also.

10 Philo, *Embassy to Gaius (Caligula)*, XXI, 145ff. (trans. E. M. Smallwood).

11 Suetonius, *Augustus*, 53, 2f. (trans. J. C. Rolfe).

12 Suetonius, *Augustus*, 89, 2 (trans. J. C. Rolfe).

13 Suetonius, *Augustus*, 71, 3 (trans. J. C. Rolfe). The *sestertius*, as incorporated in the handsome new monetary system of Augustus, was a large brass coin.

14 Suetonius, *Augustus*, 83 (trans. J. C. Rolfe).

15 Suetonius, *Augustus*, 69, 2.

16 Suetonius, *Augustus*, 79, 1f. (trans. D. Earl). Pliny the elder said his eyes were placed almost like a horse's, and that he became annoyed if people stared at them.

17 Suetonius, *Augustus*, 80–1 (trans. J. C. Rolfe and D. Earl).

18 Suetonius, *Augustus*, 82 (trans. J. C. Rolfe).

19 *Supplementum Epigraphicum Graecum*, IX, 8 (Cyrene edict 5) (trans. N. Lewis and M. Reinhold). 'Allies of the Roman people' was a euphemistic way of describing the subject communities, which enjoyed a limited autonomy. The addressee was the governor of Crete and Cyrenaica, a 'senatorial' province.

20 Suetonius, *Augustus*, 35, 2 (trans. J. C. Rolfe).

21 Horace, *Odes*, III, 6, 29ff. (trans. G. Highet).

22 Velleius Paterculus, II, 110, 6–111, 1 (trans. F. W. Shipley).

23 Velleius Paterculus, II, 119, 2f. (trans. F. W. Shipley).

24 Suetonius, *Augustus*, 23 (trans. J. C. Rolfe).

Notes

Chapter 3 *Tiberius*

1 Horace, *Odes*, IV, 14, 14ff. (trans. J. Michie). 'Nero' is Tiberius (Tiberius Claudius Nero).
2 Suetonius, *Tiberius*, 21, 4ff. (trans. R. Graves). The reference to the Muses at the beginning seems to be an allusion to Tiberius' literary tastes.
3 Suetonius, *Tiberius*, 11, 2 (trans. R. Graves).
4 Tacitus, *Annals*, I, 13, 7 (trans. M. Grant; as are other quoted passages of this work).
5 Dio, LVII, 1, 1ff. (trans. E. Cary).
6 Suetonius, *Tiberius*, 68, 1ff. (trans. P. Holland).
7 Suetonius, *Tiberius*, 29 (trans. J. C. Rolfe).
8 Tacitus, *Annals*, I, 74, 3 and 5f.
9 Seneca, *On Benefits*, III, 16 (trans. Francis Holland).
10 Juvenal, *Satires*, x, 58ff. (trans. G. Highet).
11 Juvenal, *Satires*, x, 68ff. (trans. R. Humphries).
12 Tacitus, *Annals*, VI, 51, 5f.
13 Suetonius, *Tiberius*, 57, 1; *Gaius (Caligula)*, 6, 2; *Tiberius*, 42, 1 (trans. J. C. Rolfe).
14 Dio, LVII, 13, 6 (trans. E. Cary).
15 Tacitus, *Annals*, VI, 48.
16 Tacitus, *Annals*, VI, 6, 1.

Chapter 4 *Caligula*

1 Suetonius, *Gaius (Caligula)*, 10, 2 (trans. P. Holland).
2 Suetonius, *Gaius (Caligula)*, 50, 1f. (trans. J. C. Rolfe).
3 Josephus, *Jewish Antiquities*, XIX, 208–10 (trans. L. H. Feldman).
4 Philo, *Embassy to Gaius (Caligula)*, XLV, 359 and 361 (trans. E. M. Smallwood).
5 Philo, *Embassy to Gaius (Caligula)*, III, 15ff. (trans. E. M. Smallwood).
6 Suetonius, *Gaius (Caligula)*, 53, 2 (trans. R. Graves).
7 Philo, *Embassy to Gaius (Caligula)*, VII, 42 (trans. E. M. Smallwood).
8 Suetonius, *Gaius (Caligula)*, 54, 2 (trans. R. Graves).
9 Philo, *Embassy to Gaius (Caligula)*, XXVII, 175 (trans. E. M. Smallwood).
10 Josephus, *Jewish Antiquities*, XIX, 127ff. (trans. L. H. Feldman).
11 Philo, *Embassy to Gaius (Caligula)*, II, 14 (trans. E. M. Smallwood).

Chapter 5 *Claudius*

1 Seneca, *Apocolocyntosis*, 12, 3 (trans. W. H. D. Rouse).
2 Suetonius, *Claudius*, 30 (trans. P. Holland).
3 Suetonius, *Claudius*, 4, 1f. (trans. J. C. Rolfe).

4 Suetonius, *Claudius*, 42, 2 (trans. J. C. Rolfe).
5 Suetonius, *Claudius*, 33, 1 (trans. J. C. Rolfe). The Salii were the priests of Mars.
6 *Aegyptische Urkunden aus den königlichen Museen zu Berlin (BGU)*, 611.
7 Dessau, *Inscriptiones Latinae Selectae*, 212 (trans. A. H. M. Jones; and N. Lewis and M. Reinhold).
8 Seneca, *Apocolocyntosis*, 3 (trans. W. H. D. Rouse).
9 Seneca, *Apocolocyntosis*, 12 (trans. W. H. D. Rouse).
10 Suetonius, *Claudius*, 15, 3 (trans. R. Graves).
11 Pliny the younger, *Letters*, VIII, 6, 6 and 8 (trans. B. Radice)
12 Juvenal, *Satires*, VI, 115ff. (trans. P. Green).
13 Tacitus, *Annals*, XI, 31, 4.
14 Tacitus, *Annals*, XII, 6f., 5.

Chapter 6   Nero
1 Suetonius, *Nero*, 51 (trans. P. Holland).
2 Tacitus, *Annals*, XIII, 5, 2ff.
3 Seneca, *On Clemency*, I, 2 (trans. Francis Holland).
4 Seneca, *On Benefits*, VII, 20 (trans. Francis Holland)
5 Seneca, *On Benefits*, V, 6 (trans. Francis Holland).
6 Suetonius, *Nero*, 15, 1 (trans. J. C. Rolfe).
7 Suetonius, *Nero*, 20, 1 (trans. P. Holland).
8 Dio, LXII, 13, 2 (trans. E. Cary)
9 Petronius, *Satyricon*, 132 Loeb (trans. W. Arrowsmith).
10 Tacitus, *Annals*, XIV, 14, 1f.
11 Suetonius, *Nero*, 24, 1 (trans. R. Graves).
12 Seneca, *On Benefits*, VII, 20 (trans. Francis Holland).
13 Dittenberger, *Sylloge Inscriptionum Graecarum*, 814 (trans. N. Lewis and M. Reinhold).
14 Suetonius, *Nero*, 40, 4 (trans. J. C. Rolfe). For Galba's revolt, see the next chapter.

Part III   THE CIVIL WARS

Chapter 7   Galba
1 Tacitus, *Histories*, I, 49 (trans. K. Wellesley).
2 Tacitus, *Histories*, I, 12 (trans. K. Wellesley).
3 Tacitus, *Histories*, I, 16 (trans. A. J. Church and W. J. Brodribb).

Chapter 8   Otho
1 Tacitus, *Histories*, I, 43f. (trans. A. J. Church and W. J. Brodribb).
2 Suetonius, *Otho*, 3, 2 (trans. R. Graves).

3 Suetonius, *Otho*, 12, 1 (trans. R. Graves).
4 Juvenal, *Satires*, II, 99ff. (trans. P. Green).
5 Plutarch, *Otho*, 3, 4ff. (trans. A. H. Clough, with modifications). A silver *denarius* comprised 4 *sestertii*.
6 Martial, VI, 32.
7 Tacitus, *Histories*, II, 50.

Chapter 9   Vitellius
1 Suetonius, *Vitellius*, 13, 2 (trans. R. Graves).
2 Tacitus, *Histories*, III, 86 (trans. A. J. Church and W. J. Brodribb).
3 Dio, LXIV, 6, 1ff. (trans. E. Cary).
4 Tacitus, *Histories*, III, 56 (trans. A. J. Church and W. J. Brodribb).
5 Suetonius, *Vitellius*, 7 (trans. G. W. Mooney).

Part IV   THE FLAVIAN EMPERORS

Chapter 10   Vespasian
1 Josephus, *Jewish War*, I, 4f. (trans. H. St J. Thackeray).
2 Suetonius, *Vespasian*, 12 (trans. G. W. Mooney).
3 Tacitus, *Histories*, II, 5 (trans. A. J. Church and W. J. Brodribb).
4 Tacitus, *Histories*, I, 10 (trans. K. Wellesley).
5 Tacitus, *Histories*, II, 86 (trans. K. Wellesley).
6 Suetonius, *Vespasian*, 23 (trans. R. Graves and J. C. Rolfe).

Chapter 11   Titus
1 Racine, *Bérénice*, I, 4 (trans. J. Cairncross).
2 Josephus, *Jewish War*, VI, 254ff. (trans. G. A. Williamson).
3 Josephus, *Jewish War*, VII, 37ff. (trans. G. A. Williamson).
4 Suetonius, *Titus*, 5 (trans. R. Graves).
5 Suetonius, *Titus*, 6 (trans. G. W. Mooney).
6 Juvenal, *Satires*, VI, 155ff. (trans. R. Humphries).
7 Dio, LXV, 15, 3ff. (trans. E. Cary).
8 Suetonius, *Titus*, 6 (trans. J. C. Rolfe).
9 Suetonius, *Titus*, 3 (trans. R. Graves).
10 Racine *Bérénice* I, 4 (trans. J. Cairncross).
11 Racine, *Bérénice*, IV, 5 (trans. S. Perowne).
12 Suetonius, *Titus*, 8 (trans. G. W. Mooney).
13 Edward Young (1684–1765).
14 Suetonius, *Titus*, 10 (trans. G. W. Mooney).
15 Ausonius, *Caesars*, tetrasticha 11.
16 Dio, LXVI, 18, 4 (trans. E. Cary).

Chapter 12   Domitian

1 Tacitus, *Histories*, iv, 86 (trans. K. Wellesley).
2 Suetonius, *Domitian*, 18 (trans. J. C. Rolfe).
3 Juvenal, *Satires*, iv, 81ff. (trans. P. Green).
4 Suetonius, *Domitian*, 12 (trans. R. Graves). The Jewish tax had replaced the tax formerly paid by Jews all over the empire to the Temple at Jerusalem, now destroyed.
5 Dio, lxvii, 9, 1ff. (trans. E. Cary).
6 Martial, ii, 2 (trans. J. A. Pott and F. A. Wright).
7 Tacitus, *Agricola*, 39 (trans. H. Mattingly).
8 Dio, lxvii, 1, 3f. (trans. E. Cary)

Bibliography

JULIUS CAESAR

J. P. V. D. Balsdon, *Julius Caesar and Rome*, London, 1967, 1971.

J. Carcopino, *Jules César*, revised by P. Grimal, Paris, 1968.

A. Ferrabino, *Cesare*, Turin, 1945.

M. Gelzer, *Cäsar der Politiker und Staatsmann*, Stuttgart and Berlin, 1921, translated as *Caesar: Politician and Statesman*, Oxford, 1968.

M. Grant, *Caesar*, London, 1974.

M. Grant, *Julius Caesar*, London and New York, 1969, 1972.

H. Oppermann, *Caesar: Wegbereiter Europas*, Göttingen, 1958.

R. Syme, *The Roman Revolution*, Oxford, 1939, 1971.

S. Weinstock, *Divus Julius*, Oxford, 1971.

AUGUSTUS

J. Béranger, *Recherches sur l'aspect idéologique du principat*, Basel, 1953.

G. W. Bowersock, *Augustus and the Greek World*, Oxford, 1965.

D. C. Earl, *The Age of Augustus*, London, 1968.

M. Hammond, *The Augustan Principate*, Cambridge, Massachusetts, 1933, 1968.

A. H. M. Jones, *Augustus*, London, 1970.

M. A. Levi, *Il tempo di Augusto*, Florence, 1951.

A. von Premerstein, *Vom Werden und Wesen des Prinzipats*, Munich, 1937.

P. Sattler, *Augustus und der Senat*, Göttingen, 1960.

W. Schmitthenner (ed.), *Augustus*, Darmstadt, 1969.

R. Syme, *The Roman Revolution* (see above, Julius Caesar).

Bibliography

TIBERIUS

E. Ciaceri, *Tiberio successore di Augusto*, Rome, 1934, 1944.
E. Kornemann, *Tiberius*, Stuttgart, 1960.
F. B. Marsh, *The Reign of Tiberius*, Oxford, 1931.
D. M. Pippidi, *Autour de Tibère*, Bucharest, 1944, 1965.
R. Seager, *Tiberius*, London, 1972.
E. C. Smith, *Tiberius and the Roman Empire*, Baton Rouge, 1942.

CALIGULA (GAIUS)

J. P. V. D. Balsdon, *The Emperor Gaius*, Oxford, 1934.

CLAUDIUS

A. Momigliano, *Claudius: The Emperor and his Achievement*, Cambridge, 1934, 1961.
V. M. Scramuzza, *The Emperor Claudius*, Cambridge, Massachusetts, 1940, 1971.

NERO

J. H. Bishop, *Nero: the Man and the Legend*, London, 1964.
M. Grant, *Nero*, London and New York, 1970, 1973.
B. H. Warmington, *Nero: Reality and Legend*, London, 1969.

GALBA, OTHO, VITELLIUS

G. Corradi, *Galba, Otone e Vitellio*, Rome, 1941.
B. W. Henderson, *Civil War and Rebellion in the Roman Empire*, London, 1908.
L. de Regibus, *Galba*, and L. Pareti, *Otone e Vitellio*, in *Dodici Cesari*, Rome, 1955.

VESPASIAN, TITUS, DOMITIAN

A. Calderini, *Vespasiano e Tito*, Rome, 1941.
M. Fortina, *L'imperatore Tito*, Turin, 1955.
G. Giannelli, *Domiziano*, Rome, 1941.
S. Gsell, *Essai sur le règne de l'empéreur Domitien*, Paris, 1894, 1967.
B. W. Henderson, *Five Roman Emperors*, Cambridge, 1927.
L. Homo, *Vespasien: l'empereur du bon sens*, Paris, 1944.

GENERAL WORKS

J. P. V. D. Balsdon, *Life and Leisure in Ancient Rome*, London, 1969.
Cambridge Ancient History, Vol. IX, 1932; X, 1934; XI, 1936.

Bibliography

J. Carcopino, *La vie quotidienne à Rome à l'apogèe de l'empire*, Paris, 1939, translated as *Daily Life in Ancient Rome*, London, 1941, 1964.

L. Friedländer, *Darstellungen aus der Sittengeschichte Roms*, 10th ed., Leipzig, 1922; 7th ed. translated as *Roman Life and Manners under the Early Empire*, London, 1908–1913.

A. Garzetti, *L'impero da Tiberio agli Antonini*, Bologna, 1960, translated as *From Tiberius to the Antonines*, London, 1974.

M. Grant, *The Army of the Caesars*, London and New York, 1974.

U. E. Paoli, *Vita Romana*, Florence, translated as *Rome: its People, Life and Customs*, London, 1963.

A. Piganiol, *Histoire de Rome*, Paris, 1939, 1954.

M. Rostovtzeff, *Social and Economic History of the Roman Empire*, Oxford, 1941, 1957 (ed. P. M. Fraser).

H. H. Scullard, *From the Gracchi to Nero*, London, 1959, 1970.

Also books interpreting and analysing the principal ancient writers (discussed in the Introduction and other parts of this book; cf. R. Syme, *Tacitus*, Oxford, 1958), and coins (H. Mattingly, *Roman Coins*, London, 1928, 1960; C. H. V. Sutherland, *Roman Coins*, London, 1974; M. Grant, *Roman History from Coins*, Cambridge, 1958, 1968), and works of art and buildings, and inscriptions and papyri (three volumes of *Documents*, Oxford, 1955–1967; A. H. M. Jones [ed.], *A History of Rome through the Fifth Century*, Vol. II, New York and London, 1970; N. Lewis and M. Reinhold [ed.], *Roman Civilization*, Vol. II, New York, 1955, 1966).

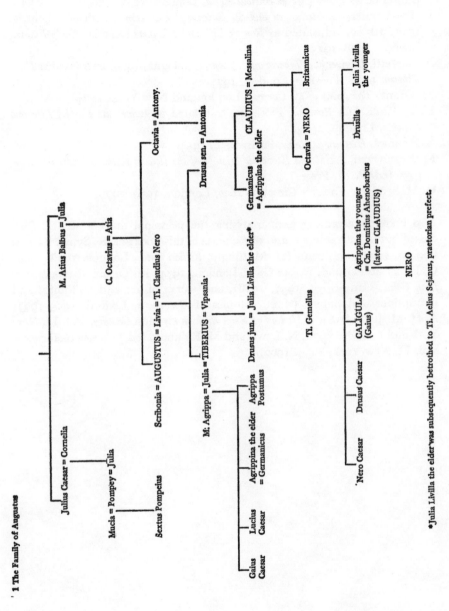

1 The Family of Augustus

*Julia Livilla the elder was subsequently betrothed to Ti. Aelius Sejanus, praetorian prefect.

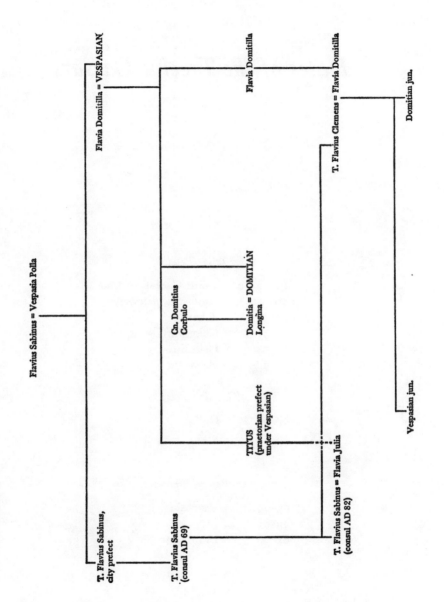

2 The Family of Vespasian

Dates of the Twelve Caesars

Dates of Subsequent Emperors

Index

Roman first names (*praenomina*) are abbreviated as follows: A.: Aulus, C.: Gaius, Cn.: Cnaeus, Dec.: Decimus, L.: Lucius, M.: Marcus, P.: Publius, Q.: Quintus, Ser.: Servius, Sex.: Sextus, T.: Titus, Ti.: Tiberius.

275